Žižek and his Contemporaries

Also available from Bloomsbury

Interrogating the Real, Slavoj Žižek
The Universal Exception, Slavoj Žižek
Slavoj Žižek: Live Theory, Rex Butler
Žižek: A Guide for the Perplexed, Sean Sheehan

Žižek and his Contemporaries

On the Emergence of the Slovenian Lacan

JONES IRWIN AND HELENA MOTOH

BLOOMSBURY
LONDON · NEW DELHI · NEW YORK · SYDNEY

Bloomsbury Academic
An imprint of Bloomsbury Publishing Plc

50 Bedford Square	1385 Broadway
London	New York
WC1B 3DP	NY 10018
UK	USA

www.bloomsbury.com

Bloomsbury is a registered trade mark of Bloomsbury Publishing Plc

First published 2014

© Jones Irwin and Helena Motoh, 2014

Jones Irwin and Helena Motoh have asserted their right under the Copyright, Designs and Patents Act, 1988, to be identified as Authors of this work.

All rights reserved. No part of this publication may be reproduced or transmitted in any form or by any means, electronic or mechanical, including photocopying, recording, or any information storage or retrieval system, without prior permission in writing from the publishers.

No responsibility for loss caused to any individual or organization acting on or refraining from action as a result of the material in this publication can be accepted by Bloomsbury Academic or the author.

British Library Cataloguing-in-Publication Data
A catalogue record for this book is available from the British Library.

ISBN: HB: 978-1-4411-1178-4
PB: 978-1-4411-0513-4
ePDF: 978-1-4411-5885-7
ePub: 978-1-4411-5395-1

Library of Congress Cataloging-in-Publication Data
A catalog record for this book is available from the Library of Congress.

Typeset by Deanta Global Publishing Services, Chennai, India
Printed and bound in India

For Eloïse

To Staš and Adam

CONTENTS

Acknowledgements ix

Introduction 1
    In the beginning 1
    Why Lacan? 6
    Development of chapters 8

1 What *was* going on in Ljubljana? 13
    'The Unconscious is Structured as Yugoslavia' 13
    Waiting for the match to be cancelled 15
    The emergence of nationalism 18
    Genealogies of philosophy in the former Yugoslavia 22
    'I Walked our Land and Got an Ulcer' 26
    'Gentlemen comrades, I don't believe you' 29
    Conclusion 33

2 The Lacan effect 39
    Introduction 39
    Interpreting Lacan 41
    Psychoanalysis and philosophy 46
    Psychoanalysis and surrealism 50
    'Kant with Sade' 56
    Lacan's *The Ethics of Psychoanalysis* 64
    Conclusion – Lacanianism via Derrida and the
    Ljubljana troika 77

3 From punk to cogito to voice: On Mladen Dolar 83

Introduction – Dolar's philosophical evolution 83
Reading Lacan-Hegel-Marx in Dolar 86
Socrates and the daemonic voice 90
'From Structuralism to Lacan' – Interview with Mladen Dolar 93
Conclusion – Dolar: Breaking through the impasse 112

4 'Learn, Learn and Learn' – On Slavoj Žižek 117

Introduction 117
The core of the Freudian revolution 120
Lacan, then and now 123
'From Lacan to Hegel' – Interview with Slavoj Žižek 125
Conclusion – 'Moving the Underground' with the NSK 146

5 'From Haso to Mujo': On Alenka Zupančič 151

Introduction 151
The ethics of the real 153
Sexuality from Plato to psychoanalysis 155
'Encountering Lacan in the Next Generation' – Interview with Alenka Zupančič 158
Conclusion – 'From Haso to Mujo' 178

Epilogue – 'We Don't Know What Will Become of This Psychoanalysis' 183

Introduction 183
Lacan 'On a Warpath from the Beginning' 185
The deadlocks of Lacanianism 188
'The New Wounded' – Žižek for and against Malabou 190
Conclusion – Enjoy your future! 194

Notes 197
Bibliography 203
Index 213

ACKNOWLEDGEMENTS

At St Patrick's College, Drumcondra, Jones Irwin would like to thank his supportive colleagues in the respective groups in Human Development and the Education Department. Thanks to the troika, that is Mladen, Slavoj and Alenka, for such (ethical-political) good will and great interviews. Thanks to Helena for starting and maintaining the whole thing with such balance. To Melissa and the gang (i.e., Eloïse, Jeremy, Gregory and Max) for inspiration. To Tom Crick and then Rachel Eisenhauer at Continuum and then Bloomsbury for editorial help and support. To Malahide library staff for a friendly space to work. Thanks also to Lenart, Pavel, Darko and Slavko who were so hospitable on my first, original trip to Slovenia (Koper and Ljubljana) in December 2008. Specific aspects of the Epilogue were originally published in the Avello journal, Issue 1, Volume 2.

Jones dedicates this book to his eldest child, his beautiful daughter Eloïse, who thinks philosophy may or may not be worth all this effort.

Jones Irwin, Dublin, 15 October 2013

Helena Motoh would like to thank the University of Primorska, where her research is based, and especially her colleagues from the Philosophy department at the Faculty of Humanities and the Institute of Philosophical Studies at the Science and Research Centre of Koper for the support and inspiration. She would like to express sincere gratitude to Jones for taking on such a large part of this project. She is joining him in expressing thanks to the three authors presented in the book, for their kind help and willingness to participate in yet another interview, and to Bloomsbury for assistance and support in the shaping of this text. A humble thanks to Miha and two little guys who are growing up in the midst of philosophical debates, which is not always an easy thing to do. To Staš and Adam she also dedicates this book.

Helena Motoh, Ljubljana, 15 October 2013

Introduction

Fucked by the Absolute/ fed up with virgins and other dying sufferers/ I love you o neighbors, meek fantasies of God the Father/ I love you o integral characters of sweet gazing/ In my mind grace yielded// O proud possessors of anxieties/ O trained intellectuals with sweaty little hands/. . . . I walked our land and got an ulcer/ Land of Cimpermans and pimply groupies/ Land of serfs myths and pedagogy// O flinty Slovenians, object of history crippled by a cold.

(ŠALAMUN DUMA [*Word*])

In the beginning

We [myself and my group] had been ultraorthodox Lacanians from roughly the mid 1970s onwards.

(ŽIŽEK AND DALY 2003: 33)

In recent years, Slovenian intellectuals with a strong (or 'orthodox') Lacanian emphasis have had a very significant influence on the international development of philosophical thinking. Led inimitably by Slavoj Žižek, this foregrounding of Slovenian thought has also been influential outside the groves of academe, with Žižek's distinctive personality in particular generating a movie in his name (Žižek 2007b) and has been the subject of much media attention.[1] However, at times, this popularity of Žižek has overshadowed or marginalized the very serious intellectual and philosophical significance of this movement or shared sensibility. Although only coming to international notice in the early 1990s, Slovenian neo-Lacanianism needs to be understood as the culmination of a whole series of intellectual and political movements inextricably connected to the quest for Slovenian national independence from Yugoslavia, especially from the late 1970s onwards. In Slovenia, these movements originated in the punk music counter-culture and evolved into a significant avant-garde and alternative movement known as *Neue Slowenische Kunst* (NSK; New Slovene Art), which included the internationally recognized group, Laibach, the visual artists IRWIN and the theatrical group Sestre Scipion Nasice. Monroe (2005) has described the latter as, for example, 'the most important avant-garde of the second half of the twentieth century' and 'the last avant-garde'. The philosophers we will be concerned with were also participants in and influential on the NSK, in various significant ways (most especially as the movement influenced the political process).

This book will attempt to do justice to this complex and fascinating history, with interviews with the leading philosophical figures of the movement (Žižek, Zupančič and Dolar) as well as an analysis of the wider new social movements in Slovenia. One of the authors, Helena Motoh, is herself a Slovenian philosopher of the younger generation and, as such, has a lot of local insight and understanding of both the political and intellectual dynamics of the development of this very specific strand of thinking. The other author, Jones Irwin, is also a younger philosopher with a specific expertise in 1960s' or 1970s' French philosophy, which was to be so influential on later Slovenian thinking. One significant factor here relates to the fact that unlike other Yugoslav republics or indeed the wider Eastern bloc, Slovenian intellectuals were allowed to travel to and study in Paris in the 1970s and 1980s, which created a greater cosmopolitanism in Slovenia than in its neighbouring countries. Additionally, many of the significant Slovenian intellectuals who studied abroad chose to return to Slovenia after their studies rather than go into exile. This latter was obviously a significant factor in the strengthening of Slovenian philosophy at home.

While our book is subtitled 'the emergence of the Slovenian Lacan', the trio or 'troika' of thinkers, who we will be most concerned with, are more specifically associated with the city of Ljubljana. Thus, their work is often referred to (by themselves also) as part of a Ljubljana School of Psychoanalysis. This is the name we will use consistently throughout the book for the activities of this group of thinkers. Nonetheless, there is also a wider focus to their work. First of all, this focus takes its cue from the national context of Slovenia as well as from the wider relationships in the former Yugoslavia, coming under the self-management socialism of Tito. We will discuss this former Yugoslavian context in most detail in Chapter 1, as it evolves from the 1970s through the controversies and Balkan wars of the 1980s and 1990s, including independence for Slovenia. One of the most curious aspects of this history is the specific orientation towards Lacanianism which we can see emerge in the Slovenian context of theory and politics. Močnik (1993) has given an excellent analysis of this evolution and spoken of it significantly in terms of the 'impasse' associated with other structuralist (and post-structuralist) philosophies, with Lacan's philosophy being designated as a 'breakthrough' moment. Not least of the dilemmas which this book will seek to address is the fact that the most enigmatic of all philosophical and theoretical systems in the twentieth century (that of Jacques Lacan, as friend and foe would agree) has come to have had such a key role in practical, political and sociocultural struggles in recent times. What is it about Lacan's philosophical system (if we can speak in such a way), which allows or enables this kind of political activism, of such a radical sort? Moreover, we will see in the context of the Ljubljana School of Psychoanalysis that they too (Žižek, Dolar and Zupančič) will come to play a crucial role in their own national, political and sociocultural struggles (leading up to independence). Also, recently, their work has taken on paradigmatic significance on a more global level, in terms, for example, of intra-leftist discussions (and diatribes) (Laclau 1989; Žižek et al. 2000) as well as discussion and inspiration around the Arab Spring and the Occupy movement in the last 2 years (Žižek 2012b). This proximity to political events is in stark contrast with many other so-called 'political philosophies' (on the surface, often far more seemingly accessible and relevant) which often inhabit a purely intra-theoretical or more rarefied academic space (having little or no impact on 'Realpolitik') (Močnik 1993; Mastnak 1988).

One of the key tensions in the book will concern the relation between, on the one hand, the very historically and culturally specific set of circumstances from which this troika of thinkers emerges, the spatio-temporal contingency of their philosophical work, and, on the other hand, the universal appeal and/or validity of the Ljubljana School of Psychoanalysis and their theoretical production. In their introduction to a joint-authored work on opera, *Opera's Second Death*, Dolar and Žižek (2002) make precisely the same point in terms of their struggle to come to terms with the meaning of opera. On the one side, opera as the philosophers see it, and here their models are Mozart and Wagner (Dolar and Žižek 2002), emerges from a specific context and set of coordinates. On the other side, the operas discussed seem to completely transcend their time and place and remain ultimately irreducible to these spatio-temporal aspects. But, of course, the demand should never be simply 'either/or' in such a context. As Žižek and Dolar (2002: vii) note here, 'if we reduce a great work of art or science to its historical context, we miss its universal dimension; apropos of Freud, it is also easy to describe his roots in fin-de-siècle Vienna – much more difficult is demonstrating how this very specific situation enabled him to formulate universal theoretical insights'.

How might we apply this logic of what Zupančič terms 'concrete universality' – simultaneously irreducibly particular and universalist (also, tellingly, her description of the movement of comedy; Zupančič 2008a) – to the work of the Ljubljana troika themselves? Žižek is always keen to undermine any univocal understanding and so we see him, for example, satirizing the international perception of the work in Slovenia, as if there was some local private joke going on. When people come to visit Ljubljana, he says, to see and understand the work of the Lacanian troika, it is 'like getting caught with our pants down': 'it is almost as if we are caught with our pants down when someone comes to Ljubljana; and then we just have to tell him nothing is happening here; there are three of us who simply meet as friends; and that's it' (Žižek and Daly 2003: 37). But simultaneously, of course, it is precisely this friendship which we should take, in a philosophical sense, seriously. Even in 2012, with his latest magnum opus *Less Than Nothing: Hegel and the Shadow of Dialectical Materialism* (Žižek 2012a), the dedication is striking – 'To Alenka and Mladen – because die Partei hat immer Necht', that is 'the Party is always right'. We could read this dedication in different ways and there is a specific reference back to the whole ideological edifice of 'the Party' under state socialism in former Yugoslavia, a history which plays a central role in the genealogy of the 'Slovenian Lacan'. But, there is also the 'party' of the troika themselves, a partnership which, in the case of Dolar and Žižek, extends all the way back to their shared undergraduate philosophy days in the late 1960s. Zupančič becomes part of this story, as a gifted student of both Dolar and Žižek in the 1980s. Since then, she has become very much part of the group in her own right through the 1990s, already publishing under Žižek as editor in English as early as 1992, for example, in *Everything You Always Wanted to Know About Lacan But Were Afraid to Ask Hitchcock* (Zupančič 1992; Žižek 1992b), a volume to which Dolar also contributed several essays. Through the anthologies in the 1990s and up to the monographs in 2000 and after, mostly under Žižek as series editor (e.g., Zupančič 2000; Dolar 2006), the Ljubljana Lacanian troika has become an internationally established entity. As Žižek has noted regarding this nomenclature, 'Here again you have your KGB Stalinist troika; you know how communists were always organised as troika, as units of three, to liquidate people? It's strictly a troika now; with Alenka Zupančič, Mladen Dolar, and myself' (Žižek and Daly 2003: 37). While Žižek remains undoubtedly the most influential and best known of this trio, at least internationally, we will explore how the narrative of the 'Slovenian Lacan' is one which can only be properly understood on a broader and more complex canvas which takes account not simply of the activities and theories of Zupančič, Dolar and Žižek, but also of the wider artistic and intellectual currents in Slovenia and the former Yugoslavia, which became inextricably connected to the political developments during the 1980s and 1990s most especially.

As with the aforementioned hermeneutic of opera then (Dolar and Žižek 2002), so too with the Ljubljana School of Psychoanalysis. We must simultaneously seek to do justice to the (extraordinary) set of particularist circumstances and events which seem to make sense of the evolution of the group's thinking, while also seeking to articulate the ways in which this thought precisely moves beyond such contingent circumstances to embrace a more wholehearted philosophical vision of the world.

Why Lacan?

One of the most interesting and perplexing questions in relation to this intellectual movement is 'why Lacan'? Given the exposure of Žižek and Dolar not simply to Lacan, but also to Althusser, Derrida, Foucault, Kristeva and the whole gamut of what they term the original movement of 'French Structuralism' (Dolar et al. 2014), why was Lacan to become such a dominant influence, to the extent that Žižek refers to his own work as an 'orthodox Lacanianism' (Žižek et al. 2014)? As Dolar has observed to us in an interview, perhaps this was because Lacan 'took it further than any other like thinker . . . brought philosophy to its ultimate conclusion' (Dolar et al. 2014). Of course, the paradox here is that such conclusiveness and orthodoxy, far from generating a sterile or closed system, have given rise to such invigorating and original readings not simply of philosophy, but of political and cultural phenomena. As Žižek observes in his short introduction to the text *Lacan's Silent Partners* (Žižek 2006b), a significant anthology of Lacan's wider philosophical context of influence which Žižek edits, 'the ultimate aim of the volume is therefore not as one usually puts it, to enable readers to approach Lacan in a new way, but rather to instigate a new wave of Lacanian paranoia, to push readers to engage in work of their own, and start to discern Lacanian themes everywhere, from politics to trash culture, from obscure ancient philosophers to Franz Kafka' (Žižek 2006c: 3). This captures the double bind of Lacan's philosophical assault perfectly. It captures the twin sense of absolute seriousness and rigor on the one hand and, on the other hand, the kind of flippant mischievousness for which Žižek (as a self-proclaimed orthodox Lacanian) has become particularly famous, seemingly more interested in causing problems in the mode of an *enfant terrible* than in any serious truth seeking. This has hugely extended the relevance and interest of Lacanianism, and has made the Slovenian school arguably the most influential and thought-provoking group of thinkers not only across the humanities today but also in political theory, psychoanalysis, theology and increasingly in the social sciences or sociology (Kay 2003).

At the same time, it has led other commentators to question the philosophical worth of the Ljubljana School of Psychoanalysis, as if this was all some kind of rather unfunny joke being played at the expense of the intellectual community.

Joking and the unconscious

Rather than po-facedly reject such an accusation outright, it seems more appropriate in this context to, precisely, tell a joke. Or more strictly, to repeat a joke. There are many to choose from in the corpus of Lacan and the neo-Lacanians and, of course, in this methodology of the satirical and the comic, Lacan is being true to his word of a 'return to Freud'. For Freud, 'the joke, like the dream and, to some degree, the parapraxis, expresses a repressed or unconscious wish' (Wollheim 1971: 97) and the significance of the topic of comedy for Freudian psychoanalysis is clear, among other places, in *Jokes and Their Relations to the Unconscious* (Freud 2002b). The texts of the Ljubljana School of Psychoanalysis are strewn with jokes and comic asides, but as Zupančič is the only one of the trio of thinkers to dedicate a full monograph to the topic (Zupančič 2008a), we will employ one of her specific jokes here to lead into some of the key issues at stake.

A man believes that he is a grain of seed. He is taken to a mental institution where the doctors finally convince him that he is not a grain of seed, but a man. No sooner has he left the hospital but he comes back very scared, claiming that there is a chicken outside the door and that he is afraid that the chicken will eat him. 'Dear fellow', says the doctor, 'you know very well that you are not a grain of seed but a man'. 'Of course I know that', replies the patient, 'but does the chicken?' (Zupančič 2008a: 15).

What is the significance of this joke for our analysis? One might link it back to Lacan's own vehement critique of idealism in Seminar XI on *The Four Fundamental Concepts of Psychoanalysis* (Lacan 1994). This is a key seminar for Lacan in several respects, as we will discuss below, but in the context of Zupančič's joke, we might say that what is especially significant is Lacan's critique of psychoanalysis as an 'idealism' or a science concerned simply with the internal effects of 'narcissism' and rather his passionate avowal of psychoanalysis as contributing to an 'encounter with the Real' (Lacan 1994). For Lacan, psychoanalysis of the most authentic 'return to Freud' is one which can and must intervene not simply in individual lives but also sociopolitically. This is also Zupančič's claim here for psychoanalysis, through the method of comedy. As she notes, 'what is at stake in psychoanalysis is not simply becoming conscious of the unconscious, and all that often painfully determines [our] actions and experiences. . . . This is insufficient: the main problem is how to shift and change the very symbolic and imaginary structures in which this unconscious is embodied outside [ourselves]' (Zupančič 2008a: 16).

It is this raison d'être of psychoanalysis which allows us to see a clear connection between Lacan's texts and the work of the Ljubljana School of Psychoanalysis. There is here, for all three thinkers – Dolar, Žižek and Zupančič – the rationale for a generalized attack on what Plato would have called *doxa*, the supposed unquestionable common sense of everyday society. As Sarah Kay (2003: 1) notes, 'what Žižek infects us with is a fundamental doubt about the very presuppositions of our social reality'.

Development of chapters

Chapter 1, entitled 'What *was* Going On in Ljubljana?' takes its cue from a significant essay by Mladen Dolar in the journal *Mladina* in 1989, a key political moment in Slovenia, where Dolar deftly interweaves psychoanalytical and political understanding in his motif or principle of 'The Unconscious is Structured as Yugoslavia' (Dolar 1989). In this chapter, we explore the complex political prehistory to the eventual break-up of the former Yugoslavia into independent states in the 1990s. We focus on the key political tensions between the state socialism of Tito and the developing opposition not only in Slovenia but also in the other federal republics. We also look at the tensions within this opposition itself, between more nationalist and leftist aspects. From a more philosophical perspective, we explore how what became known as the Ljubljana School of Psychoanalysis emerges from a very complex history of development, in relation both to the evolution of philosophy as a discipline in Slovenia and to the wider Yugoslavia and in relation to the alternative culture movements which became so important in the 1980s in Slovenia. In the first case, we trace the key distinction between 'dogmatic' and 'nondogmatic' forms of Marxism, first employed by the Belgrade and Zagreb-based Praxis school of philosophy (Motoh 2012) to distinguish between more humanist and scientific forms of Marxism but which came to be used by the Lacanian orientation in Slovenia as a distinction between Marxism that could connect to radical psychoanalysis and Marxism which could not. The high water mark for this conflict was undoubtedly the *Punk Problemi* issues which we discuss here (Dolar 1982; Žižek 1982; Motoh 2012). In the second case of the relation between the young (Lacanian) intellectuals and the emerging alternative cultures in Ljubljana, we develop the problematic as it extends from punk through to FV 112/15 and video art and finally, and more internationally, to the work of Laibach, IRWIN and the NSK (Gantar 1993; Graziano and Bilic 1993; Monroe 2005). Not the least significant of the thematics of the NSK for our purposes is its foregrounding of the specific problematic of 'Eastern Europe', understood as both an aesthetic and/or philosophical construct which has particular significance in its relation to the often diametrically opposed construct of 'Western Europe' (or 'the West') (IRWIN 1993, 2003a; Dolar 1989). We will see how this thematic is a strong link between the NSK and a similar problematic in the work of the Ljubljana School of Psychoanalysis (although the emphases and conceptual approaches often differ significantly) (Žižek 2003b, 2006c; Dolar 2003).

With this rich and broad canvas of the political and philosophical backstory of ex-Yugoslavia in mind, we then go on, in succeeding chapters, to address the specific interventions of each of the key members of the Ljubljana School of Psychoanalysis to this debate, those interventions, respectively, of Dolar, Žižek and Zupančič. But, before these specialized analyses, in Chapter 2 we explore what we refer to as 'the Lacan effect'. The interpretation of Lacan's texts is a significantly contested problematic and this chapter allows us to explore some of the key issues at stake. We address the relation between psychoanalysis and philosophy in his work, the tensions between his employment, for example, of ancient philosophical sources (going back to the Presocratics [Badiou 2006]), while simultaneously casting aspersions on what he refers to as the 'paranoia' of philosophical and speculative 'system building'. With particular reference to David Macey's controversial but brilliant text, *Lacan in Contexts* (Macey 1988), we explore the often occluded intellectual genealogy of Lacanian psychoanalysis. Here, we follow Macey's critique in his strong emphasis on the relation between surrealism and Lacan, in the varying philosophies of such figures as Bataille (2001) and Klossowski (1991), among others. This allows us to make better sense of Lacan's enigmatic text 'Kant with Sade' (Lacan 2002b) and its important relation to perhaps his most influential and paradigmatic seminar, Seminar VII on

The Ethics of Psychoanalysis (Lacan 1992). Klossowski's rereading of the Sadean legacy is crucial to understanding the complicity between Kantian ethics and Sadean anti-moralism elaborated so elegantly by Lacan. In conclusion, we also look to the affinities between Lacan and Derrida on these questions, especially because an 'ethics of psychoanalysis' as such refuses the 'moralisation of politics', while holding out for what Žižek has recently referred to as the 'political suspension of the ethical' (Žižek 2012a).

This 'Lacan in context' having been mapped out, subsequently allows us to go on to explore the developments of this legacy in each of the individual thinkers in our troika of Žižek, Dolar and Zupančič, which we do in Chapters 3, 4 and 5, respectively. In each instance, we begin our analysis with a critical introduction to the specific thinker's work, followed by an in-depth interview with the philosopher, seeking to articulate a more personal articulation of this complex of issues (with particular reference to the evolution of this complex of issues within the context of the politics of former Yugoslavia). We then follow each interview with a brief concluding analysis which, developing some of the themes raised in the interviews, allows us to contextualize these insights in relation to the philosophers' more systematic work. What emerges from these interviews and critical analysis is the sense of the importance of the work that is being done by the Ljubljana School of Psychoanalysis, its distinctiveness and immense creativity. Against accusations of dogmatism or a sterile orthodoxy, we see that while each member of the group holds to a notion of a Lacanian philosophical and/or a psychoanalytical orientation, that is much more linked to a creative understanding of such a 'positioning' in philosophy, that is, an interventionist strategy in the 'encounter with the Real'. There is also a very strong sense of a philosophical friendship between the three figures (this 'Ljubljana troika' as each describes it) which extends with Dolar and Žižek from the late 1960s right up to the present, with Zupančič's role as an initial student being superseded by her role as a 'collaborator' on equal terms since the early 1990s. This connection of friendship and philosophy (after all, going back to Pythagoras, 'philo-sophia' is a friendship) is key to understanding the work of all three thinkers and has perhaps been underplayed in analyses of Žižek as a more specific figure to date (Kay 2003; although Kay's analysis in itself is excellent). We see how strong the connection remains in the dedication on Žižek's most recent text,

Less than Nothing (Žižek 2012a) and each interview concludes with a looking forward to the 'group work together' rather than to any more isolated understanding. What is perhaps most striking in each of the thinker's work is his and her ability to combine a seemingly esoteric analysis of abstruse philosophical and psychoanalytical topics with a great sense of political and contemporary urgency, as each thinker's work continues to intervene in key (popular) cultural and political debates of great significance (Žižek 2012b), whether we are talking of the Arab Spring or the Occupy Wall Street movement (Žižek 2012b). Here, one is also reminded of the paradigmatic Marxist dimension of the troika (as Dolar notes, 'we remain and have always been Marxists of a certain kind' [Dolar et al. 2014]), of a more 'nondogmatic' than 'dogmatic' mode to reinvoke the distinction made by Dolar and Žižek during the conflicts of the 1980s (Žižek 1981).

In the Epilogue, we return to a key question of Lacan's, that is, 'what will become of this psychoanalysis?' (Lacan 2008), addressing this topic, first, in relation to the affinities between the troika of thinkers and Lacan's original legacy (in all its ambiguity and enigma). And, second, in relation to challenges to this approach of the troika from key critiques in philosophy, for example, most recently in Catherine Malabou's *The New Wounded* (Malabou 2012) and also in terms of a neo-Derridean inheritance (Derrida 2000; Irwin 2010), for example, in the work of Nancy (2005) and Butler et al. (2000). Once more, we will see how psychoanalysis, in its Lacanian version at least (which, on Lacan's terms, constitutes precisely a 'return to Freud'), remains a very significant philosophical intervention in current debates, whether of specific philosophical provenance (the nature of embodiment, sexuality etc.) or in relation to key questions connecting political crises in the world (East vs. West, liberal vs. multiculturalist, feminism, democracy, the Third World, socialism). In such debates, it is clear that the 'forces of destruction' (what psychoanalysis refers to as the 'death drive' [Freud 2002a; Lacan 1994]) may have the upper hand. But it is always to be expected, as Freud pointed out in one of his last and supposedly most pessimistic texts, *Civilisation and Its Discontents* (Freud 2002a), that that great 'adversary' of these forces of destruction, 'immortal Eros', that is Love, should make a final recovery, despite all the appearances of having been defeated: 'And now it is to be expected that the other of the two "heavenly powers", immortal Eros, will try to assert himself in the struggle with his equally immortal adversary' (Freud 2002a: 81). Freud completed these seemingly concluding words of his infamous text in 1930, but thought it imperative to add one last, haunting question in 1931: 'And who can foresee the outcome?' (Freud 2002a: 81).

CHAPTER ONE

What *was* going on in Ljubljana?

'The Unconscious is Structured as Yugoslavia'

On 29 September 1989, the alternative weekly journal *Mladina* featured a humorous half-page article, entitled 'The Unconscious is structured as Yugoslavia' (Dolar 1989). Mladen Dolar, author of the funny metaphor and the article, tried to mockingly show that a contingent selection of Yugoslav places and people contributed to the making of Freud's psychoanalysis. As Freud recalled at the beginning of *The Psychopathology of Everyday Life* (Freud 2010), it was during a debate with a fellow passenger on a train trip from Dubrovnik to some station in Herzegovina that he could not remember the name 'Signorelli'. This incident in analysis provided a key idea for both the *The Psychopathology of Everyday Life* and *The Interpretation of Dreams* (Freud 2009), published only a year earlier. A series of associations that caused the suppression of the Italian painter's name was linked to the topics of death and sexuality and with the awkward and even deadly obsession that, according to Freud, Turks allegedly had with sexual pleasures. In another case, described in *The Interpretation of Dreams* (Freud 2009), Freud recalled that in Montenegrin Kotor, he missed a wonderful opportunity (he never specified what that opportunity was) and the memory of this led him to recall a thought from his dreams that 'one shouldn't miss any opportunity'. There is another reference to the 'locale' in a further analysis of these dreams, namely, Freud recalls an awkward reaction of a certain 'Popović' when he had to present himself with the surname that obviously sounded amusing to a German speaker and linked these dreams to anal connotations. 'Last, but not least', adds Dolar in his article (Dolar 1989), after Turks, Dalmatia, Herzegovina and a Popović, we also find a Slovenian in Freud's biography. In a letter to Weiss, Freud mentions a patient whom Weiss treated for impotence, but eventually realized that he was only pretending to have a problem in order to make some profit. Freud advises Weiss not to waste effort on people like that, for they cannot be analysed, their psyche being led by dynamic relationships that even psychoanalysis was not yet able to understand. The missed opportunity in Montenegrin Kotor, the unanalysable Slovenian imposter and the section of the Herzegovian railway trails, where Freud got his key idea – all these contributed to the system that Freud, a fellow Austro-Hungarian citizen, set up in his subsequent texts. Even more, says Dolar, Yugoslavia and the Balkans *were* in a sense, the unconscious of Freud's Europe, 'a locus of Freudian suppression, a place where everything that a "normal European" must suppress, returns; a weird place of forgotten things and missed opportunities, secrets of sexuality and death, things obscene and anal . . .' (Dolar 1989: 16).

A similar metaphor can be used for the purpose of this book. It cannot be claimed that the making of the Ljubljana School of Psychoanalysis was somehow predetermined by the contingencies of time and place in which it developed. Socialist Yugoslavia has, however, with its own missed opportunities, funny surnames and railway journeys, doubtlessly contributed to the making of the Ljubljana school. The introductory chapter will thus provide a brief overview of the events and trends on the Slovenian cultural scene before and during the intellectual ferment that brought about the Ljubljana School of Psychoanalysis.[1] The heterogeneity of different literary scenes, the intellectual clashes between journals, the sporadic translational undertakings, the variety of cultural happenings and, last but not least, the subtle differences in different kinds of relationships to the official politics and its institutions, all constitute a background from which the Ljubljana School grew.

The choice of the time span in this introduction is, first and foremost, biographical. It begins with the first published articles by

Slavoj Žižek, the oldest of the three protagonists of the Ljubljana School, and ends in the early 1990s, with the first publications by Zupančič on Lacanian topics. In between these two temporal boundaries, the social and political reality in Slovenia had fundamentally changed. The fact that, on the way from the late 1960s to the early 1990s, one state gradually replaced the other might be the most obvious and well known of these changes, but for our intended topic it isn't the most important one. The changes that caused and accompanied the dismemberment of the Yugoslav state also had other consequences; they profoundly changed the cultural and intellectual sphere and their relations to what was going on in Europe and the world.

Waiting for the match to be cancelled

The 1950s and early 1960s in Yugoslavia were a period of economic prosperity and considerable political liberalization. The system of self-management, which differed from the Soviet model of central planning and state ownership of industry, endured through its first decade with reasonable success. The Yugoslav economy also profited from its political position between the two sides of the 'Iron Curtain', being able to export its produce to and establish good economic cooperation with countries from both sides. Yugoslavia started to consolidate its place in the global balance of powers and attempted to become a key member of the Non-Aligned Movement, established in the early 1960s. One of the last obstacles on the path of the political and economic liberalizers was removed in 1966 with the fall from power of their chief opponent, the Minister of the Interior and head of the military intelligence and secret police, Aleksandar Ranković (Pirjevec 1995).

This brief period of liberalization and prosperity ended in the mid-1960s, when – as result of a series of inadequate measures and interventions – an economic crisis began to emerge. Mammoth state firms were unable to survive without extensive funding from the state and many collapsed under the increased pressure of the liberalized economy. Their failure and the stress it placed on the state economy resulted in inflation, a rise in prices, a series of strikes and increasing unemployment rates. During the same period, new political processes started to take place. In the spring and early summer of 1968, in addition to the internal crisis, two international episodes rattled the political scene: the May events in France and the Prague Spring. In July 1968, in response to these international stimuli and as a criticism of the situation within the country, a series of student demonstrations overtook the Yugoslav universities. Students were critical of the negative effects of the economic liberalization, the increasing social differentiation and unemployment rates, a situation that was especially difficult for socially underprivileged students and new graduates. In the capital cities of the federal republics, students took to the streets and occupied universities, establishing autonomous academic zones. Building on the topics that these early demonstrations invoked, a group of intellectuals, gathered around the Praxis movement in Zagreb and Belgrade, began to give the student revolt a larger ideological meaning. The Praxis movement was a group of intellectuals that successfully led the famous Korčula Summer School (1963–74), witnessed the core of the crisis in the bureaucratization of Yugoslav socialism and advocated for the return to the 'young Marx' (Marx 1992a, 1992b) and the idea of praxis. They also strongly opposed the newly emerging nationalisms – although a few decades later, some of them unfortunately changed their mind. The protests against the 'red bourgeoisie' met the fiercest police reaction in Belgrade when in an incident at a 'podvožnjak' (underpass), a couple of students were killed and many were left wounded. The student movement was finally addressed by Tito who managed to calm the students with a (false) promise to consider their proposals.

Another obvious trend during the late 1960s was an increasingly strong emphasis on issues of ethnicity. Allegedly loyal to the official principle of 'brotherhood and unity', nations and nationalities[2] started to emphasize their nationhood and to strive for equal participation in the political sphere – although they did not always agree on how this equality should be achieved. As early as 1966, linguistic movements started to appear; Slovenians and Macedonians opposed the use of Serbo-Croatian as the operational language of the federation, while both Serbs and Croats struggled to achieve a separation of the two languages that were previously considered to be two dialects of the same Serbo-Croat language. The conflicts escalated during 1969, when the Slovenian government first protested against the federal budget priorities in the so-called 'highway affair' and next it was Croat and Serb intellectuals and politicians who got involved in a long series of mutual accusations of burgeoning nationalism. The state also progressively began to be governed according to the nation principle, each nation and nationality being given an equal share of votes, regardless of the difference in their population size (Pirjevec 1995).

Both of the problematic issues, the increased ethnic tensions and the worsening of the economic crisis, were exacerbated during the early 1970s. As we will see, this was a crucial period in the formation of the 'Slovenian Lacan' for both Dolar and Žižek (Dolar et al. 2014). The decade, however, began on an optimistic note. For a while, it seemed that Tito had managed to consolidate the Yugoslav position in world politics. The Lusaka conference of the Non-Aligned Movement established the doctrine of peaceful coexistence that was later accepted by the United Nations (UN) General Assembly in autumn 1970. The importance of the Yugoslav position seemed further confirmed by Nixon's visit and Tito's trip to five European Economic Community (EEC) countries and subsequent visits by Willy Brandt and Queen Elizabeth. Trouble in the internal affairs of Yugoslavia, however, continued to worsen.

Party politics started to change dramatically and, in the first half of the 1970s, it began to shift back towards the centralized model of government and the principle of state control over the economy. A new organizational principle in the economy, that is, 'associated labour', started to emerge in order to counter the liberalized 'firms', and the protagonists of liberalization were progressively being accused of ruining the economic and sociopolitical situation of the state and perverting the system of self-management. Confrontation with the liberals began in 1972 and in the process the leaderships of Slovenia, Serbia, Bosnia and Herzegovina, Vojvodina and Macedonia were replaced. Later, we will see how this return to centralized politics affects Dolar and Žižek's work in the university (Dolar et al. 2014).

The new Socialist Federal Republic of Yugoslavia (SFRY) constitution, ratified in 1974, confirmed the shift towards 'Basic Organizations of Associated Labour' (TOZD) that became the organizational building blocks for the entire political and economic system and also had an electoral function. The 1974 constitution also confirmed the equal representational system for the republics and the collective presidency with a rotating presidency. After the constitution was ratified, the League of Communists of Yugoslavia (LCY) began to reaffirm its central position at the Xth Congress, while also strengthening its link with the army. In preparation for the 'match to be cancelled' – as was the high officials' code for Tito's death (Pirjevec 1995), for the first time after Ranković's fall, the state security agency also started to regain its importance and power. In 1975, a new, stricter penal code was issued, including the much disputed Article 133, concerning so-called 'hostile propaganda' and 'counterrevolutionary activity', euphemisms that served as a pretext for the persecution of political opponents throughout the 1980s. We will see this impacting directly on our philosophical protagonists during the so-called '*Punk Problemi*' affair between 1981 and 1983, with accusations and charges of propagandizing for 'neo-Nazism' (Žižek 1981; Dolar 1982; Motoh 2012).

The mid-1970s brought a new set of problems at the international level. Yugoslav relations with both the USSR and the USA started to deteriorate and the stability of these relations was further shaken by the re-establishment of Yugoslav relations with China, after the end of the Cultural Revolution. Yugoslavia, acting in accordance with its newly established friendship with Hua Guofeng's China, fiercely opposed the Vietnamese invasion of Pol Pot's Kampuchea and thereby provoked the USSR. In his last year of life, Tito tried to settle the dispute with the Soviets, but his May 1979 visit to Moscow was unsuccessful. In the late 1970s, the Non-Aligned Movement also started to be affected by the Soviet–Yugoslav struggle. The rivalry between Tito and Castro, the latter acting on behalf of the Soviet side, escalated at the 1979 Non-Aligned conference in Havana, where the Soviet cause prevailed and the inter-block neutrality of the organization was irretrievably lost (Pirjevec 1995).

The emergence of nationalism

Early in 1980, Tito fell very ill and, in preparation for his death, additional measures were taken to ensure a stable period of transition. The army and the security service were geared up and a 'committee for the defense of the constitutional order' was established to prevent either a foreign intervention or an inside coup. Tito died on 4 May that same year and after his death – and spectacular mourning procedures – old problems started to resurface. The economic crisis worsened and the International Monetary Fund conditioned the new package of loans with demands for harsh economic measures that were largely unsuccessful. One of these was the devaluation of the Yugoslav currency, the *dinar*, against the US dollar, which only further divided the country. The saving measures, however, were not successful and the economic crisis progressively worsened. Different diagnoses were given for the situation: some accused the decentralization process established by the 1974 constitution, some blamed it on the inequalities between the federal republics, some accused the liberalizers' reforms etc. In the early 1980s, nationalist tendencies within the federal republics radicalized, openly nationalistic demonstrations occurred and several books on the topic were published – and consequently banned. Tensions in Kosovo, which at the time was one of the two independent regions within the Serbian federal republic, also started to worsen soon after Tito's death. The demonstrations of Albanians in March 1981 demanded equal rights for the Albanian minority and the change of their status into one of the nations of the federation. The situation got even worse in 1985 when tensions became openly violent in Belgrade and Kosovo. The crucial shift for both Serbian nationalism and the situation in Kosovo happened in February 1986, when Milošević succeeded in taking over the Serbian League of Communists (LC) leadership. The former leadership, which was very critical towards Serbian nationalism, was removed from power and the new orientation in Serbian LC politics became evident in the second half of the decade (Pirjevec 1995; Repe 2002).

In the months following Tito's death, critical intellectuals started to raise the issue of censorship and Article 133 of the penal code that criminalized any so-called 'verbal act' against the integrity of the state. The censorship of publications, however, started to loosen. First, critical books were published on issues such as the post-war labour camps for political prisoners and the role of the Communist Party in the struggle with other political parties during and after World War II. Political critics of the 1950s, such as Djilas, became active again and the first open criticisms of the Yugoslav National Army appeared, combined with the demand for the possibility of an alternative service to the 1-year-long military conscription. In May 1985, at the parade on the 40th anniversary of the establishment of the SFRY, another signal was given to the emerging political and cultural movements: a group of anti-militarist demonstrators showed up at the parade while the state organs refrained from sanctioning their protest (Pirjevec 1995).

While the economic crisis worsened, nationalist tensions grew and emerging alternative political and cultural movements started to appear, which we will see is a crucial aspect of our story about the 'Slovenian Lacan'. As Močnik (1993) and others have described, it was the relationship between the 'alternative culture' (bypassing 'civil society') and the 'younger intellectuals' which, in effect, gave rise to the emergence of Lacanianism as the distinctive aspect of the Ljubljana scene. This Lacanian orientation is present not simply in the philosophical approaches but also, as we will see, in the alternative culture phenomena, most especially and explicitly in Laibach, IRWIN and the Neue Slowenische Kunst (NSK) (Monroe 2005), as well as more implicitly in the earlier punk movements and the FV 112/15 art scene (Motoh 2012).

An important shift marked the official politics of the mid-1980s as well. Within the LCs of the federal republics, most notably in Slovenia and Serbia, a generational shift took place among the high party officials. The new generation of leaders, such as Slobodan Milošević in Serbia and Milan Kučan in Slovenia, grew up after the war and hadn't participated in the partisan movement or in the controversies of the 1940s and 1950s. At the same time, the intellectual elites of the federal republics started to openly promote national issues. Milošević, newly affirmed president of the Serbian LC, managed to turn the orientation of the Serbian LC from a more centralist towards a more nationalist direction. While a more nationalist orientation prevailed in Serbia, political changes started to happen in Slovenia as well. The first attempts at forming political parties (at the time still called 'unions') resulted in the establishment of the Slovenian Peasant Union (SKZ; later to become the Slovenian People's Party) in May 1988, and other similar associations soon followed, all in the space of 2 years. Some of these – the Social Democrats, Democratic Union, Christian Democrats and partly Peasant Union – later joined to form a coalition of oppositional parties, called DEMOS. This restructuring was enabled by the changes made by the Slovenian LC, from the beginning of 1989 onwards. They officially accepted the interpretation according to which the crisis in Yugoslavia was only a symptom of the general crisis of the European socialist countries and they expressed their willingness to give up their political monopoly and introduce political pluralism in order to achieve the democratization of the state and society. The existence of political parties was officially confirmed by the Slovenian parliament in the last days of 1989.

These changes, among other reasons, also increased the tensions between Slovenia and the federation. If, in the late 1980s, it still seemed that the national and inter-federal squabbles could be solved by either centralist intervention – advocated by the Serbian LC – or by confederalist reforms – advocated by Slovenian politics – in 1990, it became painfully clear that a solution to the conflicts was very unlikely. New political parties started to emerge in other republics as well, first in Croatia, where the most prominent of those became the conservative and nationalist Croatian Democratic Union (HDZ), then in Bosnia and Herzegovina, Macedonia, Montenegro and finally even in Serbia, where Milošević's Socialist Party of Serbia became the most prominent. Milošević is a constant reference point for the later philosophical analyses of the Ljubljana School of Psychoanalysis, for example, in Dolar's (2006) paradigmatic text on the 'voice', where Milošević's manipulation of the Serbian mass rally is interpreted as a crucial index for the relation between psychoanalysis and sociopolitical critique (Dolar 2006).

The April elections in Slovenia were won by a coalition of oppositional parties, called DEMOS with Prime Minister Lojze Peterle from the Christian Democrat Party. While former oppositional parties got the majority in the assembly, it was a candidate of the former LC, Milan Kučan, who became the president of the Republic of Slovenia (Žižek never actually ran for the position of president, as is often erroneously supposed).[3] The Slovenian elections were followed by those in Croatia the same month and, later in the year, in all other federal republics. At the end of December 1990, Slovenia held a plebiscite on the question of whether the Republic of Slovenia should become an independent and sovereign state. The result was almost unequivocal: of all Slovenians eligible to vote, 88.5 per cent voted for independence. In January, Slovenia also started to apply measures to cut financial ties with the federal reserves and federal banks and to separately run their tax system and customs (Repe 2002).

The first half of 1991 was marked by preparations for the official proclamation of independence, but at the same time, the first serious ethnic conflicts started to occur all over the SFRY. The proclamation of independence of the Serbian minority in Croatian Krajina in February and the incident in Plitvice in March were followed by the Slovenian refusal to send its soldiers to the Yugoslav Army. These events were a forecast of the armed conflict that started with the short intervention by the Yugoslav People's Army (YPA) in Slovenia in late June of the same year and the following long years of war in Croatia (1991–95), Bosnia and Herzegovina (1992–95), Kosovo (1998–99) and the events in Serbia in 1999. This tragic final phase of the history of the SFRY ended with the Dayton Agreement in 1995 and the UN peacekeeping mission in Kosovo after the North Atlantic Treaty Organization (NATO) intervention in 1999. The former state dismembered to form seven new political entities: Slovenia (1991), Croatia (1991), Federation of Bosnia and Herzegovina (1994), Macedonia (1991), Serbia (2006), Montenegro (2006) and Kosovo (2008).[4]

Genealogies of philosophy in the former Yugoslavia

The political changes during these turbulent years also, unsurprisingly, had a huge impact on the academic institutions and theoretical production. From the first years after the establishment of the Ljubljana University in 1919, philosophy was taught at the Faculty of Arts and this remained the only faculty in Slovenia where it was possible to study philosophy until the establishment of other Slovenian faculties for humanities at the end of the century. The end of World War II and the establishment of the SFRY brought radical changes to the Department of Philosophy, which at the time only consisted of two professors and one teaching assistant. The curriculum included the history of philosophy from ancient Greece to the early modern authors, Slovenian philosophy and noetics (epistemology). Interestingly, it was not until 2 years later, in autumn 1947, that Marxist topics entered the curriculum and were taught by young Cene Logar. After the subsequent imprisonment of Logar during the *informbiro* period, Marxist topics were condensed to form a single course of dialectical materialism and they stayed this way until the early 1950s. During this period, the curriculum thus consisted of the history of philosophy and dialectical materialism, and had not changed much until the mid-1950s when the philosophy department had transformed into the Department for Philosophy and Sociology and some philosophical courses had to give way to sociological ones. The latter also doubled for the courses in Marxism, while explicit dialectical materialism disappeared from the curriculum. This third period ended with the separation of the two departments, which deprived the philosophy department of one of its teachers. This was followed by a period of even greater difficulty for the philosophy department. In 1959/1960, two of its assistants, Taras Kermauner and Veljko Rus, were sanctioned for having participated in the publication of *Revija 57* (*Journal 57*). The journal was confiscated and subsequently forbidden from publishing critical opinions on the official politics and culture in Slovenia and Yugoslavia. Having thereby lost two teachers, and having two more retire in protest at the events, in 1960 the philosophy department was on the verge of being closed down and its students redirected to other faculties in the SFRY. The situation finally started to turn for the better in 1962/1963, when new teachers and assistants took over the courses and the curriculum changed again. Apart from the history of philosophy and philosophical anthropology and/or epistemology, the curriculum also started to include courses in logics and neopositivism and some fairly controversial additions: courses in existentialism and the philosophy of Jean-Paul Sartre. Moreover, the curriculum also started to show the impact of the early 1960 schism that had split the Yugoslav Marxist philosophers into two groups. Namely, at the Fourth Meeting of the Yugoslav Philosophical Association in Bled (Slovenia), the orthodox, dogmatic interpretation of Marxism was confronted with the opinions of the younger generation of Marxists who advocated for the interpretation of Marx through his earlier works, the concepts of alienation and of praxis being thus closer to the ideas of the Frankfurt school. This second group then formed *Praxis*, an association and a journal that was also important for having organized the Korčula Summer School (1963–74). Although the teachers from the Ljubljana Department of Philosophy ended up supporting the 'dogmatic' side of the debate in Bled, the curricular changes still reflected the change of climate in Yugoslav Marxist theory. The dogmatic course of dialectical materialism was replaced by courses in Marxism, Marx's critique of Hegel, the imperative of changing the world in Marx's philosophy etc.

This complex philosophical (but also political) issue of the relation between so-called 'dogmatic' and 'nondogmatic' Marxism returned as a key point of contestation between Dolar, Žižek and the state authorities during the 1970s and 1980s, for example, in relation to the controversy around Žižek's master's thesis (Dolar et al. 2014) and the *Punk Problemi* affair (1981–83) (Motoh 2012). In their editorial for *Problemi* during the crisis with the authorities, entitled 'Punk is a Symptom' (Žižek 1981; Motoh 2012), Dolar and Žižek had actually foregrounded this precise distinction between 'dogmatic' and 'nondogmatic' Marxism in relation to their more affirmative interpretation of the punk movement. This 'nondogmatic' approach to Marxism had also been a perspective which called for a more Lacanian orientation in Marxist analyses, what might be termed Lacanian–Marxism (Žižek 2010; Laclau 1989; Žižek 1989), whereas the 'dogmatic' Marxism (of the state and 'Party') saw the Lacanian method (and French structuralism, more generally) as dangerously heterodox.

In the mid-1960s, Vojan Rus from the Belgrade Institute for the Research of the Workers' Movement came to join the faculty and his tenure also enabled other members to obtain their PhDs and become university teachers. He introduced courses in general dialectics, ontology, gnoseology, anthropology etc., while other new members of the faculty also revived the old courses (e.g. the history of philosophy) and started new ones (e.g., philosophy of the twentieth century and ethics). It was during this period that Slavoj Žižek enrolled in the Faculty of Arts and started his studies. During his pregraduate years, other new courses were also introduced to the philosophy curriculum, most importantly, courses on Husserlian phenomenology and German idealism. Exceptionally, in 1969/1970 a course on structuralism was taught by Boris Majer, but it wasn't repeated until 1975/1976, and this is especially important for our purposes in the light of the very significant influence of 'French structuralism' in the early self-identification of the Ljubljana school (Dolar et al. 2014). In the mid-1970s, the reform of the Yugoslav economy, the 'associated labour system', reached the universities and the departments were renamed 'Pedagogical and Research Units'.

Throughout the 1970s, when Žižek was already a postgraduate and Dolar was doing his pregraduate studies, the curricular changes remained small and subtle. Marxist topics were mostly limited to one or two courses of 'The Introduction to Marxology', courses in early modern philosophy began to be consistently taught almost every year, courses in logics, methodology and positivism were expanding and so were the courses on the philosophy of the twentieth century, sometimes also with additional seminars on chosen topics, for example, on Gramsci and Althusser in 1971/1972 and on Deleuze in 1976/1977. In the late 1970s, Heidegger's work also entered the curriculum explicitly, being first taught in relation to Kant's aesthetics in 1978/1979. All through the 1970s and 1980s, new teachers were joining the faculty but the curriculum remained largely the same, although – interestingly enough – the number of Marxist courses started to rise again steadily through the 1980s. In the mid-1980s, first Dolar and then Žižek started to teach at the department,[5] Dolar as an assistant to the lectures of Božidar Debenjak on Marxist topics and German idealism and Žižek (who had already defended his PhD) at the lectures of early modern philosophy. In addition to the university, many other research institutions also gave jobs to philosophers, sociologists, politologists and the like, the most notable of these being the Marxist centres,[6] institutes of the university and institutes at the Slovenian Academy of Sciences and Arts (SASA). In 1979, the Marxist Institute was founded at the SASA, later (1988) to be renamed the Institute of Philosophy at the Scientific Research Centre of SASA. It gradually became one of the most important institutions for the development of the Ljubljana School of Psychoanalysis (with Žižek and Zupančič particularly being associated with it) (Kalan 2009a, 2009b).

As is evident from this overview, although academic life, especially at the philosophy department (although the same held true for most of the humanities) was under the direct impact of the current politics and the shifts in official ideology in the former Yugoslavia, at the same time it also represented a determined struggle to distance academia from these currents. The purges after the war and during the *informbiro* period and the dismissal of teaching assistants during the *Journal 57* affair in 1959/1960, were juxtaposed by a surprisingly liberal choice of course topics: existentialism in the early 1960s, Husserl in the late 1960s, structuralism in the mid-1970s and Heidegger in the 1980s. It was also crucial that the academic staff that carried out the teaching and research at the philosophy department was at the same time active in translation and journalism and also intertwined with the newly emerging literary, artistic and civil society movements. Whereas the translations were significant from an intra-philosophical perspective (engendering a constant dialogue in Slovenia with contemporary thinking abroad), the journals are especially important in relation to the key connections between the 'young intellectuals' and the successive 'alternative culture' in Slovenia (Močnik 1993), which can be seen in three important phases: punk, FV and the NSK (Motoh 2012).

'I Walked our Land and Got an Ulcer'

In post-war Slovenia, the main open public space for the introduction of new ideas and trends was literary journals. Allegedly focused on literature – or even on youth writing only – these journals soon started to include a more varied selection of genres and topics and reached a much wider readership. One of the first journals of such importance was *Beseda* (*Word*) that was published from 1951 till 1957, when it was suppressed and forbidden. The same group of critical authors started publishing a new journal later the same year, called *Revija 57* (*Journal 57*), only to be forbidden a year later, because of the publication of critical theoretical texts by Jože Pučnik. The third in the series of critical journals, *Perspektive* (*Perspectives*), was first published in 1960, bringing together authors from the two previous journals. Famously, the combination of political critique and contemporary literature managed to endure for 4 years – when it was forbidden – because of the intended publication of some critical texts on the conditions of the Slovenian peasantry and some literary pieces that crossed the line of tolerated criticism, for example, the poem that contained the line 'socialism à la Louis XIV'.[7] When *Perspektive* was suppressed, another journal that had previously stayed mostly within the confines of allowed literary production, *Problemi* (*Problems*), welcomed the group of writers from *Perspektive*. Around 1968, this group – along with a few critical authors from the younger generation – took over the editorial board of *Problemi* and transformed it into the most important journal of its time, introducing avant-garde literature trends (reism, ludism) and establishing links with contemporary artists. Two of the most notable early cooperations of this kind were the late 1960s' publication of OHO-Katalog movement's edition of *Problemi* and the early 1980s' publication of three 'punk' issues of the journal (*Punk Problemi*), where the newly emerging music, art and social movement was given a platform to present its ideas, while being criticized by the mainstream official media (Žižek 1981; Motoh 2012). They also included presentations of other new art groups (i.e., theatre Group 442/443 and their Pupilija Ferkeverk projects) and a special issue presenting the NSK in 1985. In the mid-1970s, the editorial team started to diverge, a trend that became evident during the 1974 polemic between Ivo Urbančič, a thinker of Heideggerian provenance, and Žižek, who at the time had already distanced himself from Heideggerianism and started his work in a Lacanian direction. The loosely defined Heideggerian group left the journal in the early 1980s to establish *Nova revija* (*The New Journal*), while *Problemi* was progressively shifting towards structuralism and – later – a specifically Lacanian orientation (Dolar et al. 2014). Especially during the 1970s, the membership of the editorial boards of the few critical journals greatly overlapped, of which Žižek's and Dolar's participation in that decade are very good examples. They both participated in the publication of *Problemi*, Žižek since the late 1960s, Dolar since the mid-1970s; they were active in the publication of the Ljubljana students' journal *Tribuna*; they joined the newly established journal *Časopis za kritiko znanosti, domišljijo in novo antropologijo* (*Journal for the Critique of Science, Imagination and the New Anthropology*) in the mid-1970s; and they published their articles in many other journals. The Institute of Marxist studies/ Institute of Philosophy at the Scientific Research Centre of SASA also published a journal, called *Vestnik* (later *Filozofski Vestnik*), in which Zupančič and other authors, who were associated with the Ljubljana school (Riha et al.) were very active as well. While it is often thought that the 1989 publication of *The Sublime Object of Ideology* (Žižek 1989) represents the virgin moment of the Ljubljana School of Psychoanalysis, we see here that the translation into English, at this time, of their work was already somewhat of a late development, with a significant pre-history (Dolar et al. 2014; Žižek et al. 2014).

In the late 1970s, after the divergence from the Heideggerian group, *Problemi* became the key journal for the new structuralist and Lacanian tendencies. They published translations and articles by a wide group of authors, which gradually started to differ in their interpretations of these new trends. It wasn't until the mid-1980s, however, that the Lacanian group started to publish their work in a separate yearly journal, called *Razpol*, with the subtitle *The Journal of the Freudian Field*. The first editions, published from 1985 on, gathered a wide group of authors but were already edited by what was later to be considered a part of the core group of Lacanian authors: Slavoj Žižek, Mladen Dolar, Rado Riha and Miran Božovič. Apart from these four editors, the journal regularly published articles by Jelica Šumič-Riha, Eva Bahovec, Renata Salecl, Alenka Zupančič, Marcel Štefančič, Stojan Pelko and Zdenko Vrdlovec. The whole list of authors who published in the *Razpol* issues before 1991 is much longer, but the number and array of authors rapidly decreased in the process of shaping the core group within the Ljubljana School of Psychoanalysis. A diverse group of authors focused on a very varied range of topics and decades later they ended up pursuing very different careers. Apart from Žižek, Dolar and Zupančič, some of the *Razpol*'s authors stayed in the academy, while others continued their work in other spheres.

It was around these journals that the new generations of thinkers gathered and introduced ideas of existentialism, critical theory, structuralism, psychoanalysis and many other new philosophical and cultural trends. It was the publication of these ideas that provided a public space, where almost complete freedom of expression was sporadically allowed, although on occasions severely supervised and criticized by the regime. The relationship that the journals had with the official line after the persecution of *Perspektive* was very complex, but mostly they managed to keep a fine balance, being sometimes sharply critical, but still avoiding direct persecution or prohibition. This strategy did not, however, always succeed, and the official structures used many different tactics to obstruct their work. *Problemi* and *Tribuna* were repeatedly criticized for engaging with the new critical movements. *Tribuna* was targeted after the student demonstrations in 1971, when one of its authors, Frane Adam, was accused of having displayed an anti-regime slogan. Subsequently, the publication of the journal was obstructed for a few months.[8] In the early 1980s, *Problemi* and its editor Mladen Dolar were accused of having supported the alleged Nazi-punk movement by publishing *Punk Problemi* (Dolar et al. 2014). We will return to the question of this specific situation later, in the discussion of Dolar's philosophy.

The publication of these critical journals was also of great importance because they regularly included translations of foreign authors, often long before they were published in book format. The first wave of such translations was done in the 1960s with the translations of the still partly controversial existentialist authors, Sartre and Camus. The most important wave of translations, however, followed from 1970 onwards. That year alone brought the translations of texts by Horkheimer, Marcuse, Althusser, Husserl, Heidegger, Saussure, Derrida, Orwell's *Animal Farm* and also the first post-World War II translation of Nietzsche (*Birth of Tragedy*).[9] Even before these texts were translated into Slovenian, some of them were available in other Yugoslav languages, notably in Croatian, Serbian and Bosnian editions. Throughout the 1970s and 1980s, these translations were followed by those of Foucault, Deleuze, Guattari, Adorno, Gramsci and Balibar and by a whole range of translations of Freud, Lacan and Alain-Miller.

'Gentlemen comrades, I don't believe you'[10]

The journals also provided a link that proved crucial for the development of critical thought from its beginnings in the 1950s to the development of structuralist, post-structuralist and Lacanian theories, namely, a link between theory and literature/arts. The critical journals of the 1950s, 1960s and 1970s all began as literary journals and then opened to topics of literary theory and criticism, philosophy, art theory and, finally, socio-political discussions. More importantly, the same authors were often active in many of these genres.

The *Problemi* group stayed true to the paradigm of cultural involvement of their predecessors, but took it even further. It was not only literature that they included, but they also connected with the new developments within the art scene, the first example of which was the cooperation with the OHO group in the 1960s. In very broad terms, in the history of Slovenian art, the OHO group marks the shift from modernism to avant-garde, the same change being represented in the differences between the journals *Perspektive* and *Problemi*. Žižek also contributed his texts to these publications.

These journals and their editorial boards were also active in the next great wave of alternative culture movements of the early 1980s, which can be schematically divided into three interconnected trends: the punk movement, FV 112/15 and Laibach/NSK (Motoh 2012).

All happening at the same time, in the early 1980s, these three trends were not only a sharp break with the avant-garde movements of the 1960s and 1970s, but also a unique reflection of the contemporary Yugoslav political, economic and social crisis. In the second half of the 1970s, as a reflection of the current political and economic issues and only a few years after the first British punk bands, a group of youngsters gathered to form the first Slovenian punk band, *Pankrti* (Bastards). Provoked by openly critical songs such as *Comrades, I don't believe you* or *Total revolution (. . . is not a solution)* and by the provocative behaviour of young punkers, the state organs started to repress, censor and persecute the protagonists of the movement. This repression reached its peak in 1981 with the 'Nazi-punk affair', when a group of youngsters were arrested under fabricated charges of having established a national socialist party, and many more were questioned and harassed. Nevertheless, in the few years following *Pankrti*'s first concert in 1977, many new groups sprung up and, by the early 1980s, the punk movement was widespread in Ljubljana and other cities. In the same year, the new movement was given space to present themselves in the journal *Problemi*, in the aforementioned special edition called *Punk Problemi* (Dolar 1982; Žižek 1981; Motoh 2012). The second of the three special editions, issued in 1982, caused great upheaval, when the editors of the issue refused to quietly censor parts of the lyrics that were printed in the journal, but instead published pages with black spots marking the censored parts. This was simply too provocative for the official line, and Dolar, the editor of *Problemi* at the time, was accused of having allowed the publication of pornographic material, and forced to pay a fine (Dolar et al. 2014). Judged as an anticultural phenomenon by the right-wing opposition and as a fascist and destructionist tendency by the left-wing pro-regime literati, the punk movement functioned as a more radical version of the newly emerging social movements that sought reforms and change with their pacifist, ecological, feminist and other programmes (Močnik 1993).

While the punk movement consisted mostly of very young people, another related art and cultural movement, represented mostly by students, appeared at the same time. Group FV 112/15 started off as an alternative theatre and allegedly got their enigmatic name by randomly choosing among slogans from the dictionary of loan words (known by the name of its author as 'France Verbinc') and ending up with 'c'est la guerre', printed in France Verbinc (thus 'FV') on page 112, line 15. Soon, this group – Neven Korda, Zemira Alajbegović, Marina Gržinić, Dušan Mandič, Aldo Ivančić, Dario Sereval et al. – managed to take over a students' disco club in Ljubljana for one night per week. On Tuesdays, and gradually on all other days as well, they replaced rock music of the 1960s and 1970s with the current trends in punk and new wave. Mixing music with video production, this club became the hub of the new alternative production and an instant hit among the young alternative crowd in Ljubljana and remained an important platform for new art and culture, although it frequently came under official pressure and was forced to move locations. Different alternative movements started to appear in connection with FV 112/15, most notably the movement against the discrimination of homosexuals, a unique phenomenon in Yugoslavia and the communist part of Europe at the time. Apart from special gay/lesbian nights in Disco FV, they also organized Magnus, a festival of gay and lesbian film in 1984. At the time, homosexual sex was still illegal in some parts of Yugoslavia and taboo in others. Disco FV and its activities also provided a space for the development of new art genres, specific for this generation of artists: they introduced video art and graffiti art, while also exploring the relation between art and pornography and introducing pornographic material into art forms. Some members of the FV group also formed an alternative music band, *Borghesia* that defined itself as a multimedia project, combining music with video art, using new tools such as video home systems (VHS) and computers. It was, however, video art that determined most of the activities of this generation of artists. Other genres included Xerox collage and graffiti, both frequently subversive in their form and content.

The third movement that shocked Slovenia and Yugoslavia at the time was the new music group Laibach, started in 1980 (Monroe 2005). Later, it joined its affiliated groups, the painters' collective IRWIN, the group of designers Neue Kunsthandlung/Novi kolektivizem and the Sisters Scipion Nasice Theatre to form the NSK in 1984 (Monroe 2005). If FV was subversive for its popularity, choice of video genre, use of pornography and its affiliation with the gay movement, and punk was subversive for its youth rebellion, Laibach and later the whole NSK were considered the most dangerous because of their deliberate use of Nazi symbolism, an act that went against the total prohibition of Nazi symbols in post-war

Yugoslavia. The name Laibach was already indicative, for they had chosen the name that was used for Ljubljana during its occupation by the Germans in World War II. Questioning the interlacing of art and ideology, they played with the old symbols in completely new contexts, thus inventing the alleged new art movement, called retrogardism. We will see below how this approach to Slovenian art, just as with the Ljubljana School of Psychoanalysis, broadly follows a Lacanian orientation (Močnik 1993).

Their first performances, using forbidden symbols, German phrases, army smoke bombs (in Belgrade in 1982) and other provocations, provocatively caused criticism among the state organs and resulted in a series of measures being taken against the Laibach activities, most notably from early 1983 onwards. The City committee of the Socialist Union of Working People of Ljubljana demanded that Laibach should obtain permission from the city of Ljubljana to use its German name, which de facto meant that Laibach was officially forbidden to perform in public. The same year, marked by a deliberately arrogant television interview that caused another wave of criticism, also saw the beginning of two affiliated artist groups, designers' Neue Kunsthandlung (also known as *Novi kolektivizem* [New collectivism]) and a theatre group *Gledališče sester Scipion Nasice* (Scipion Nasice Sisters' Theatre). In 1984, all these joined to form a collective and gave it a provocatively German name *Neue Slowenische Kunst* (Monroe 2005). The Scipion Nasice Sisters' Theatre, which borrowed the name from the Roman consul who had allegedly abolished theatre, also planned for its own dissolution 4 years later, and had in the meantime staged four major 'retrograde' theatre events. The first two, *Hinkemann* (1984) and *Marija Nablocka* (1985), staged in private apartments in Ljubljana, were followed by *Krst pod Triglavom* (1986) and the last one, *Day of Youth* in 1987, which was a reference to the widely criticized official celebrations of Tito's birthday. All through the early 1980s, following Tito's death and the overblown official mourning, young intellectuals, particularly in Slovenia, started to question the meaning of perpetuating the annual Day of Youth celebration that consisted of a rally of youth, a ceremony of a torch being carried all over Yugoslavia, and a final colossal celebration in a stadium in Belgrade. In 1987, during a wide debate on the proposals for the abolishment of the Relay of Youth ceremonies, another scandal broke out in connection with the NSK collective. Its designers' subgroup, Neue Kunsthandlung/Novi kolektivizem, participated in a competition for the poster for the 1987 Relay of Youth and won with a poster that was actually a remade version of a Nazi propaganda poster by Richard Klein. The initial enthusiasm of the selecting commission was overshadowed when the reference was revealed by an unknown Serbian engineer, and the group, together with the Slovenian Youth organization leaders that initially chose the poster, became targets of a widespread attack against 'fascist elements', a sort of repetition of the Nazi-punk affair and the initial criticisms of Laibach in the early 1980s.

Conclusion

The story of the break-up of the former Yugoslavia is a story that is only told here through a very selective and narrow lens, with the particular focus on the Ljubljana School of Psychoanalysis and their connection to the specific alternative culture in Slovenia, from the punk movement through to the NSK (Motoh 2012; Monroe 2005). Tracing some of the key political factors which eventually led to the independence of each of the former federal republics of Yugoslavia, we have seen how these were accompanied by acute cultural and philosophical developments and here our focus has been mainly on the interpretation of the 'Slovenian Lacan'. Following Rastko Močnik's (1993) analysis, it is clear that this Lacanianism emerges as the distinctive feature of the political–intellectual landscape in Slovenia, and is accompanied by the unusual relationship between alternative culture and civil society, as well as the almost unique relationship between a generation of young intellectuals and the alternative cultures, whether of punk, FV or the NSK.

Močnik's meta-level analysis of the relation between theory and politics is crucial here. We should note Močnik's own seminal role in the developments in Ljubljana, being originally the very last co-editor with the poet Tomaž Šalamun (author of the infamous counter-cultural poem *Duma*) of the journal *Perspektive* before it was shut down by the Communist regime. After doing a PhD in Paris, Močnik returned to Ljubljana, becoming editor of the journal *Problemi* and working closely with both Dolar and Žižek, to whom he remains a close collaborator. Močnik's text in this context, entitled 'How we were fighting for the victory of reason and what happened when we made it' (Močnik 1993) is very instructive in this regard, again pointing to the specificity and peculiarity of some of the Slovenian responses to the problematic, very much focusing, at a certain point, on the Lacanian philosophy as crucial to their purposes. As Močnik observes, 'the theoretical history of the last two decades can be represented by a series of dichotomies (represented by their main authors) that led to a dead-end, and the dead-end was again broken by the discontinuous intervention of a subversive text' (Močnik 1993: 89). What is interesting especially about this perspective is the way that it foregrounds the theoretical history as so key, a thematic we also see in Gantar (1993), Motoh (2012) and Mastnak (1988). In the Introduction, we asked what seemed to us a decisive question in this intellectual history: 'Why Lacan?'. Here, with regard to the intra-theoretical conflicts within the original take-up of French structuralism in Ljubljana, which Dolar will refer to in detail in his interview (Dolar et al. 2014), Močnik argues as follows: 'For instance, Derrida falls short of his critique of Husserl; he is unable to valorise the formalistic dimensions of phenomenology; in this way his anti-metaphysical verve makes him overlook the very nonmetaphysical moments in Husserl. Derrida fell victim to his own activism, we could call it "theoretical leftism"' (Močnik 1993: 89). This rather peculiar take on Derrida is somewhat shared by the troika of thinkers, Dolar, Žižek and Zupančič. They see something different in Lacan, something unique, which is where the affirmation of an 'orthodox Lacanianism' (so strange to non-Lacanians) becomes clearer and somewhat more understandable. What is key here is also the manner in which Derrida's work (and the wider movement of French structuralism), both philosophically and politically, is seen as leading to a 'dead end' (Močnik 1993: 85). In contrast, Lacan and Lacanianism are seen as leading beyond this impasse and paralysis. Močnik's description here is paradigmatic to understanding the move made by Žižek and Dolar in the 1970s towards Lacan, but it also shows how this Lacanian movement was more generalized in the alternative theoretical circles in Slovenia: 'the intervention of Lacan was decisive; it enabled us to reformulate in a theoretically productive way the seeming dead-ends of the previous theories. Against the dead-end formulas, I put first the Lacanian concepts that break the dead-end, and then the positive reformulation of the impasse' (Močnik 1993: 88). This is brilliantly and decisively expressed here; breaking through the dead ends and reformulating the impasse; and this was only possible through Lacanianism. Significantly, Močnik opposed the dissolution of Yugoslavia and independence for Slovenia and the other federal republics in 1991, but precisely on Lacanian grounds.

But how did this Lacanian intervention, so radically and persuasively articulated here, work in the longer term? As Gantar has powerfully shown, the complex relation between civil society and alternative culture was to have an influence even beyond independence. For Gantar, going all the way back to the late 1960s' eruption of dissent (and even through the political journals of the 1950s and 1960s), there was a sense of a 'legitimate' space for criticism of state socialism. This 'liberalizing' tolerance towards dissent was meant to be a sign of the greater political freedoms available under the Yugoslav regime of Tito (e.g., as compared to the Soviet bloc). There was, of course, a partial truth to this liberalization; as Dolar puts it in his later essay on punk and civil society (Dolar 2003), 'we cannot pretend we were Czechoslovakia'. The 1968 and 1971 university struggles were examples of this relatively liberal tolerance in Ljubljana (Dolar et al. 2014), as well as the 'critique of the red bourgeoisie' (Gantar 1993) which seems to have come from civil society movements.

However, this appearance of the liberal civil society in Yugoslavia also masked what Gantar (1993) refers to as the attempted 'colonisation of the life world'. In other words, even the possibility or conditions of dissent were kept under strict regime control and 'civil society' became the receptacle for such forms of resistance which could then be effectively 'colonised' by the state. Gantar, for example, in his 'Discussions on Civil Society in Slovenia' speaks of the political colonization of the life world in Yugoslavia, which 'effectively obliterated civil society' (Gantar 1993: 358). According to Gantar, 'they [the regime] were not satisfied with economic and political subordination of the population but set about cultural subordination and the capturing of souls, bedrooms and social life as their next goal' (Gantar 1993: 357). In such a context, the new forms of social movement or alternative culture 'actually signified a new form of society, not infected by official ideology and politics' (Gantar 1993: 357).

This interpretation (important in understanding the pre- and post-independence contexts) is articulated by Gantar, Močnik and also by others such as Mastnak (1988) in his theory of 'social implosion' and Zgaga (1991) in his critique of 'politics as domination' under so-called democracy. Each of these readings, in different ways, foregrounds both the importance of the space of a genuinely 'alternative culture' not reducible to civil society (Motoh 2012), while also calling attention to some of the limitations of the 'national independence movements', which in the case of Slovenia, were to lead to official nationhood in 1991. In the measure to which these movements, which explicitly sought independence and foregrounded the 'nation', stemmed more from civil society than from the alternative culture (the latter, for example, the NSK [Monroe 2005], being famously more ambivalent on the values of socialism and/or nationalism), we can perhaps foresee some of the political, cultural and philosophical issues which would remain after the break-up of the former Yugoslavia. In the conclusion to his important essay, Gantar (who was to go on to have an important role in independent Slovenia as a politician) also looks at the more long-term picture of the relation between state, civil society and the other space inhabited by some aspects of the counter-culture, reflecting on the processes after 1991 independence: 'civil society has not disappeared since independence but come more to the fore . . . we can say that there are dangerous pitfalls when civil society initiatives "unmediated" become the ruling idea in politics' (Gantar 1993: 365).

Tomaž Mastnak, in his influential essay, 'The implosion of the social' (Mastnak 1988) connects this thematic of the limits of civil society in the former Yugoslavia to the question of the whole construct of 'Eastern Europe' as it is viewed by Western intellectuals, right or left. This thematic of 'Eastern Europe' is, of course, also key for the NSK, and especially in the cases of Laibach and IRWIN (Monroe 2005). 'My question is how does Eastern Europe function in a particular Western European discourse? What kind of constellation produces such functioning and what are the theoretical implications [which] such functioning of Eastern Europe has?' (Mastnak 1988: 113). Mastnak thematizes again some of the distinctions made between alternative culture and civil society, here offering some criticism of what he sees as the avant-garde opposition for opposition's sake. As Mastnak notes, 'what must become fundamental for us is initiation, not dissidence; that is, we should consider ourselves first and foremost as initiators of future possibilities and not as subversives; dropouts, rebels who are anti-a, anti-b and anti-c' (Mastnak 1988: 124). Again, in a manner related to the criticism of the 'colonisation of the life-world' (Gantar 1993) in the former Yugoslavia, including its supposed spaces of resistance and system critique, which Gantar, among others, has put forward, Mastnak seems to be looking for other alternatives here: 'We should leave resistance and repression to the ruling powers and transform our opposition into an increasingly clear position' (Mastnak 1988: 124). Strikingly, it is the Lacanian philosophy which provides this Slovenian political intellectual with his framework for transformation. Mastnak here is more vehement than the other critics cited in his critique of 'socialism' as such, but he shares the Lacanian perspective: 'In order to escape the split in the Real, we struggle in reality. . . . Socialism is an almost perfect example of a political project or system which cannot face its own limitations and incapacity . . . and which almost pathetically takes refuge in struggles in reality; a symptom of this pathology is the continual invention of internal and external enemies; enemies are the only true love of socialism' (Mastnak 1988: 124). There is a great irony here if we think back to the previous attempts by the state to interpret alternative culture, whether punk, FV or the NSK, as a 'symptom' of 'fascism'. Now the symptom critique is turned back against the system itself.

Of course, as we have seen, this critique and wariness of the 'official' civil society (under state socialism) was the very driving force of the Slovenian alternative culture from the beginning. As Dolar observes about the NSK, and he might equally have said this of punk, 'the NSK equally scoffs at socialism and the dissenters' (Dolar 2003). Crucially for our purposes, Dolar might equally have said this of the political–philosophical perspective of the Ljubljana School of Psychoanalysis. As we will see in the following chapters, which focus on interviews and critical analysis with Dolar, Žižek and Zupančič, each of these thinkers in their own way is alert to the simultaneous limitations of state socialism and contemporary, supposedly 'democratic', global capitalism. For each of the thinkers, Lacanianism provides the privileged philosophical perspective to deconstruct the 'short circuiting' (Žižek 2005) of the system, what Močnik has spoken of more generally as the 'breakthrough' of Lacan, working through the 'impasse' of French structuralism (Močnik 1993). For the respective thinkers, different concepts become foregrounded: for Dolar, cogito and voice; for Žižek, ideology;

and for Zupančič, ethics and comedy. But each of these individual intellectual journeys testifies to the fecundity of psychoanalysis as a philosophical and a political-cultural framework for understanding both our contemporary malaise and how we have come to be in such a malaise. Here, we can see the problematics of the Ljubljana School of Psychoanalysis come full circle from the work and the crises with the alternative culture in the 1970s and 1980s. We can relate this problematic back to the 'Nazi scandal' of the *Punk Problemi* issues we discussed above, for which Dolar as editor was charged with publishing pornography and supporting Nazi or 'fascist propaganda' (Motoh 2012). This attempt by the state to 'stigmatise' the punk movement with the accusation of fascism would eventually fail. As Gantar notes, 'the attempt to stigmatise punk with fascism was never successful, even though Igor Vidnana was imprisoned for 30 days' (Gantar 1993: 362). With reference to the role of Dolar (who had to appear and speak in court) and Žižek, among others, Gantar clarifies that 'the reason for the failure was a specific liaison between the punk alternative scene and the younger intellectuals' (Gantar 1993: 361–2).

In a philosophical text on fascism published during this period, Dolar notes strikingly that the historical heritage of fascism is preserved 'not in those movements or regimes that seem most similar by their appearance, but lives on in late capitalism as such' (Dolar 1982: 31; Motoh 2012). The key question, according to the author, is thus: 'how does fascism continue today with different means?' (Dolar 1982: 31). And if we can say that fascism is a metaphor for capitalist society, what metaphor is socialism reflected in? (Motoh 2012: 292). We could argue that these remain the key questions today for the Ljubljana School of Psychoanalysis, both as political questions and as questions with regard to the psychic register of the enigmatic subject.

CHAPTER TWO

The Lacan effect

Introduction

Even respected commentators on the original work of Jacques Lacan admit that, at least to the uninitiated, his writings can appear almost impossibly daunting (Homer 2005; Bowie 1991; Macey 1994). His contemporary, Jacques Derrida, in an infamous exchange of essays, portrayed Lacan's work as systematically hermetic, interpreting the labyrinthine Lacanian prose as a protection against reductionistic meaning and epistemology (Derrida 1988). For Derrida, whose own reputation for difficulty is significant, what lies behind the Lacanian question of style is a 'critique of semanticism' enacted through the text: 'The general question of the text is at work unceasingly in his [Lacan's] writings, where the logic of the signifier disrupts naive semanticism and Lacan's style was constructed so as to check permanently any access to an isolatable content, to an unequivocal, determinable meaning beyond writing' (Derrida 1988: 176).

Given this fact, one of the most curious aspects of the subsequent influence of Lacan's work is that such an esoteric example of the original movement of French structuralism (the term constantly invoked by Žižek et al. to denote that emergent philosophy of the 1960s) (Žižek et al. 2014) will come to have such a significant impact not simply intra-theoretically but also in a practical-political context, on succeeding thought and history. The influence of Lacan and Lacanianism on succeeding radical political thought in France and beyond has been immense. From within France, there are the influences, for example, on Badiou, Balibar and Rancière (Badiou

2009; Balibar 2007). Within the ambit of post-Marxist theory, there is the influence on Mouffe and Laclau, among others (Laclau 1989). And, finally, among our troika of thinkers, we also see this influence which, as Močnik has shown very well, also extended to an interventionist relation to the wider political and social movements in Slovenia (Močnik 1993).

How can such a paradoxical 'Lacan effect' be understood? In this chapter, we will set the scene for the microanalysis of each of our troika of thinkers and interviews with Žižek, Dolar and Zupančič which follows, by contextualising this moment of Lacanianism within the work of Lacan's own thought. Here, we will make reference not only to commentators on Lacan (Homer 2005; Bowie 1991; Macey 1988, 1994) but also to Lacan's own texts, most notably Seminar VII, *The Ethics of Psychoanalysis. 1959–1960* (Lacan 1992), Seminar XI, *The Four Fundamental Concepts of Psychoanalysis* (Lacan 1994) and Seminar XX, *On Feminine Sexuality. The Limits of Love and Knowledge, 1972–1973. ENCORE* (Lacan 1998). In particular, we will focus on Seminar VII, arguably Lacan's most important and influential work in the longer term, as well as the latter's relation to Lacan's enigmatic essay on ethics published in the *Écrits* (Lacan 2002a), entitled 'Kant with Sade' (Lacan 2002b). We will see, in the interviews, that each of our troika of thinkers privileges not only the sense of an orthodox Lacanianism but also the sense that psychoanalysis, as one understands it, is first and foremost a kind of philosophy (Dolar et al. 2014). This will also highlight Freud's original sense of psychoanalysis and its already problematic relation to philosophy, which we will discuss in brief. We will also look to a later relation, that between Lacan and Derrida (a famously problematic relation), to foreground some of the meta-level issues between philosophy and Lacanian psychoanalysis (Derrida 1988; Hurst 2008).

In conclusion, we will speak to the original development of Lacan in Slovenia, the emergence of the Slovene Lacan. We have already looked at this issue in the first chapter from a more sociopolitical and culturalist perspective. In the discussion of the Neue Slowenische Kunst (NSK), we also developed some key points about how this thematic was developed in a more artistic context. But philosophically and conceptually, the Slovenian troika or the Ljubljana School of Psychoanalysis brings something new to the table. Their elaboration of Lacanian concepts and a conceptual framework is thus faithful to Lacan, while it is also developing in originally important directions.

Interpreting Lacan

We will see in the next three chapters the crucial conceptual interpretations of Lacan provided by our troika of thinkers, Žižek, Dolar and Zupančič. But we will also see how specific this interpretation is and how it evolves to a great extent from the particular dynamics of the Ljubljana and Slovenian contexts of politics and interpretation. We have seen in Chapter 1, in a different way, how the NSK evolve a version of Lacanian analysis more suitable to the artistic context of activity, and how this becomes simultaneously, especially polemical and complex (the 'interrogation machine' of the NSK as Monroe well describes it, becoming an 'interrogation of interrogation' [Monroe 2005]).

But the influence of Lacan extends beyond the Ljubljana troika and the NSK, and, in contemporary philosophy, it is perhaps surprising that this influence has been so strong. One key figure in contemporary French philosophy, whose influence has also extended more globally in recent years, is Alain Badiou (2009). Although not an orthodox Lacanian in the same manner as the troika, Badiou's work demonstrates a powerful Lacanian element which, not unlike the troika, also sees this emphasis as compatible with a radical form of contemporary Marxism and political analysis.

In his passionate obituary of Lacan, Badiou helps us to understand what for him are the most radical moments of Lacan, which (in Badiou's eyes) remain both repressed and misunderstood at the time of his death, but which also point the way to the future development of this thinking (with or perhaps beyond Lacan) (Badiou 2009). Indeed, especially with reference to Badiou's discussion of 'ethics' in Lacan's work, which he sees as paradigmatic in its 'intractability', we see the way forward for the elaboration of Badiou's own seminal text, *Ethics* (Badiou 2000). This latter text can also be seen to intersect in its interests and problematics, some of the very themes which have been elaborated by Žižek, Dolar and Zupančič in their more politically oriented work. In his most recent text, for example, *Less Than Nothing: Hegel and the Shadow of Dialectical Materialism* (Žižek 2012a), and with specific reference to the troika as a group and to an affinity between the troika and Badiou, Žižek refers to the need for a 'political suspension of the ethical' (Žižek 2012a). We can see this as a reading which shows the influence of Lacan's *The Ethics of Psychoanalysis* (Lacan 1992), on Žižek, as well as the influence of Kierkegaard's three stages of existence, a Kierkegaardian dialectic which is becoming increasingly significant for Žižek (2012a).

What, therefore, represents for Badiou the key intervention of Lacan, what we are calling the 'Lacan effect'? Peter Hallward, for example, has elaborated the complexity of Badiou's lineage in his philosophy, drawing on many sources in philosophy and mathematics, but the influence for Hallward of Lacan is clear (and Hallward's introduction to Badiou's ethics is also useful in this regard) (Hallward 2000, 2003). In the first case, and against much of the popular view of Lacan as a kind of obscurantist, Badiou makes the claim for Lacan as a radical, a genuinely radical thinker, 'on the warpath from the very beginning' (Badiou 2009: 1): 'it is a fact that Lacan was on the warpath right from the start, denouncing the illusory consistency of the "ego", rejecting the American psychoanalysis of the 1950s which proposed to "reinforce the ego" and thereby adapt people to the social consensus and arguing that, because it is symbolically determined by language, the subject is irreducibly the subject of desire, and as such cannot be adapted to reality except perhaps in the imaginary' (Badiou 2009: 1).

We will see, in succeeding chapters, that the thematic of 'desire' is crucial for Lacan's early work and it is perhaps the most important theme in psychoanalysis more generally. However, we will also see that the concept of 'desire' shifts in importance and interpretation from the early to the later Lacan texts. This rereading of desire will have a very significant bearing on, for example, the status of what becomes known as the 'ethics of psychoanalysis', referring back to Lacan's seminar of the same name, Seminar VII (Lacan 1992). We will also see this crucial relation between 'desire' and the later developing concept of 'drive' as central to the Ljubljana troika's understanding of the relation between ethics and psychoanalysis. This is especially the case, for example, with Zupančič's work on the 'ethics of the Real' (Zupančič 2000). The discussion of the relation (a relation of irreducible tension) between 'desire' and 'drive' is also central to Lacan's development of thought from Seminar XI, *The Four Fundamental Concepts of Psychoanalysis* (Lacan 1994) to Seminar XX, *On Feminine Sexuality. The Limits of Love and Knowledge, 1972–1973. ENCORE* (Lacan 1998).

Here, in his obituary of Lacan, Badiou gives a helpful contextualization of the rereading of desire in the later texts of Lacan, against his earlier thinking. Badiou tells us that 'desire has no substance and no nature; it has only a truth' (Badiou 2009: 2). One of the aspects of this analysis which is also highlighted, for example, by Terry Eagleton in his *Figures of Dissent* text (Eagleton 2003), is that the message which Lacan is putting forward is not a harmonious one for the 'human condition'. Eagleton refers to it as a kind of 'secularisation of the original sin notion' (Eagleton 2003). Badiou, for his part, concurs with Eagleton, referring to Lacan's specific reinterpretation of Freudianism as a 'particularly bleak vision of psychoanalysis': 'his particularly bleak vision of psychoanalysis in which it is the truth and not happiness which is in play' (Badiou 2009: 3). This meta-level reading of Lacanianism will also be important for us in terms of situating Lacan's psychoanalysis and his renewed interpretation of an 'ethics of psychoanalysis' in the context of a more traditional genealogy of ethics, starting paradigmatically with Plato and Aristotle. Lacan's own thematics constantly foreground this relation to ancient philosophical and metaphysical sources, and indeed Badiou writes additionally of the Lacanian relation to the Presocratics, especially Empedocles and Heraclitus (Badiou 2006), a thematic we will return to below.

In the work of both Freud and Lacan, there is a complex relation between psychoanalysis on the one side and the epochal history of thought on the other, extending from the premodern Hellenic period through early and late medieval metaphysics (itself dominated by monotheistic borrowings from Platonic Aristotelianism) and through to the moderns. On one level, psychoanalysis owes a significant debt to the ancient sources. Freud, for example, as we cited in our Introduction, invokes especially the Platonic theory of 'Eros' in his seminal writings on sexuality (Freud 1977, 2002a) and the question of an 'ontological' crisis (Zupančič 2008b). Lacan similarly pits Heraclitus firmly against the edifice of Aristotelianism at crucial junctures of his thinking on both 'ethics' (Lacan 1992) and on 'drive' (Lacan 1994). We will see this gesture repeated in our troika, and, for example, we will discuss in succeeding chapters the brilliant exposition of Plato's *The Symposium* (Plato 1961) in Zupančič's *The Odd One In: On Comedy* (Zupančič 2008a), which allows her to recast the Freudian/Lacanian conception of sex in classically Platonic terms (albeit as refracted through the enigmatic and comedic figure of Aristophanes).

Alongside this avowed classical (and particularly Heraclitean–Platonic as opposed to Aristotelian) inheritance in psychoanalysis, there is nonetheless a simultaneous disavowal of premodern metaphysics as 'naive' or merely 'figurative' and the avowal of psychoanalysis as an irreducibly modernist phenomenon. Even Descartes' *Meditations* (and thus the paradigm of Cartesianism) is seen as overly influenced by a residual metaphysics in this regard and if the concept of the 'cogito' is to be reclaimed, it can only be done so as the 'cogito of the unconscious' through a properly Kantian moment, as Dolar eloquently argues (Dolar 1998). Psychoanalysis is thus, by definition, post-Kantian. Indeed, we can go further and say that, from the orthodox Lacanian position adopted by the troika of the Ljubljana school, that 'philosophy begins only with Kant' (Žižek et al. 2014).

At issue here, then, is also a radical rereading by Lacan of the Freudian inheritance. Lacan is constantly the one to reiterate his being a 'Freudian', as he does polemically (and infamously) against any attempt to instigate a 'Lacanian' psychoanalysis in his name at his last talk in Caracas in 1981. 'It is up to you to be Lacanians if you wish. I am a Freudian' (Macey 1988: 257). Similarly, Lacan is insistent in his emphasizing of the motto of 'a return to Freud' to describe on a meta-level his interpretation of psychoanalysis as such in the seminars and the *Écrits* (Lacan 2002a). Nonetheless, these pronouncements only intensified the censure of much of the psychoanalytical community against Lacan, both in France and abroad, especially in America where his disdain for the 'ego psychology' interpretation of Freudianism was so controversial. It is in this context, for example, that we can best understand the title of his opening essay in Seminar XI, on *The Four Fundamental Concepts of Psychoanalysis* (Lacan 1994), called 'Excommunication'. As Macey (1994) and Badiou (2009) make clear, this conceptual title refers also to the very real excommunication of Lacan from the standard psychoanalytical associations: Lacan was 'excommunicated by the psychoanalytic international' (Badiou 2009: 2). Such gestures of iconoclasm against the established authorities are very much also a part of the philosophical style of the Ljubljana School of Psychoanalysis. In his important introduction to his first major monograph in English, *The Sublime Object of Ideology*, Žižek launches a comparable attack on the attempt by Herbert Marcuse to combine critical theory and Freudianism, lambasting it as 'psychoanalytical essentialism' (Žižek 1989).

Alongside the conceptual developments and intricacies, we can also say that there is a crucial political dimension to the whole relation to psychoanalysis. This politicized aspect to Lacanianism is one of its most influential and significant contributions to contemporary thought. Freud was already well aware, for example, of the sociopolitical implications of bringing his psychoanalysis to a wider audience; witness his infamous quip on arriving in the United States that he was bringing the 'plague' (Bowie 1991). Lacan's own relation to an explicit politics was always highly ambiguous. As Badiou (2009) states, for Lacan, political ideology is often misconceived and naive from a psychoanalytical perspective. In a related key, we might cite Lacan's criticism of the most significant explosion of leftist politics in the 1960s, the moment of May 1968, when he offers warnings concerning the psychological motivations of the young protestors (indicating their desire for a 'master' figure) (Bowie 1991).

But alongside this explicit political reticence, a more vehement politicization emerges from within Lacan's thinking, especially as it develops from early to late. Perhaps the most striking example of this is the increasing significance which the concept of the 'Real' is given in Lacan's philosophy in his later works, coming to be increasingly at odds with (and subversive of) the earlier hegemonic register of the 'symbolic' (Bowie 1991; Homer 2005). We can see this exact thematic (as well as its overt political resonances) being taken up by the succeeding thinkers who invoke Lacan, from the case of Badiou's own militant politics (Badiou 2009) to the nuanced philosophical leftism of the Ljubljana School of Psychoanalysis (Žižek 2000). In his obituary of Lacan, this is one of the key points which Badiou takes up. What Badiou finds striking as we have described it, is not simply the political dimension of Lacanianism but rather the juxtaposition of the critique of political ideology (which appears to rule out a political position tout court), alongside such a radical political aspect.

Part of this issue of politics relates back to the previous discussion of Lacan's 'excommunication' from the orthodox Freudian schools. Lacan's alternative 'ethics of psychoanalysis', at odds with the therapeutism of the ego psychology interpretation, thus culminates in a new school, 'his own school'; 'The need to organise the transmission of his thought and to train analysts who would work in accordance with what he believed to be the ethics of psychoanalytic practice, led him to found his own school' (Badiou 2009: 3). But this new ethics is also a new *politics* of psychoanalysis, and Lacan's criticisms of therapeutism are not simply on issues concerning the intra-textual readings of Freud. At issue, as stated by Badiou, is also a whole politics of 'transmission', where therapeutic practices are seen as simply justifications for the political status quo. It is the antagonism to precisely this sociopolitical conservatism which is at the heart of Badiou's reference to Lacan 'being on the warpath from the very beginning' (Badiou 2009). We will return to this issue in a moment in exploring how Badiou addresses the problematic of the Marxist relation to Lacan's thought (and here Badiou, in 2009, is very much thinking of the relation to a contemporary Marxism). We will also see this Marxist dimension ('Lacan and Marx') addressed by each of our troika of thinkers in their respective interviews. Laclau, in his preface to Žižek's *The Sublime Object of Ideology*, set the scene for this reception of the 'Lacan and Marx dimension' in the English-speaking world (Laclau 1989). But we have seen, in Chapter 1, how this evolution of the problematic was already very well developed in Slovenia through the early 1970s and early 1980s. It is also precisely this radical political edge of Lacanianism which constitutes the lever for the moment of 'breakthrough', as, for example, Močnik (1993) describes it. We have also seen how this was far from being simply a contribution to academic discourse on the political. In the former Yugoslavia at least, and especially in Slovenia, Lacan and Lacanianism came to have a highly significant impact on the politics of everyday life as well as more centralized institutionalized political questions, as Slovenia developed these latter problematics both before and after national independence (Močnik 1993; Gantar 1993; Žižek 1997).

Psychoanalysis and philosophy

Alongside the political importance of psychoanalysis, and despite the protestations of Lacan to the contrary, there is the complex question of the relation between philosophy and psychoanalysis. Macey's seminal (but also highly controversial) interpretative text on Lacan and Lacanianism, entitled *Lacan in Contexts* (Macey 1988), is one of the most interesting attempts to provide a genealogy of the evolution of Lacan's thinking. It is controversial for one reason, because it accuses much so-called Lacanianism of deliberately forgetting the developmental aspect of psychoanalysis and focusing instead on a counter-productive and obscurantist 'myth of the hero': 'For a long time, the reader of Lacan has been faced with a stark dilemma: total acceptance or total rejection. In one sense, this is a reflection of the fierce loyalties and hatreds inspired by a redoubtable individual, and of the sectarian affections that are so often inspired by psychoanalysis. But it is also an effect of the illusion that Lacan's work is a whole which is entire unto itself, that it has no basis in five decades of French intellectual life, that it is the result of some immaculate theoretical conception. If his work is to be evaluated critically, rather than being rejected out of hand or reproduced with filial piety, that illusion must be dispelled' (Macey 1988: x).

Rather than being a creation ex nihilo ('some immaculate theoretical conception'), then, Macey powerfully maps out the coordinates of Lacan's thought, as it draws from a history of French psychiatry, from Freud, from surrealism and from the history of philosophy. In the latter case, the thematic of the relationship between philosophy and psychoanalysis, which will become a crucial theme for the troika of Ljubljana thinkers in its own right, is foregrounded (Zupančič 2008b). As Macey demonstrates, the relation between psychoanalysis and philosophy is problematical from the inception of Freud's thinking onwards. For example, Macey notes that 'Freud's epistemologically and metapsychologically based suspicions of philosophy are voiced on a number of occasions, but rarely more clearly than in the *New Introductory Lectures* of 1932–33. Here, he explicitly argues that psychoanalysis is antithetical to the elaboration of a specific *Weltanschauung*' (Macey 1988: 76). Nonetheless, despite this suspicion (voiced even more vehemently in Freud's diagnostic of the illusory satisfactions of the 'total philosophical system' as a form of 'paranoia' and an 'overevaluation of the magic of words' [Macey 1988: 77]), we have nonetheless seen in the Introduction that Freud often relies on philosophical sources. The most obvious case in point is the example of Plato's philosophy of the erotic, which Freud draws on crucially in his early lectures on sexuality (Freud 1977) as well as in later key texts such as *Civilisation and Its Discontents* (Freud 2002a).

The relationship between philosophy and psychoanalysis, in the case of Lacan, is perhaps more complex again. Badiou (2006), for example, has drawn attention to the strong Presocratic philosophical influence on Lacan, most notably in the case of Heraclitus, who Lacan explicitly posits against what he sees as the diametrically opposed philosophical influence of Parmenides. Similarly, Badiou makes reference to the influence of Empedocles on Lacan's conception of an intractable 'strife' in life, which will go on to influence his later formulations of the concept of the 'Real' (Badiou 2006). In Seminar XI, for example, *The Four Fundamental Concepts of Psychoanalysis* (Lacan 1994), the notion of 'drive' (in effect, 'death drive') is seen as connecting back to the figure of Heraclitus and his image of a bow in tension between life and death (Lacan 1994).

But, as with Freud, Lacan can also be very vehement in his more explicit rejections of philosophical influence. As Macey notes, in both cases 'the critique of philosophy is also a defence of psychoanalysis' (Macey 1988: 78). We know that there is a very tense relation between philosophy and psychoanalysis in university settings, and for example, in France, the development of the Department of Psychoanalysis at Vincennes is an interesting case in point (Macey 1988: 90), with Lacan's daughter Judith and son-in-law Jacques-Alain Miller being at the helm. Miller especially, and his very particular reading of Lacan (in addition to him being the authorized and exclusive editor of the seminars), has been a very significant influence on the Ljubljana School of Psychoanalysis. Both Žižek and Dolar studied closely with Miller in Paris (Žižek et al. 2014) and Zupančič also refers to his specific readings of Lacan. But Miller is also far from being a universally accepted figure, even within Lacanian circles, and there has been much controversy surrounding the politics of psychoanalysis, and the legacy of Lacan, in this regard (Macey 1988).

Going back to 1975, for example, two key philosophers at Vincennes perceived the situation at the Department of Psychoanalysis to be sufficiently acute as to require a very strongly worded riposte and intra-institutional critique. In the wake of several staff 'firings', Jean Francois Lyotard and Gilles Deleuze in a short piece entitled 'Concerning the Vincennes Psychoanalysis Department' (Lyotard and Deleuze 1993: 69) say the following: 'What psychoanalysis presents as its knowledge is accompanied by a kind of intellectual and emotional terrorism that is suitable for breaking down resistances that are said to be unhealthy. It is already disturbing when this operation is carried out between psychoanalysts, or between psychoanalysts and patients, for a certified therapeutic goal. But it is much more disturbing when the same operation seeks to break down resistances of a completely different kind, in a teaching section that declares itself to have no intention of "looking after" or "training" psychoanalysts'. Lyotard and Deleuze go on to specifically identify Lacan's position as a supposed authority in this seemingly malignant context: 'A veritable unconscious blackmail is directed against opponents, under the prestige and in the presence of Dr Lacan, in order to impose his decisions without any possibility of discussion' (Lyotard and Deleuze 1993: 69). We can also note the polemical atmosphere in French philosophy with regard to Freud and Lacan, for example, in highly charged anti-psychoanalytical texts such as Deleuze and Guattari's (2004) *Anti-Oedipus*. We will return below to the related example of the inter-textual communications between Lacan and Derrida (Hurst 2008).

With this background in mind, it is hardly surprising that Lacan should oftentimes seek to defend psychoanalysis against philosophical attack. As Macey notes, one can also argue that this critique of philosophy on behalf of Lacan goes significantly beyond a localized dispute: 'Lacan clearly does not subscribe to Freud's tacit positivism but he does display the overt distrust of philosophy, arguing that the very term "world-view" is antithetical to psychoanalytic discourse and even that all "philosophical – ologies (onto, theo, cosmo and psycho alike) contradict the basic tenet of the existence of the unconscious"' (Macey 1988: 81). One of the complexities of this situation is the way in which this 'overt distrust' of philosophy is not something in any way shared by the later Lacanian development. The so-called 'Slovene Lacan' as evolved from the Ljubljana School of Psychoanalysis is a Lacan completely at home with philosophy, this variant of (non-clinical and 'theoretical') psychoanalysis being one which, while remaining a distinct discipline, is nonetheless in constant dialogue with philosophical concepts and the philosophical tradition. Again, we can say that Lacanian orthodoxy as understood by Žižek, Dolar and Zupančič is far from being literalist, and rather constitutes orthodoxy as 'transformation' (Dolar et al. 2014). Despite the different conceptions of the exact relation between philosophy and psychoanalysis, however, (and Macey also notes how Lacan's conception of the history of philosophy is naively 'traditionalist'), there is also a strong continuity in relation to a certain illusion of 'mastery' which the philosophical tradition often posits. As Macey observes, 'his (Lacan's) objections to the project of totalisation crystallize in the critique of the "discourse of the Master", one of the four discourses . . .' (Macey 1988: 81). Thus, the overt distrust of philosophy also relates back to Freud's diagnostic reading of some of the intentionality behind philosophical and metaphysical system building in the history of thought. In his later seminar, Seminar XX, *On Feminine Sexuality. The Limits of Love and Knowledge, 1972–1973. ENCORE* (Lacan 1998), Lacan powerfully parodies this system building in a punning sentence which draws on the French literary tradition, from *Cinna* (Corneille's heroic drama of 1640): 'Je suis m'être, je progresse dans la m'etrise, je suis m'être de moi comme de l'univers' ('I am my-being: I progress in my-being/mastery; I am master/my-being of myself and of the universe') (Macey 1988: 82). This attempt at universalizing mastery is seen as characteristic of philosophy as a discipline and at the root of the overt distrust from psychoanalysis vis-à-vis such philosophy.

Significantly, the Ljubljana School of Psychoanalysis vehemently continue this disavowal of system building and overarching or totalizing philosophies. However, where they discontinue with Lacan's reading of philosophy is in their precise affirmation of a non-totalizing philosophical practice. A recent powerful example of this simultaneous critique and affirmation of philosophy is Zupančič's text *Why Psychoanalysis?: Three Interventions* (Zupančič 2008b). There, invoking both Freud and Lacan, Zupančič attempts to demonstrate how even the most seemingly anti-philosophical of psychoanalytical concepts, for example that of 'sexuality', can be seen as precisely inaugurating a renewed philosophical epistemology and ontology, sensitive to the gaps and aporias of a more authentic existence (Zupančič 2008b). Here, philosophy seems to have completely rejected the 'discourse of the master' on Lacan's terms and sought to work through some of the 'paranoia' which Freud seems to ascribe to the philosophical will to system building (Macey 1988).

Psychoanalysis and surrealism

The tendency to see Lacan's psychoanalysis in terms of a 'for' or 'against' mentality has already been described, and Macey describes how this is at least partly the result of a tendency to occlude the real genealogy of influence on French psychoanalysis (Macey 1988).

In such a context, Lacan's thought takes on the appearance of pure autonomy and independence. Pointing rather to the complexity of influence which is present in Lacan's thought allows us not only to see his borrowings and dependencies, but also to see that the weaknesses and strengths of his approach are not simply his weaknesses and strengths, but partly at least are shared by other movements and schools of thought. Nonetheless, this is not to say that Lacan's thought is wholly unoriginal and certainly, as we will see, there are particular aspects and interpretations which are quite unique to him.

One aspect of his genealogy which demonstrates both these facets, his borrowings and his originality, is his relation to surrealism. As Bowie (1991) and Macey (1988) describe in some detail, the relation to surrealist thought and art is very significant in Lacan's work. Nonetheless, he is far from being an orthodox surrealist and if he does utilize many surrealist motifs and ideas (not always explicitly), it can also be said that he redeploys these conceptions in a very different context from their original one. In this, we might argue that he has far more in common with so-called 'dissident surrealists' such as Georges Bataille and Pierre Klossowski (Irwin 2010) than he has with more orthodox surrealist figures such as Breton (Macey 1988). As Macey (1988: 45) notes, 'surrealism is the only identifiable "school" to which Lacan refers so consistently'. But what does Lacan define as surrealism? Typically, he gives a very idiosyncratic and provocative definition of the latter: '[surrealism is] a tornado on the edge of an atmospheric depression where the norms of humanist individualism founder' (Macey 1988: 46).

As Irwin (2010) has argued in his book on Derrida, *Derrida and the Writing of the Body*, the French avant-garde of the 1920s and 1930s remains a very underestimated source for later philosophical thinking. It is clear, for example, in a crucial Derridean text like *Writing and Difference* (from 1967), that the influence of this avant-garde is far stronger on Derrida than the simultaneous influence of phenomenology; nonetheless, commentators tend to emphasize the latter at the expense of the former. In Derrida's case, the main influences can be said to be Artaud and Bataille, among others (Irwin 2010). The situation with Lacan is not dissimilar. As Macey (1988: 47) notes, 'the inflections of his discourse are profoundly marked by his encounter with the tornado of surrealism'. This influence of surrealism is both artistic and philosophical. In the case of art, we might note among many others the influence of the work of Salvador Dali and André Masson on Lacan. Indeed, in the former case, there was also a very strong relationship between Freud and Dali, although Freud was far more suspicious of the general surrealist movement led by Breton (Macey 1988). But what of surrealist philosophy? Here, we can look ahead in order to look back. One of the key questions which we will pose to the Ljubljana troika of thinkers, Žižek, Dolar and Zupančič, is precisely 'why Lacan?'. That is, in the context of the wider influence of what Žižek et al. (2014) refers to more generally as 'French structuralism' on earlier 1970s Slovenian thought, what were the factors which led to the more specific and singular commitment to Lacanianism from the late 1970s onwards? We have seen how this commitment to Lacan was not simply exclusive to our troika of thinkers under discussion, but it was part of a wider 'Slovenian Lacan' which was to have a very significant impact on the relationship between theory and political life in Slovenia leading up to independence (Močnik 1993). This Lacanianism went beyond the philosophers and also came to be central to the avant-garde and artistic movements, brought together under the banner of the NSK (Močnik 1993; Motoh 2012).

One way to understand the specificity of Lacan vis-à-vis the other main structuralist thinkers (Althusser, Foucault etc.) is to see his work in the context of the very particular influence of surrealist thought and philosophy. As Macey makes us aware, the surrealists are misunderstood if one sees them simply as an aesthetic phenomenon. Instead, the 'intellectual breadth' and philosophical radicalism of their work is perhaps the most striking aspect. 'These manipulators of signs and symbols irrevocably altered the intellectual landscape of France' (Macey 1988: 49). In the 'Surrealist Manifesto' of 1924, Breton defines surrealism in a 'once and for all' manner as: 'pure psychic automatism, by which we propose to express the real functioning of thought, verbally, in writing, or by any other means. The dictation of thought, in the absence of any control exercised by reason and regardless of any aesthetic or moral preoccupations' (Macey 1988: 51). Breton goes on to magnify the definition and more in philosophical or conceptual terms: 'a belief in the higher reality of certain forms of associations which have hitherto been neglected, in the omnipotence of dreams and in the disinterested play of thought' (Macey 1988: 51).

The influence among the surrealists of Bataille on Lacan is perhaps more striking than that of Breton, as Bataille rejects what he sees as the 'residual idealism' of Breton's approach to the notion of 'Eros' in surrealist thought (Mundy 2006; Bataille 2001). This leads to Bataille being referred to as a 'dissident surrealist' in philosophical terms (Ades and Bradley 2006: 11). We will see a similar critique of idealism coming from Lacan in his Seminar XI, *The Four Fundamental Concepts of Psychoanalysis* (Lacan 1994). Additionally, the close and rather bizarre family ties linking Bataille and Lacan (with Lacan marrying Bataille's ex-wife Sylvia and adopting Bataille's daughter Laurence to whom he will become very close) have been well documented and are another key feature of their relation (Macey 1988). It is clear that while Bataille seems to have overtly avoided reading Lacan, that Lacan was a close and highly influenced reader of Bataille. The lack of explicit acknowledgement of this element by Lacan is significant in itself.

The strong connections to Bataille's thinking, as well as to related dissidents such as Pierre Klossowski (1991), bring Lacan into dialogue with a very particular tradition of French thinking, going back at least to Sade (and we will see the importance of Sade's philosophy to Lacan below). Charles Taylor (2007), in his recent text *A Secular Age*, has foregrounded another possible way of interpreting this line of intellectual development. Here, Bataille and Lacan can be seen to have inherited the spirit of what Taylor refers to as the 'immanent Counter-Enlightenment' in French literature, the poet *maudits* or damned poets, such as Rimbaud, Baudelaire, Lautréamont and Mallarmé espousing an 'immanent transcendence' (Taylor 2007). This is also very much the key thematic of Macey's analysis of Lacan's version of psychoanalysis, which he views as having been decontextualized from this pre-history (Macey 1988).

Another reinforcement of this view can be claimed from the rereading of Sade practised within this tradition, which is clearly borrowed by Lacan (2002b) in his reading of 'Kant and Sade', as we will see below in more detail. Susan Sontag (2001), in her essay 'The Pornographic Imagination', foregrounds this reinterpretation of the Marquis De Sade (Sontag 2001: 96) after World War II: the crucial 'importance of the reinterpretation of Sade after World War II by French intellectuals . . . a crucial point of departure for radical thinking about the human condition' (Sontag 2001: 102). She notes what she terms 'the prevailing view of sexuality as a perfectly intelligible source of emotional and physical pleasure' (Sontag 2001: 102). It is 'these assumptions [which] are challenged in the French

Sadean tradition' (Sontag 2001: 102). Here, the link ahead to Lacan is undeniable but, as Lacan tries to show in 'Kant with Sade', there is also a strong connecting link between this avant-garde tradition and Freud's own original insights. In this context, the rereading of Freudian texts such as *Three Essays on the Theory of Sexuality* (Freud 1977) and *Civilisation and Its Discontents* (Freud 2002a) in light of this avant-garde would be especially important. This, perhaps surprisingly, is not a line of interpretation which has been developed directly by the Ljubljana School of Psychoanalysis, although Žižek especially has been explicit in connecting Lacan with surrealism (Žižek 1997). Here, the reference to surrealist cinema has been especially important for Žižek, whether in the shape of earlier surrealists such as Luis Buñuel, or later in the evolution of a more differentiated surrealism in auteurs such as Alfred Hitchcock or David Lynch (Žižek 1997). Hitchcock's cinema has taken on paradigmatic significance not simply for Žižek but for the Ljubljana School of Psychoanalysis as such, for example in their important collection of essays from 1992, edited by Žižek and containing several contributions also from Žižek, Dolar and Zupančič, entitled *Everything You Always Wanted to Know About Lacan But Were Afraid to Ask Hitchcock* (Žižek 1992b).

The final reference to surrealism which we can make in this context vis-à-vis Lacan and Lacanianism, is in relation to the reading or reinterpretation of Hegel during the period of surrealism (Baugh 2005). Bruce Baugh, for example, in his seminal text, *French Hegel: From Surrealism to Postmodernism* (Baugh 2005), provides some very helpful historical contextualization of this problematic and begins by complicating 'the notion that Kojève's lectures brought Hegel to France' (Baugh 2005: 1). This argument with regard to Kojève underestimates the influence of surrealism, Marxism and also Jean Wahl, whose book on the 'unhappy consciousness' in Hegel precedes Kojève by a decade, beginning in 1929/1939.

We know that Lacan did diligently attend Kojève's lectures on Hegel, although we also know that, in many respects, the interpretation of Hegel which he developed on this basis has been significantly criticized by recent commentators. Indeed, this is one of Dolar's key points in his discussion of the Hegel and Lacan relation in his interview (Dolar et al. 2014). Briefly put, Kojève, according to Dolar, misreads Hegel as an 'anthropological thinker', and accords too much significance (almost exclusive significance) in his reading of Hegel's texts specifically to the *Phenomenology of Spirit*. In broad outline, Lacan follows Kojève in his analysis of Hegel. But Dolar's claim will be that the strong influence of Hegel on the Ljubljana School of Psychoanalysis is not a Hegel understood through this line of thought. Rather, for Dolar and the troika, here Lacan must be read somewhat against Lacan, so as to delineate a reading of Hegel (and indeed of Lacan) which is 'orthodox' but not literalist. Another feature here of this scene of interpretation concerning surrealism which is significant is the relation between these early readings of Hegel in 1920s and 1930s France and the philosophy of Kierkegaard. The philosophy of Kierkegaard is often presented as completely opposed and mutually exclusive with the Hegelian system, but during this period, as Baugh (2005: 5) shows, the interpretations of Hegel by the 'neo-Kierkegaardian' Jean Wahl also developed a penetrating analysis of 'a self divided against itself, an internally divided and self-alienated subject; a subject that strives vainly for synthesis but instead oscillates between self and non-self, being and nothingness'. The description here of this divided self (with its hybrid of Hegel and Kierkegaard's philosophies) strikingly anticipates some of Lacan's own pronouncements on the notion of the 'subject' (for example, Lacan 1994). The early work of the Ljubljana School of Psychoanalysis certainly seemed to favour a strong relation between Lacan and Hegel (but without explicit reference to Kierkegaard). However, it is perhaps unsurprising, given the reference to Wahl and surrealism, that more recent works of the troika have seen Kierkegaard's philosophy take on a more important role in breaking through some of the remaining philosophical 'deadlocks', most notably in one of Žižek's most substantial and important recent texts, *Less Than Nothing: Hegel and the Shadow of Dialectical Materialism* (Žižek 2012a). We will return to this thematic in the chapter on Žižek and also in our Epilogue.

In the next two sections, having previously explored some of the key influences on Lacan in relation to philosophy and surrealism, we will turn to the more specific detail of Lacan's own texts and his foregrounding of paradigmatic concepts and thematics. Here, we will take the crucial thematic of 'ethics' or 'the ethics of psychoanalysis' as it is developed especially in Seminar VII, *The Ethics of Psychoanalysis* (Lacan 1992) but also as it relates to the important essay in the *Écrits* (Lacan 2002a), entitled 'Kant with Sade' (Lacan 2002b). We will begin with an analysis of the latter, moving back to its connections with the former work. We will also attempt to briefly trace some of the key developments of this thematic as it relates to two important seminars: Seminar XI, *The Four Fundamental Concepts of Psychoanalysis* (Lacan 1994) and Seminar XX, *On Feminine Sexuality. The Limits of Love and Knowledge, 1972–1973. ENCORE* (Lacan 1998). As we will see in succeeding chapters on our troika of thinkers, Žižek, Dolar and Zupančič, this thematic and these specific Lacanian seminars will also play a pivotal role in the evolution of the 'Slovenian Lacan'. We will briefly return to this question of the relation between the seminars (Lacan 1992, 1994, 1998) and the more contemporary philosophical concepts of the Ljubljana School of Psychoanalysis, in the conclusion to this chapter.

'Kant with Sade'

Lacan's infamous and provocative essay 'Kant with Sade' (Lacan 2002b), published in the *Écrits* (Lacan 2002a), was originally intended to serve as a preface to a new edition of the Marquis de Sade's own *Philosophy in the Bedroom* (Sade 1980). It was eventually published in the journal *Critique*, a journal with strong surrealist associations, having been founded and edited for a long period by Bataille. The essay shows definite surrealist influences, not least in its very juxtaposition of two intellectual figures from very different worlds; Kant, the arch-figure of dutiful Germanic morality, and Sade, the paradigm figure of French libertinage and rabid anti-moralism. In this section, we will employ some of the detail of this curious Lacan text to explore some of the philosophical problems which will be more systematically developed by Lacan in his seminars, and especially in Seminar VII, *The Ethics of Psychoanalysis* (Lacan 1992).

What Lacan's essay 'Kant with Sade' does first of all is to rehabilitate the figure of Sade philosophically. Against the view that Sadean thought is simply a catalogue of the perverse (Lacan 2002b: 765), Lacan is keen to stress a certain philosophical lineage, extending all the way back to the Platonic Academy: 'I, on the contrary, maintain that the Sadean bedroom is of the same stature as those places from which the schools of ancient philosophy borrowed their names: Academy, Lyceum and Stoa. Here as there, one paves the way for science by rectifying one's ethical position'

(Lacan 2002b: 765). What Lacan has added here, then, is a sense of philosophical importance as well as a more specific intervention: the rectification of one's ethical position. Ethics, from a psychoanalytical perspective, consequently, will involve a revolution in how we think ethically, in how we position ourselves ethically.

As Lacan notes, there is a process of 'subversion' going on here in relation to both the history of philosophy and the history of ethics. But the subversion is not simply from the Sadean side. Against appearances, Kantian ethics is also, for Lacan, subversive. Moreover, it is subversive in a way which brings it into close proximity with the thought of Sade. This is the shocking aspect of Lacan's essay, most of all that Sade and Kant would somehow be in philosophical and 'ethical' complicity in their simultaneous critique of the tradition. Lacan notes the originality of this thesis: 'Sade represents here the first step of a subversion of which Kant, as piquant as this may seem in light of the coldness of the man himself, represents the turning point – something that has never been pointed out as such, to the best of my knowledge' (Lacan 2002b: 645). For Lacan, Sade in this text can be said to 'complete' the meaning of the Kantian ethical critique but the latter is here understood in terms of an unconventional 'subversive core' which leads the reader to an 'incredible exaltation' (Lacan 2002b: 646), although Lacan is also clear that this radical experience is not open to those who view Kant with the usual 'academic piety' (Lacan 2002b: 646). This opening section of Lacan's essay thus claims to be about an extraordinary story about ethics and philosophy, a story which might seem to turn all the usual moral understandings on their heads. Again, in this very moment of 'subversive' thinking, we are reminded precisely of the revolutionary aims of Breton as the originator of surrealism, for example, in his claim that the most exemplary surrealist act would be to run out into the street and fire a gun at passers-by at random (Macey 1988).

As Walter Benjamin puts it in his essay 'Surrealism: The Last Snapshot of the European Intelligentsia' (Benjamin 1979: 236), 'since Bakunin, Europe has lacked a radical concept of freedom. The Surrealists have one'. Benjamin's essay is also instructive for us in the measure to which it takes direct aim at what it calls the complicity between 'idealistic morality' and (leftist) 'political practice' (Benjamin 1979: 234). At stake for both Benjamin and Lacan here is an attempt to subvert the residual moralism of supposedly radical philosophy and/or psychoanalysis. We have already seen this in terms of Lacan's being (in Badiou's phrase) 'on the warpath from the very beginning' (Badiou 2009) against, for example, ego psychology. But this attack on ego psychology is misunderstood if it is simply understood as a localized spat between psychoanalysis and more conservative psychology. Rather, what is at stake here is a whole politics of knowledge and the way in which certain kinds of knowledge can be used to reinforce the status quo. This is precisely Lacan's concern – that the radical implications of Freudianism are being domesticated and used in the service of a therapeutic culture which will only succeed in reinforcing the very same conventions which Freud (2002a) exposes as a lie. It is the same point which Žižek makes against Marcuse's 'psychoanalytical essentialism' in his introduction to *The Sublime Object of Ideology* (Žižek 1989). In the supposed radical Marcuse texts surrounding 1968 and the student revolts, Žižek can only detect a ruse for a domesticating conservatism.

In his obituary of Lacan, Badiou (2009) takes this radical critique one stage further, and here he is directly in accordance with Benjamin's reading of surrealism. What differentiates Badiou's reading of Lacan here is that he applies it directly to the hypocrises (as he sees them) of contemporary leftist or supposedly emancipatory 'Marxist' thought. We will see in later chapters that Žižek also directs his attention towards such supposedly 'revolutionary' political discourse (Žižek 1989). Against all appearances to the contrary for Badiou, Lacan (in his very disavowals of political ideology) is precisely offering the most radical critique of ideology. Such a critique of ideology, to be pertinent in a very complex contemporary scene of interpretation, will have to invoke not simply the 'political' but also the notion of the 'ethical'. In relation to the notion of both, no conventional understandings will be possible but each conception (or process) will have to be radically reworked. Here, we see the direct connection back to Lacan's thematics in 'Kant with Sade' and in Seminar VII, *The Ethics of Psychoanalysis* and succeeding seminars. As Lacan puts it there, 'one paves the way for science by rectifying one's ethical position' (Lacan 2002b: 765).

The detail of the discussion in 'Kant with Sade' is too intricate to describe in total but here we can perhaps focus on one aspect of it which is particularly relevant to our thematic of the 'Lacan effect'. That is, Lacan's rereading in this context of the Sadean inheritance, the philosophical framework of Sade's work, which he cites as having been completely misunderstood. Although Macey (1988) is right to point to an obscurantist tendency in Lacan (and Lacanianism) which tends to obscure the genealogy of Lacan's influences, in this case it is interesting that he does cite one significant precursor. Near the conclusion of 'Kant with Sade' (Lacan 2002b), Lacan refers to Pierre Klossowski's work, *Sade, mon prochain* (*Sade, My Neighbour*) (Klossowski 1991), as particularly important for the rereading of Sade that he is proposing. We have already mentioned Susan Sontag's foregrounding of this dissident surrealist reinterpretation of Sade in the 1930s and 1940s, and her key point of reference was Bataille (Sontag 2001). But Klossowski's reading is as important if not more important to Lacan than that of Bataille. In his footnotes to the essay, Lacan comments that: '*Sade, mon prochain* is the title of Klossowski's work that was published by Seuil in 1947. It is the only contemporary contribution to the Sadean question that does not strike me as marred by the tics of the highbrow literati' (Lacan 2002b: 668). A brief exploration of Klossowski's rereading of Sade will thus allow us to understand somewhat more precisely what Lacan means by the notion of 'rectifying one's ethical position' (Lacan 2002b: 765). We will also see how this relates to Badiou's reading of Lacan's critique of ideological Marxism in the obituary (Badiou 2009). At stake here is the relation between 'ethics' and 'politics', and a refusal of the tendency, in Mouffe's terms, to bring about a 'moralisation' or a 'moralising' of the political sphere (Mouffe 2005). Instead, we are seeking here rather what Žižek refers to as a 'political suspension of the ethical' (Žižek 2012a).

But what of Klossowski's rereading of Sade? What is crucial to understand here is the recontextualization of Sade's work, outside the traditional reading of his work as a wild, naturalized 'liberation of desire' (Lacan 1992). This, of course, was also the dominant reading of psychoanalysis and Freudianism, not just from its opponents, but also from its supposed defenders such as those in 'ego psychology' who would seek to overcome traditional prohibitions, especially of the sexual kind. Understood in this way, psychoanalysis is about becoming at ease ('becoming natural') with one's sexuality. Sade would obviously represent a more radical version of this ideology than Freud, but still, Sade too is interpreted traditionally in this way. But when Lacan tells us in his introduction to *The Ethics of Psychoanalysis* that 'the liberation of desire has failed' (Lacan

1992), he is already indicating that his 'return to Freud' will not be on such terms.

In Sontag's terms, we can refer to the liberationist reading as 'the prevailing view of sexuality as a perfectly intelligible source of emotional and physical pleasure' (Sontag 2001: 102). However, for Sontag as for Lacan, it is 'these assumptions [which] are challenged in the French Sadean tradition' (Sontag 2001: 102). This alternative tradition is where we can also authentically locate Freud and Lacan and the psychoanalysis of sexuality, or to use Freud's preferred term 'psychosexuality' (Freud 1977). In this alternative tradition, the obscene is a primary notion of human consciousness, human sexuality is a highly questionable and contested phenomenon and there are extreme and demonic forces in consciousness which are linked to the desire for death. Of course, the latter notion especially will increasingly come to dominate discussions of sexuality and the erotic in psychoanalysis, in Freud's later work and in Lacan's work from the beginning (Freud 2002a). Nonetheless, as we shall see, the emphasis on death drive and simply on 'drive' (Lacan 1994) should not be seen as excluding the emphasis on 'eros' or 'desire'. This has also been a key point of contestation for the Ljubljana School of Psychoanalysis, as we shall see. If their early work, especially that of Žižek, can be seen as somewhat overstressing the notion of 'drive' (also the related notion of the 'Real'), more recently the work of Dolar and Zupančič (Zupančič 2008a) can be seen as redressing this imbalance, with a renewed stress on the concepts of 'love' and a notion of 'drive' mediated by 'desire' (e.g., through the notion of comedy in Plato's *The Symposium* [Zupančič 2008a]).

Lacan's very affirmative comments on Klossowski's reading of Sade can be read in the specific context of Klossowski's 1947 essay 'Under the Mask of Atheism', which is included as part of his text *Sade, My Neighbour* (Klossowski 1991). In a highly idiosyncratic and original reading of Sade, Klossowski argues that the Sadean system which appears focused on the concepts of 'Nature' and 'perpetual motion' is, in fact, a transposition of themes connected with that which works 'against nature'. Here, we can refer back to what we discussed above concerning Lacan's critique of what he termed the 'natural liberation of desire'. Just as psychoanalysis (whether of Freud or of Lacan) is completely misunderstood if it is seen as advocating some kind of 'free desire', so too in the case of Sade. At least on Klossowski's terms (and in 'Kant with Sade'

Lacan follows Klossowski's analysis more than any other), Sade's philosophy operates in the exact opposite manner with regard to desire and sexuality: 'The terms *Nature* and *perpetual motion* have served only to transfer the mystery and incomprehensibility of God into metaphysical entities, without resolving or exhausting that mystery of being which is the possibility of evil and of nothingness' (Klossowski 1991: 99).

The problem with the notion of 'nature' or 'what is natural', then, is that it simply repeats the very metaphysics from which it is supposedly attempting to liberate us. Against such notions of 'nature' or 'natural sexual desire' (or related Enlightenment ideas such as 'freedom', 'autonomy' etc.), Klossowski instead foregrounds completely antithetical concepts in his analysis of what is crucial in Sade's discourse on sex: 'the possibility of evil and of nothingness' (Klossowski 1991: 99). Far from being the ultimate modernist, Sade is rather pre-modern, invoking concepts and experiences which constitute a reawakening of the most ancient sources: 'In the soul of this libertine great lord of the century of Enlightenment, very old mental structures are reawakened; it is impossible not to recognise the whole ancient system of the Manichean gnosis, the visions of Basilides, Valentinus, and especially Marcion' (Klossowski 1991: 100). As Klossowski interprets Sade consequently (and Lacan follows more or less exactly), the Sadean system, far from being some kind of hyper-Enlightenment project, is one of the most exemplary cases of a radical 'counter-Enlightenment' perspective. Again, what is crucial for our purposes here is to realize that this is also Lacan's way of repositioning not simply Sade (or indeed Kant) vis-à-vis the Enlightenment but psychoanalysis itself, as a discipline of thought and a practice. Psychoanalysis, for Lacan, in its authentic Freudian vision, would be radically counter-Enlightenment, anti-Enlightenment. But what would this mean for any possible notion of the 'ethical', or indeed of the 'political', two key notions often crucially reclaimed by the Enlightenment from premodern metaphysics?

In the next section, we will explore this issue in terms of Lacan's most direct analysis of the problematic, in Seminar VII, *The Ethics of Psychoanalysis* (Lacan 1992), a seminar which will have a formative influence on the work of the succeeding Ljubljana School of Psychoanalysis. But here, to conclude this section, let us just say something about how these conceptions of ethics and politics might be conceived through the rereading of Sade in 'Kant with Sade', and also with brief reference to the earlier discussion of Badiou's understanding of the radicalism of Lacan's politics (Badiou 2009).

Under the mask of being an atheist modernist, in fact of being *the* atheist modernist, and some kind of Enlightenment libertine, Sade is rather an opponent of modernism. Klossowski compares Sade to Baudelaire, figures looking back from modernity to premodern themes, and also looking forward to post-modernity, to the demise of modernity; caught temporally in what Lyotard has referred to as the 'future anterior'. Sade has been so misinterpreted because he has been looked at exclusively through a modernist lens, on both Klossowski and Lacan's terms. Judged by the values of rational morality and social conscience representative of modernity (Klossowski 1991: 108), Sade's work can only be misread. 'Everything in Sade will thus predispose him, in these last years of the century of Voltaire, to speak the language of a latent Jansenism' (Klossowski 1991: 106). The religious reference is obviously important here (the interpretation of Sade as a non-atheist, 'under the mask of atheism') but in this context, the crucial implication for our reading concerns the relation to ethics and politics. Here, in Lacanian terms, Klossowski's foregrounding of the concept of 'sin' is especially significant (Klossowski 1991: 108ff). The key to understanding Sade, according to Klossowski, is the medieval Christian conception of *delectatio morosa* or 'morose delectation' (also 'morbid pleasure') (Klossowski 1991: 112). In Klossowski's analysis, this concept serves an analogous function to Bataille's use of the concept of *felix culpa*. 'Morose delectation consists in that movement of the soul by which it bears itself voluntarily towards images of forbidden carnal or spiritual acts in order to linger in contemplation of them' (Klossowski 1991: 113).

Again, we can return to Sontag's contextualization of the problematic (Sontag 1981). Sexuality is not something 'natural' to be 'liberated' or made more 'permissive'. For Sade (and also for Lacan/Klossowski), this is to misrecognize a more 'morbid' dimension of the sexual. This then allows us to make better sense of Lacan's often misunderstood disavowal at the beginning of his seminar, *The Ethics of Psychoanalysis* (Lacan 1992) of the 'libertine' project to emancipate desire from societal and/or traditionalist shackles. The libertine project to naturalize desire, to free desire, 'has failed', Lacan tells us. Instead of such notions as 'freedom' being foregrounded, what interests Lacan in Sade's discourse is precisely (through the reading of Klossowski) the reintroduction of premodern concepts such as 'evil' and 'nothingness'; 'the possibility of evil and of nothingness' (Klossowski 1991: 99). Of course, despite Lacan's provocative disavowals of modernist notions in this essay, we must be careful not to simply interpret his reading of Sade's or Klossowski's concepts as simply those of psychoanalysis. Rather, in their employment by Lacan, there is also a recontextualization of these concepts (concepts such as 'sin', 'nothingness', 'evil', 'delectatio morosa' etc.).[1]

But, if such a recontextualization is the case, where does this leave either the notion of the 'ethical' or the conception of the 'political', on Lacanian terms? Below, we will turn to a closer analysis of Seminar VII to understand Lacan's approach to this problem (Lacan 1992). But Badiou's obituary of Lacan, in its points concerning the ethical–political, already gives us some direction in advance (Badiou 2009). For Badiou, what is crucial to understand with regard to an interpretation of Lacan, is the latter's fundamental 'materialism' (Badiou 2009: 4). Again, we can stress here the critique of idealism in Seminar XI as paradigmatic (Lacan 1994), where Lacan laments the complete misconstrual of psychoanalysis as some kind of therapy for 'narcissism'. The attack on (American) ego psychology is also close to this argument and it allows Lacan to introduce the notion of the 'Real', which enables Lacan to reassert the commitment of psychoanalysis to 'experience' (Lacan 1994). At the same time, any notion of the political based on such materialism must also take account, Badiou warns us, of Lacan's suspicion of the very notion of the sociopolitical. As Badiou (2009: 4) notes, 'he [Lacan] used to say that "the social is always a wound" and yet it so happens that even a Marxism in crisis cannot avoid making reference to the dialectic of the subject that he outlines'.

This last statement captures the ambiguity of the Lacanian (political) position perfectly. Lacanianism undermines any simple objectivist notion of the 'social' or the 'political' (and by implication of the 'ethical') but by the same token, more typically, objectivist accounts of the political (such as Marxism) are in 'crisis'. It is here that Lacan's far more fragile or traumatic conception of the 'political' (which Badiou also refers to here as 'the product of a break' [Badiou 2009: 4]) can come into its own. Thus, Badiou concludes, we can say that Lacan developed 'an ethics of thought that is highly unusual' which he contrasts with the 'platitudes and relative self-abasement of our [public] intellectuals' (Badiou 2009: 7). But there remains a significant work of interpretation (or reinterpretation) to be done. For Badiou, there is an 'almost incalculable import' (Badiou 2009: 7) to such a Lacanian ethics. In the next section, we will look at Lacan's own most systematic attempt to come to terms with the implications of this enigmatic and revolutionary 'ethics of psychoanalysis' (Lacan 1992).

Lacan's *The Ethics of Psychoanalysis*

Given what we have explored in terms of Lacan's revolutionary understanding of the Sadean system (and what he has referred to as the rather shocking 'complicity' of the latter with Kantianism), one might expect Lacan to jettison the conception of 'ethics' entirely.[2] Indeed, looking back to Freud's approach to these issues, especially in his later work, it is far from clear that Freud is interested in salvaging any notion of the ethical. If we look, for example, at one of the key texts of Freud's later period, *Civilisation and Its Discontents* (Freud 2002a), this polemical work may be perceived as a work of 'destruction' more than any attempt at rehabilitation. Leo Bersani's reading of this work is a case in point. Briefly, Bersani (2002) reads Freud's text as a powerful and singularly uncompromising descent into a kind of joyous nihilism. The concept of the 'death drive' is central to how Bersani reads this text, although he also uses this notion to reread Freud's earlier texts, especially the texts on sexuality (Freud 1977), in an analogous manner. On this interpretation, Freud would be a vehemently anti-ethical thinker, and psychoanalysis would be intent on dismantling the fearful pretensions of traditional morality. Lacanianism, as viewed by Bersani, constitutes simply an ever more intensified version of such original Freudian ethical–political nihilism (Bersani 2002).

There is certainly some substance to Bersani's textual reading. *Civilisation and Its Discontents* (Freud 2002a), as the work of the elder Freud, is stark in its assessments of the self-deceptions at the heart of the human condition. As Bersani notes, the foregrounding of the notion of the 'death drive' is uncompromising in this text and, for example, Freud's reading of religion here is vehement (he describes religion, as such, as a form of 'psychic infantilism' [Freud 2002a]).

The text seems intent on not simply deconstructing what Sartre was later to refer to as the 'bad faith' of human illusion, but on *destroying* in as casual a manner as possible this very self-deception. Similarly, it is difficult to disagree with Bersani's analysis of some of the more destructive aspects of the development of Freudianism by Lacan. If the 'death drive' is emphasized more in the later Freud, it is also true that Lacan seeks to assert its destructive force all the more unequivocally. Here, for example, one can cite Lacan's Seminar XX, *On Feminine Sexuality. The Limits of Love and Knowledge, 1972–1973. ENCORE* (Lacan 1998) as some kind of ultimate rebooting of *Civilisation and Its Discontents* (Freud 2002a). Moreover, taking this meta-level reading of Lacanianism one stage further, the works of the Ljubljana School of Psychoanalysis become the contemporary, ever more nihilistic versions of the same (with Žižek as the high priest of such anti-ethical carnage). One can find these readings of Žižek, for example, in a text such as *The Truth of Žižek* (Bowman and Stamp 2007).

But there is also a very different reading of the original and later Freudian project possible, one which similarly connects this project organically to that of Lacan and the later Ljubljana School of Psychoanalysis, but which avoids such negative conclusions. Here, while all the ambiguity and inherent tension of Freud and succeeding versions of psychoanalysis are stressed, nonetheless this pessimistic version of interpretation is seen as far too one-sided and reductive. Instead, there are far more possibilities of affirmative ethical and political understanding present in this second interpretation. Here, the Lacanian text *The Ethics of Psychoanalysis* (Lacan 1992) becomes particularly important.

In his 'Translator's Note' (Porter 1992) to this latter text, Dennis Porter speaks to the complex question of Lacan's 'style'. We have mentioned above the important discussions in relation, for example, to Derrida and Lacan, deconstruction and psychoanalysis, with regard to style (Derrida 1988; Hurst 2008). There, Derrida speaks of Lacan's 'critique of semanticism' as being at the foundation of Lacan's approach to the organization of his texts. Our discussion above of the essay 'Kant with Sade' (Lacan 2002b) came from the *Écrits* (Lacan 2002a), which, although itself a diverse collection, nonetheless involves essays completed by Lacan's own hand. However, in the case of the editing and publication of the seminars, we are dealing with a more complex (and, for some, far more controversial) hermeneutic situation. Macey (1988), for example, is highly critical of the process by which the seminars have come to be published, arguing that this process itself has engendered the kind of 'myth of the hero' reading of Lacan which is averse to proper critical discussion. Here, the role of Jacques-Alain Miller is heavily criticized by Macey, although the reading of Miller through the Ljubljana School of Psychoanalysis is far more positive (Žižek et al. 2014).

Whatever the truth of this politicized process, perhaps a more important point, as Porter notes, is the more positive pluralism of the Lacan seminars in and of itself. As Porter observes here: 'the experience of those who read the seminar is in the experience of a thought in the making; . . . a captivating spoken word that sometimes meanders, throws out asides. Refers backwards or anticipates future problems, moves through passages dense with difficult ideas, narrates an illustrative comic anecdote, draws out the forgotten etymological significance of a word or resorts suddenly to popular speech' (Porter 1992: viii). We referred above to the comparison one can make between the Lacanian seminar and the seminars of Kojève. Both were informal, written up not by the speakers but by those who attended, and both were an extraordinary influence on a whole generation of thinkers. As we saw, the Kojève seminars were crucial to Lacan's own understanding of Hegelianism, as well as his own self-understanding and development as a thinker. But another comparison, equally apt, might be made to the process of Plato's dialogues (Plato 1961). These dialogues often become congealed into a certain univocal hermeneutics, referred to as 'Platonism'. But reading the dialogues in and of themselves, one can only be struck by the seemingly endless semantic ambiguities and textual suggestivity. It is striking, for example, how Plato's dialogues become such an important resource for both Freud (1977) and Lacan (1992). Oftentimes, as we suggested above, this more ambiguous reading of Plato is employed against the more traditionalist approach of Aristotelianism (we will see this again in the discussion of 'ethics'). Indeed, one of the most powerful developments of the Platonic legacy in recent years has precisely been Zupančič's (2008a) radical reinterpretation of the discussion of 'eros' in *The Symposium* (Plato 1961). Once more, the connections between Plato and psychoanalysis (this time, through the Ljubljana school) remain strong.

When we come to the seminar itself here, on *The Ethics of Psychoanalysis*, we see that Lacan precisely does want to foreground a robust enough 'ethics' to properly deal with the challenge which we have seen him outline already in the essay 'Kant with Sade'. These texts are both from roughly the same period of Lacan's work and we can see the shared thematics. In his 'Outline of the Seminar' (Lacan 1992: 1), Lacan delineates the substantive issues to be addressed. It is hardly surprising given what we have discussed above in relation to 'Kant with Sade' (Lacan 2002b) that his first main topic is what he describes as 'the attraction of transgression [la faute]' (Lacan 1992: 1). As Porter notes, the translation of 'la faute' is not straightforward. 'Lacan's word here "la faute" translated as transgression, has a great range of potential equivalents; from wrong, error, mistake, to blame, misconduct, and offense; "the fault" also' (Porter 1992: 1). What is perhaps most significant for our purposes is that the notion of 'transgression' which is how Lacan seems to mean the term here more or less, is tied very intimately to the tradition of thinking which we saw expressed above through Klossowski (1991) (and also Bataille). In other words, in seeking to reground the notion of the 'ethical', Lacan is intent on drawing on a precisely counter-Enlightenment tradition very much at odds with earlier (and more conventional) conceptions of the moral or the 'Good'. The latter notion especially comes under direct fire from Lacan (we might compare this also with Badiou's *Ethics* [Badiou 2000] where the notion of the 'Good' is vehemently undermined). At the same time as thus critiquing the more traditional understandings, while drawing on the resources of surrealism and the avant-garde, Lacan is also keen to stress that there is something originally new in what he is terming the 'ethics of psychoanalysis': 'what is new in both Freud's thought and in the experience of psychoanalysis that derives from it. The experience of psychoanalysis is highly significant for a certain moment in the history of man' (Lacan 1992: 1).

What is Lacan claiming here? His reference to a 'certain moment' suggests that something occurs with the advent of Freud's thinking and the origins of psychoanalysis as such, which is historically unprecedented in the tradition of philosophy. We will see in the interviews how the Ljubljana School of Psychoanalysis, while drawing on ancient and premodern resources philosophically (both Hellenic and medieval), nonetheless also associate psychoanalysis with an irreducibly modernist moment. On Dolar's et al. (2014) terms, for example, there are cases where earlier thought can really only offer 'metaphoric approximations' of later insights derived, for example, from the transcendental philosophy of Kant. Indeed, Žižek similarly in his interview, speaks of philosophy 'beginning with Kant' (Žižek et al. 2014).

Here, in this context, we can also see how this reading of certain epochal shifts in philosophical thinking can also apply directly to the history of thinking on ethics. Zupančič's work is especially instructive in this regard; for example, her text *Why Psychoanalysis? Three Interventions* (Zupančič 2008b), where she discusses the whole relation between psychoanalysis and philosophy, but crucially her first monograph in English, *The Ethics of the Real: Kant, Lacan* (Zupančič 2000). In this latter text, the world of traditional philosophical ethics is turned upside down and made to see its affinities with, of all people, Sade's discourse (Zupančič 2000), precisely following Lacan's 'Kant with Sade' (Lacan 2002b). As Zupančič notes here, 'the concept of ethics, as it is developed throughout the history of philosophy, suffers a double "blow of disillusionment" at the hands of psychoanalysis' (Zupančič 2000). How so? Zupančič goes on: 'the Freudian blow to philosophical ethics can be summarised as follows: what philosophy calls the moral law – and more precisely what Kant calls the "categorical imperative" – is in fact nothing other than the superego' (Zupančič 2000: 1). The second blow follows from Lacan's extension of the Freudian moment to make Kant complicit with Sade: 'the thesis of "Kant with Sade" is not simply that Kantian ethics has a merely "perverse" value. It is also the claim that Sade's discourse has an ethical value; that it can be properly understood only as an ethical project' (Zupančič 2000: 2). It is this latter conception which is perhaps the most shocking in Lacan's approach, at least from the point of view of conventional morals – Sade as an ethicist. This was certainly Lacan 'on the warpath' against conventional morality, society and the repressive psychic register (Badiou 2009).

Lacan, in his outline for the seminar *The Ethics of Psychoanalysis* (Lacan 1992: 2), foregrounds what he sees as a key distinction between the notion of 'ethics', on the one side, and the notion of 'morality' on the other. As Lacan notes in this context, 'in speaking of the ethics of psychoanalysis, I might have said morality instead' (Lacan 1992: 2). But, of course, the key point being made by Lacan here is that there is a world of difference between the two, ethics and morality. Lacan gives an indication of what he understands by such an 'ethics' when he refers to the notion of 'transgression', 'the attraction of transgression' or what he here now calls 'the morbid universe of transgression' (Lacan 1992: 2). Again, we can relate this problematic back to our earlier discussion of Klossowski's theoretical framework, in relation to the essay 'Kant with Sade' (Lacan 2002b). There, we explored Klossowski's radically heterodox reinterpretation of Sade, reading the latter very much against the standard modernist approach and foregrounding the medieval Christian conception of *delectatio morosa* or 'morose delectation' (also 'morbid pleasure') (Klossowski 1991: 112). 'Morose delectation consists in that movement of the soul by which it bears itself voluntarily towards images of forbidden carnal or spiritual acts in order to linger in contemplation of them' (Klossowski 1991: 113). In his seminar on *The Ethics of Psychoanalysis* (Lacan 2002a), and in a more systematic fashion than in the essay from the *Écrits* (Lacan 2002a), Lacan once again refers to the 'morbid universe of transgression' (Lacan 1992: 2).

We should be careful of simply equating Klossowski's heterodox reading of Sade with that of Lacan, although Lacan affirms the former reading as very significant (Lacan 2002b). One of the key questions for us will be where we might see Klossowski and Lacan diverge? In seeking to develop what he terms an 'ethics of psychoanalysis', Lacan wants to show affinity but also some independence from the position of Klossowski. For example, we have seen him refer at the beginning of his 'Outline of the Seminar' (Lacan 1992: 1) to 'what is new in Freud and from the experience of psychoanalysis'. Certainly, in Klossowski's reading of Sade in *Sade, My Neighbour* (Klossowski 1991), there is, at times, simply too much of the logic of an inverted Christian ethic. This becomes clearer in his important *Appendix* to the text (Klossowski 1991: 137ff), where Klossowski affirms the notion of 'sin'. Klossowski clarifies the genealogy of this faith in sin through a discussion of Carpocrates, whom he describes as a 'Gnostic sectarian' (Klossowski 1991: 138). The Carpocratian sect of the Gnostics gave an especial emphasis to Matthew 5.25-26; 'agree with thine adversary' (Klossowski 1991: 138). On their interpretation, this passage involved an acceptance of the adversary of sin: 'crime is a tribute paid to life, they say, a tribute demanded by the creator of this life. It is necessary, then, that the soul delivers itself over to sin as soon as temptation presents itself' (Klossowski 1991: 138). The Sadean crimes against humanity are thus interpreted by Klossowski as intrinsically religious acts; they are perpetuated not against the sacred but precisely in the name of the sacred against the rational morality and social solidarity of modernity. Sade thus becomes an unlikely advocate of religiosity and the sacred, albeit in an unorthodox key and under the 'mask of atheism'.

This Klossowskian interpretation lies behind much of the discussion of ethics in Lacan, during this period of his work especially and in the essay 'Kant with Sade' (Lacan 2002b). We will see that the emphases change in, for example, some of the later seminars, such as Seminar XI on *The Four Fundamental Concepts of Psychoanalysis* (Lacan 1994) and Seminar XX, *On Feminine Sexuality. The Limits of Love and Knowledge, 1972–1973. ENCORE* (Lacan 1998). However, even here in the earlier texts on ethics, there are different issues at work for Lacan (and his reformulated psychoanalysis) than there are for Klossowski. Most especially, Lacan wishes to draw out the ethical significance of Freud's work, as he says 'In Freud, a body of thought and development; the importance of the ethical dimension' (Lacan 1992: 2).

In relation to the reading of Freud, Lacan has two major aims. To demonstrate, first of all, what we have seen Zupančič describe as the 'blow of disillusionment at the hands of psychoanalysis' (Zupančič 2000) which Freudianism inaugurates. And second, that this experience of disillusionment, this 'undergoing' is not simply an end in itself for Freud. This kind of nihilistic teleology is the meta-level interpretation of Freud (and Lacan) which we have discussed in relation to Bersani's controversial reading of the late Freud text *Civilisation and Its Discontents* (Freud 2002a). But it is precisely this nihilistic reading which Seminar VII is set up against, which it sets out to contest. In his 'Outline of the Seminar' (Lacan 1992), Lacan makes clear that this is one of his two main targets, which he associates here with a reading of psychoanalysis as a 'naturalist liberation of desire' (Lacan 1992: 3), Freud as connecting back to a tradition of 'eighteenth century' libertinage. As he notes here, 'A certain eighteenth century philosophy; the naturalist liberation of desire has failed' (Lacan 1992: 3).

Just as in 'Kant with Sade', where Lacan seeks to extricate Sade from this tradition of libertinage, now he also seeks to extricate Freudianism and psychoanalysis from such a mistaken (modernist libertarian) permissiveness. We might note in passing here the strong connections between this argument and Bataille's arguments in his important text, *Eroticism*, published a few years earlier in 1957 (Bataille 2001). But Lacan also has an equally important target in mind in this text; the tradition of a certain supposed authentic psychoanalysis which, on Lacan's own terms, quite distorts the Freudian legacy. Here, in a striking and complex passage from the 'Outline', Lacan directs his ire. He notes, 'A general tendency to reduce the paradoxical elements which might bring about a harmonious conclusion; . . . it is worth asking if this theoretical progress was not leading in the end to an even more all embracing moralism than any that has previously existed. Psychoanalysis would seem to have as its sole aim the calming of guilt, the taming of perverse *jouissance*' (Lacan 1992: 4).

Although he doesn't name it here, the ideology of 'ego psychology' and its attendant therapy, attempting to transmit a very different Freudianism from that of Lacan, is what is at issue. Lacan is very direct and simple in his opposition to the 'general tendency' which is described as being reductionistic and attempting to do away with the 'paradoxical elements', so as to bring about 'harmony'. Lacan also associates this supposed harmony with an 'all embracing moralism'. It is clear, then, that when Lacan wishes to instigate an 'ethics of psychoanalysis', he has no intention of reinstituting such a 'moralism'. This brings us back to the earlier discussion – Lacan has chosen the concept of 'ethics', but not that of 'morality'. Here, the latter concept of 'morality' is indistinguishable from its pejorative expression as a 'moralism', which is seen as reducing paradox amidst its generalizations of the 'Good', in the name of a false kind of 'harmony'. In contrast, we can deduce that Lacan's more authentic 'ethics of psychoanalysis' will seek to affirm rather than reduce paradox and will be less directed by a teleology of 'harmony'.

For Lacan, as he now clarifies, this latter logic of harmony has come to define the moral–ethical tradition as we have known it, which Lacan interprets in strongly negative terms as a reductionistic 'moralism'. Aristotelianism comes to take on a paradigm status once more for Lacan in this context, this time in terms of its moral expression as a teleology of 'eudaimonia' (happiness or flourishing). In very direct and militant terms, Lacan contextualizes this seminar in terms of a powerful opposition between this latter eudaimonistic Aristotelianism and a specific Freud – the Freud of *Civilisation and Its Discontents* (Freud 2002).

The key problem as Lacan sees it in relation to the Aristotle/Freud dualism is summed up in his closing phrase to this key passage: 'Psychoanalysis would seem to have as its sole aim the calming of guilt, the taming of perverse *jouissance*' (Lacan 1992: 4). What is at stake then is not simply an abstract matter of the history of philosophy and the reading of an age-old Aristotelian discourse on flourishing. Rather, what is at stake is the matter of now, here today, the contemporary interpretation of psychoanalysis. In brief, psychoanalysis (in the guise, for example, of 'ego psychology') would have become indistinguishable from Aristotelianism as an ethics, as a 'moralism'. As against the heterodox interpretations of, for example, Klossowski (1991) which we described above, which provide the impetus for Lacan's rereading of the essay 'Kant with Sade' (Lacan 2002b), there would rather be an attempt to domesticate Freudianism as a therapy for perversion and 'jouissance' (Lacan 1992: 4). 'Jouissance' is the term here which comes to stand for 'excessive pleasure' in Lacan's discourse – he will return to it in Seminar XX, *On Feminine Sexuality. The Limits of Love and Knowledge, 1972–1973. ENCORE* (Lacan 1998). It is also a concept which becomes increasingly important for the Ljubljana School of Psychoanalysis. Here, in an earlier Lacanian seminar, we have a key index of why it does become so important. In effect, 'jouissance' in Seminar VII stands for the impossibility of psychoanalysis becoming a therapy of happiness or Aristotelian 'eudaimonia' ('flourishing'). In her later text on comedy, *On Comedy: The Odd One In* (Zupančič 2008a), Zupančič will refer pejoratively to this reductionistic psychology which has become ever more hegemonic in contemporary society as a 'bio-morality'. Again, as with Lacan in this context, we should note the key distinction between 'ethics' and 'morality'. Lacan, in Seminar VII, wishes to mark this clear distinction of an authentic psychoanalysis from Aristotelianism: 'How subversive our experience is; since it serves to render his (Aristotle's) theory surprising, primitive, paradoxical and in truth incomprehensible' (Lacan 1992: 5).

Developing this distinction between Aristotle and Freud on ethics, and seeking to reformulate psychoanalysis as an ethics against the false moralism of ego psychology, Lacan draws explicitly on the later Freud in this context, with special reference to the text *Civilisation and Its Discontents* (Freud 2002a). As Lacan observes: 'And in order to draw attention immediately to the work in which we will take up the problem, I refer you to *Civilization and Its Discontents* published in 1922, and written by Freud after working out his second topic, that is to say, after he had placed in the foreground the highly problematic notion of the death instinct' (Lacan 1992: 6).

Lacan's oft-quoted 'return to Freud' is thus of a very specific sort. We should note the explicit clues that Lacan gives us here, as to his overall meta-level reading of the Freudian legacy for contemporary psychoanalysis. First, *Civilisation and Its Discontents* (Freud 2002a) will be at the heart of the overall interpretation, which as a work of the later period suggests already a certain progressive or developmental interpretation of Freud. A little further on, in case there was any doubt, Lacan will refer to this text as 'an indispensable work unsurpassed for an understanding of Freud's thought and the summation of his experience' (Lacan 1992: 6). Second, for Lacan, what is particularly foregrounded in this reading is the 'death instinct' or 'death drive'. This becomes a key notion for the Ljubljana School of Psychoanalysis as we shall see, but we must be wary of an overly simplified reading of this concept. For example, above we spoke of Bersani's preface to the most recent edition of this text as adopting what we might call a 'literalist' understanding of the death drive (Bersani 2002). For Bersani, the death drive equals unabated nihilism. However, this is not the reading which Lacan puts forward here. Aside from the necessary contextualization of this being a text on 'ethics', Lacan also warns the reader against literalism by referring to this notion of the 'death drive' as 'highly problematic' (Lacan 1992: 6). This problematicity goes to the heart of the interpretative enterprise, as it calls into question whether there is a unified meta-level psychoanalysis as such. We will return to this question below with regard to the Lacan–Derrida encounter (Derrida 1988; Hurst 2008) and we will also see it recur more recently in the debate between Žižek (2010) and Catherine Malabou (2012) on the projected future of psychoanalysis (e.g., for Malabou, in relation to critiques coming from neuroscience). We will explore this current debate in the Epilogue (Žižek 2010; Malabou 2012).

More specifically, in this context, Lacan uses this hermeneutic ambiguity to reformulate one of the central Freudian ethical propositions, which Lacan regards as having been fatally misrecognized by ego psychology. In Freud's principle of 'Wo Es war, soll Ich werden' (usually translated as: 'where the id was, the ego shall be'), there has been an apparent justification for the therapy of 'happiness' which we described above. But as Porter notes, Lacan begs to differ: 'Rather than strengthening the ego as the great intellectual and ideological rival of Lacanian psychoanalysis, *ego psychology*, encouraged the patient to do, Lacan claims that the analysand must [engage in] . . . modifying the moorings that anchor his being' (Porter 1992: 7). This relates back to Lacan's earlier statement that ethics requires of the subject a kind of revolutionary transformation or 'rectification' (Lacan 1992: 1). As with the notion of the 'death drive', such a process would be far from linear and straightforward. At the very least, it would be 'highly problematic' (Lacan 1992: 6). In the same way, then, that the subject must undergo an ambiguous and highly problematical process to be ethical, so too must the very meta-level understanding of what an 'ethics of psychoanalysis' is remain irreducibly problematic. This is where the critique of the more univocal (Cartesian) semantics of ego psychology is unequivocal. It is also where we can see the 'critique of semantics' integral to Lacan's very textual style (which we saw Derrida [1988] describe) dovetail with and provide an authentic philosophical expression for the very 'ethics of psychoanalysis' (Lacan 1992). It is in its failure to come to terms with such a philosophical and ethical complexity that ego psychology (and mistranslated contemporary versions of Freudian 'therapy') can be said by Lacan to 'shirk [their] tasks' (Lacan 1992: 7).

This, then, is precisely the task at hand for the future, not to be 'shirked', as envisaged by Lacan's 'ethics of psychoanalysis'. Again, Lacan wishes to stress that although the foundation for ethics was provided by the Aristotelian tradition and although it might appear that he is seeking to continue this tradition, rather something else is taking place. 'Insofar as Freud's position constitutes progress here, the question of ethics is to be articulated from the point of view of the location of man in relation to the "real". To appreciate this, one has to look at what occurred in the interval between Aristotle and Freud' (Lacan 1992: 7). This 'interval' between Aristotle and Freud should not be underestimated – it is, in effect, unbridgeable. What Lacan (and Freud) mean by ethics is unrecognizable to an Aristotelian. This at least is the claim being made in Seminar VII: 'since Aristotle's time, we have experienced a complete reversal of point of view' (Lacan 1992: 7).

From 'Kant with Sade' (Lacan 2002b) then to Seminar VII on *The Ethics of Psychoanalysis* (Lacan 1992), there is a clear outline of a trajectory for a new interpretation of psychoanalysis. However, we might say that what this psychoanalysis rails against is far clearer than what it exactly constitutes in terms of positive content. Lacan, in both these texts, clearly opposes two main traditions of thinking, as we have elaborated. On the one side, he attacks the traditional form of metaphysics, the science of being, and especially the mode in which this metaphysics is articulated through an 'ethics' of 'happiness', 'harmony' etc. This metaphysical ethics, the paradigm for Lacan being the Aristotelian eudaimonistic approach, constitutes a reductionism in relation to human life and possibility for Lacan. It has also, on his interpretation (and this view will be continued by his successors in the Ljubljana School of Psychoanalysis, such as Zupančič [2008a]) had a pernicious effect on societal norms around the desire to be happy and the failure to come to terms with a darker side of the human condition (a key concept for Lacan here being 'jouissance' or [excessive/deficient] enjoyment). Lacan captures what he sees as this integral instability in the human condition and desire for pleasure in the phrase 'plus de jouir', meaning both 'more pleasure' and 'no more pleasure' (Lacan 1998).

On the other side, Lacan's key opponent comes from within the psychoanalytical school itself. This opposition, which is even more vehement than in the first instance, is towards what is referred to as 'ego psychology' and the attempt to defend a culture of therapy (not dissimilar to the Aristotelian cultural politics just described) precisely in the name of Freud and Freudianism. This is why Lacan is so keen to pinpoint what he refers to as the 'interval' between Freud and Aristotle: 'since Aristotle's time, we have experienced a complete reversal of point of view' (Lacan 1992: 7). The difference between Aristotle and Freud is not simply a localized one, but rather a fundamental discord, an irreducible conflict.

Not the least interesting question here as an implication of this fundamental conflict is what it can tell us about the relation between philosophy as such and psychoanalysis. As described by Lacan (1992) in *The Ethics of Psychoanalysis*, for example, the so-called irreducible 'interval' between Freud and Aristotle might also be affirmed by an Aristotelian. On this reading, one might argue, as an Aristotelian, that what we have here in effect are two different disciplines of thought, on the one side philosophy (represented by Aristotle) and on the other psychoanalysis (represented by Freud). For the Aristotelian, then, the interval which separates Aristotle and Freud would point to the distorting nature of psychoanalysis as a hermeneutic lens. Consequently, the whole attempt to make Kant complicit with Sade would be an example, for the Aristotelian, of the complete failure of psychoanalysis to understand the nature of authentic ethical practice and reflection.

As we discussed earlier, there is also a sense in which Freud and Lacan would agree with this meta-level reading of the relation between psychoanalysis and philosophy, but of course understood from the opposite side. Both thinkers (and especially Freud) tend towards a very suspicious view of philosophy as a discipline and its attempts at 'system building'. While this view has its merits and its justifications, there are also difficulties attached to it. In many respects, it significantly weakens the case for psychoanalysis if it simply generalizes the whole history of pre-psychoanalytical thought as some kind of reductive and aberrant mistake. Here, as Macey (1988) has suggested, there is also the risk of underestimating the debt which psychoanalysis owes (in the cases of Freud, Lacan and others) precisely to the philosophical tradition. Their significant recourse to Platonism (as in the case of Freud's theory of Eros) would be just one example of such a debt having to be repaid (Freud 1977).

However, there is a more significant problem for our purposes with this analysis, that of a complete 'interval' between Freudian–Lacanianism and the history of philosophy. What such a binarism fails to do is explain in any convincing way the immense influence which Freudian–Lacanian thinking has had, not simply on contemporary culture, but also on succeeding philosophical and political thought. One of the major themes of this book is precisely the question of how Lacanianism, most especially Lacanian psychoanalysis, has had such a singular philosophical and political influence on the former Yugoslavia and Slovenia. But we can only understand this influence by moving beyond the terms of reference which Lacan himself set for his work, especially with regard to the relation between psychoanalysis and philosophy. In an analogous way to the mode in which Lacan sought to sometimes interpret 'Freud against Freud' so to speak, so too it would seem that if we are to properly understand the full significance of the 'Slovenian Lacan', we will also have to read, in some instances, 'Lacan against Lacan'. This, then, is where our story moves from Lacan's original trajectory to a trajectory of the Ljubljana School of Psychoanalysis. While, in principle, as we shall see, this evolution of the Lacanian discourse is described by its proponents as 'orthodox', it will also become clear that this is no literalist orthodoxy. Rather, as Dolar puts it succinctly in his interview, 'orthodoxy is transformation' (Dolar et al. 2014).

Conclusion – Lacanianism via Derrida and the Ljubljana troika

In our discussion of Lacan's Seminar VII, *The Ethics of Psychoanalysis* (Lacan 1992) above, we foregrounded Lacan's emphasis on Freud's concept of the 'death drive'. But we also noted how commentators such as Bersani (2002) have been far too quick to assimilate such a framework to a 'nihilism'. Instead, Lacan is far more cautious in his reading of Freud, citing the concept but also referring to a reading of it as 'highly problematic'. This hermeneutic reticence of Lacan has been much criticized, as it is often perceived as a kind of obscurantism or conceptual and philosophical weakness. For example, even in the case of Badiou (2009), who praises highly the Lacanian approach to thought, there is the description of Lacan's thinking as an 'antiphilosophy'. We have also seen that even in Lacan (and Freud's) self-descriptions as thinkers, there is some evidence to suggest that this anti-philosophy perspective might be a valid interpretation.

What is interesting, however, as we go on to develop our reading of this narrative of the 'Slovenian Lacan', is that the Ljubljana School of Psychoanalysis, which will take up this reading of Lacan, reject tout court this interpretation of an 'anti-philosophy'. In this concluding section to the chapter, and before looking in more detail at the individual philosophical systems of Žižek, Dolar and Zupančič, we will briefly look at some of the dilemmas surrounding this question of the relation between psychoanalysis and philosophy. Beginning with an exploration of the infamous encounter between Derrida and Lacan (Derrida 1988; Hurst 2008) and developing through reference to some of the Lacanian aspects of the NSK art practice, I will conclude with a brief anticipation of how the Ljubljana School of Psychoanalysis can be seen as evolving this problematic. Of course, the answers suggested, or sometimes simply the way the questions are articulated, tend to differ across the examples of the three individual thinkers, Žižek, Dolar and Zupančič, respectively.

First, then, let us refer to the Derrida–Lacan encounter. It is perhaps not coincidental that the encounter should primarily take place around a contested analysis of one of the stories of Edgar Allen Poe, the enigmatic narrative of 'The Purloined Letter'. Poe's work, both his gothic narratives and his poetry, can itself be situated in a very close relationship with the avant-garde of French surrealism which we discussed earlier as having such a strong influence on Lacan's thinking (Macey 1988). Here, we can refer again to Benjamin's extraordinary essay, 'Surrealism: The Last Snapshot of the European Intelligentsia' (Benjamin 1979) for some context. Benjamin makes one reference in this essay to Poe, speaking of the 'depth of the insights of Poe' (Benjamin 1979: 236) in relation to what Benjamin sees as the genuinely subversive politics (and 'poetics') of surrealism: 'they are the first to liquidate the sclerotic liberal-moral-humanistic ideal of freedom' (Benjamin 1979: 236). In Lacanian terms, we might say that this puts them on the side of psychoanalysis over against 'ego psychology', on the side of an 'ethics of psychoanalysis' as against the 'moralism' which Lacan is so weary of in Seminar VII (Lacan 1992). Benjamin also attacks exactly the combination of this moralism with politics: 'characteristic of this whole left-wing bourgeois position is its irremediable coupling of idealistic morality with political practice' (Benjamin 1979: 234).

Benjamin anticipates the critique of the 'moralisation of the political', of which Mouffe (2005) has been such a powerful example. In stressing the notion of ethics, psychoanalysis must be careful to avoid becoming complicit with conservative and reactionary moralism. This is Lacan's point in *The Ethics of Psychoanalysis* (Lacan 1992) and it explains why he seeks to make the moral assurance of Kantianism uneasy with a juxtaposition against a far more decadent counter-example (of Sade) in 'Kant with Sade' (Lacan 2002b). It is also Benjamin's exact critique of bourgeois leftism in his seminal essay on surrealism and we will see a very similar unease recur in the Slovenian context in the subversive art practice of the NSK. There is a strong connecting line between the subversions of surrealism and the 'unbearable' art practices of Laibach, IRWIN and the NSK as described by Žižek in Ljubljana through the 1980s (Žižek 2003b).

There is also a strong connecting line between surrealism and the Derrida–Lacan encounter (Irwin 2010). In her important text, *Derrida vis-à-vis Lacan: Interweaving Deconstruction and Psychoanalysis*

(Hurst 2008), Andrea Hurst argues that the philosophical and stylistic approaches of Derridean deconstruction and Lacanian psychoanalysis, after a detailed analysis, are far more congruent than one might imagine on first inspection: 'Derrida, it would seem, loves Lacan. It is, he insists, "for the love of Lacan" that he emphasises the important political obligation to embrace a difficult thinking that rebels against normalisation' (Hurst 2008: 2). Much has been made, as Hurst also shows, of the seeming ideological rift between the two thinkers, but here we should note the 'political' dimension which Derrida foregrounds. Alongside the 'ethics of psychoanalysis' there would also be a 'politics' of psychoanalysis, and on Derrida's terms, it would be a politics contra 'normalisation'. We have seen this viewpoint also articulated strongly by no less a radical political thinker and activist than Badiou, in his obituary of Lacan (Badiou 2009): 'Lacan was on the warpath from the very beginning'.

This is also the related thematic of Benjamin in his essay on surrealism: against all appearances to the contrary, surrealism would be far more politically subversive than the kind of 'moralism' associated with 'bourgeois leftism' and egalitarianism. The latter political ideologies remain complicit with the worst kind of naive utopianism concerning the 'good' (or, even more farcically, the 'Good') of human nature: 'how naive is the view of the Philistines that goodness, for all the many virtues of those who practice it, is God-inspired' (Benjamin 1979: 234). In another great and revealing phrase, Benjamin refers to the 'helpless compromises of sentiment' (Benjamin 1979: 234), the reality being of course that such egalitarian 'sentiment' is mostly simply self-serving and self-justifying, reinforcing the privileges of the status quo.

It is precisely in this context that we can better understand Lacan's recourse to Sade, to Klossowski and to the rather enigmatic notion of 'evil' in the essay 'Kant with Sade' (Lacan 2002b). Again, in Benjamin's terms, this is an 'evil' which 'stems entirely from our spontaneity, and in it we are independent and self-sufficient beings' (Benjamin 1979: 234). The notion of the 'good' and the related notions of 'flourishing' and 'eudaimonia' (or 'happiness) in Aristotelian terms point towards an objectivist well-being, however ultimately self-deceptive this perspective may be in Lacanian terms. In contrast, the emphasis on 'evil' through surrealism, Sade and Klossowski points rather to existential and sociopolitical crises: 'the Surrealists have understood its present commands. They exchange, to a man, the play of human features for the face of an alarm clock that in each minute rings for sixty seconds' (Benjamin 1979: 239).

In such a context, it is hardly surprising that in *The Ethics of Psychoanalysis* (Lacan 1992), Lacan should focus in on the later Freud and especially the Freud of *Civilisation and Its Discontents* (Freud 2002a). But if this is true, and if the notion of the 'death drive' is foregrounded there by Freud (which is then precisely re-emphasized by Lacan against ego psychology), it is also true that this should not be overstated. Rather, an irreducible equivocality regarding the death drive remains in Freud (and thus by implication in Lacan). If Lacan describes the matter as 'highly problematic', Freud had already gone one stage further, by reinvoking the drive of Eros as a counterpoint to Thanatos: 'And now it is to be expected that the other of the two "heavenly powers", immortal Eros, will try to assert himself in the struggle with his equally immortal adversary', with the one last, haunting question added in 1931: 'And who can forsee the outcome?' (Freud 2002a: 81).

This, of course, is also a question or an ambiguity concerning the very status of psychoanalysis itself: 'we don't know what will become of this psychoanalysis' (Lacan 2008). Rather than this being some kind of localized hermeneutic error to be remedied or tightened up, it is a systemic ambiguity, a structural and fundamental feature of this philosophical and psychoanalytical perspective. As Lacan says in relation to his reading of Freud: 'all of us share an experience based upon a system of concepts to which we remain faithful, partly because this system was developed by the man who opened up to us all the ways to that experience and partly because it bears the living mark of the different stages of its elaboration. That is to say, contrary to the dogmatism that is sometimes imputed to us, we know that this system remains open both as a whole and in several of its articulations' (Hurst 2008: 2). This is a powerful meta-level statement from Lacan (which he sees as precisely being faithful to Freudianism): 'we know that the system remains open as a whole'.

In the development of this Freudian–Lacanianism by the Ljubljana School of Psychoanalysis, there is one significant shift. Lacan and Freud saw this systemic openness as characteristic of psychoanalysis but oftentimes (at least in principle) as being at odds with the method of philosophical speculation (Macey 1988). In the case, however, of Žižek, Dolar and Zupančič, this systemic openness is shared by both psychoanalysis and philosophy. Where psychoanalysis ends and philosophy begins becomes increasingly hard to decipher, the borderlines being impossible to clearly and distinctly maintain. In the next three chapters, and dealing with each of these individual thinkers in turn, I want to explore how this Lacanian legacy is both adapted and continued.

CHAPTER THREE

From punk to cogito to voice: On Mladen Dolar

Introduction – Dolar's philosophical evolution

Although it is Slavoj Žižek's work in philosophy which has received the most attention internationally (Kay 2003), the genealogy of his Lacanian approach cannot be separated from the seminal figure of Mladen Dolar. Indeed, Žižek has constantly been the first to acknowledge Dolar's influence (Žižek et al. 2014). In our interview with Dolar et al. (2014), what becomes clear are the powerful ties of culture and friendship which bind the latter and Žižek, from the late 1960s onwards. As Dolar et al. (2014) observes, "71 was our '68'. Developing their work from this period onwards, one also sees significant philosophical commonalities, their both being influenced powerfully by the wider movement of French structuralism, a 'unity in difference' in the early 1970s, from Derrida to their fellow Eastern European, Kristeva. Their going to Paris, for example, in the late 1970s, their taking on a certain 'ultraorthodox' perspective in Lacanianism, the evolution of their work simultaneously in the local environs of Ljubljana and internationally. Finally, we see this philosophical and psychoanalytical duo develop into a troika with the emergence of Alenka Zupančič as a thinker in her own right, having been a gifted student of both Dolar and Žižek (Zupančič et al. 2014; Žižek et al. 2014).

Dolar's philosophical evolution, as we will see him describe it in the interview below, begins with the advent of a French structuralist influence, understood in a broad sense, through the 1970s to a more specific Lacanian orientation. In the 1980s, Dolar's editorial work with *Problemi* (through some of its most acute controversies) is noteworthy, foregrounding his important interpretations of the concept of fascism (Dolar 1982). This latter work is best understood as the beginning of the more advanced political critique of state socialism in the former Yugoslavia, which will find an international audience in Žižek's *The Sublime Object of Ideology* in 1989. Dolar continues this political critique in his significant monograph *A Voice and Nothing More* (Dolar 2006), which reads the advent of Milošević, in the former Yugoslavia, in relation to a whole psychoanalytics of inauthentic 'voice'. Here, he focuses on the employment of the enigma of the 'voice' by Milošević at political rallies in Serbia early in the conflict (Dolar 2006: 189).

Thus, we can read Dolar's work here alongside that of the work of Slovenian commentators such as Močnik (1993), Mastnak (1988) and Gantar (1993), as was discussed in Chapter 1, although Dolar's work remains perhaps less politically compromised than any of the latters' work. Here, his reading of Marx and the subtle reinterpretation of Marxist concepts such as ideology, the symptom and materialism in his work are crucial to his original contribution (Marx 1992a, 1992b; Balibar 2007). Dolar's work on the Neue Slowenische Kunst (NSK) and Laibach also brings out this crucial reinterpretation of ideology (Dolar 1989, 2003, 2006).

His work since the 1980s has seen a growing conceptual sophistication and development, with strong affinities to the work of Žižek, while remaining distinctive in its own specific philosophical concerns. In terms of the Lacanian perspective, it is perhaps Lacan's (1994) Seminar XI on *The Four Fundamental Concepts of Psychoanalysis* which is most evident in Dolar's reading, with special emphasis on the 'object voice' and the concept of the 'drive' (Dolar 2006). Dolar's work brings out the properly surrealist constitution of the drive, a connotation which Lacan constantly plays with in Seminar XI. One striking example of this more surrealist reading in Dolar's work is the employment of Kafka and what Dolar refers to as 'Kafka's Voices' (Dolar 2006) to explore the sheer absurdity of the drive, which nonetheless somehow ends up as a justification for psychoanalysis as a 'science of freedom' (Dolar 2006), albeit the only freedom available to us, a 'wretched freedom'.

Here, we can reinvoke Benjamin's understanding of freedom as it is articulated through surrealism (Kafka being another in a long line of dissident surrealists). Benjamin says: 'Since Bakunin, Europe has lacked a radical concept of freedom. The Surrealists have one' (Benjamin 1979: 236). And in a key which anticipates Dolar's analysis to come: 'They are the first to liquidate the sclerotic liberal-moral-humanistic ideal of freedom, because they are convinced that "freedom, which on this earth can only be bought with a thousand of the hardest sacrifices, must be enjoyed unrestrictedly in its fullness without any kind of pragmatic calculation, as long as it lasts"' (Benjamin 1979: 236).[1]

If there is a key Freudian text for Dolar, it is perhaps *Civilisation and Its Discontents* (Freud 2002a), with the emphasis on thanatology and an overarching 'death drive', a surging Thanatos having the upper hand on a defeatist Eros. Here, Dolar's work would seem to be in line only with the most radical of neo-Freudians, such as Leo Bersani (2002), who see this late Freudian text as apocalyptically jettisoning all anthropomorphic false hopes and cares. In Bersani's analysis, what becomes crucial to understand is the redirection which psychoanalysis takes 'against ego psychology' (Bersani 2002: xxi). But this critique, sometimes associated with Lacan (as against Freud), is here reread by Bersani as precisely a 'return to Freud', that is, to the later Freud and *Civilisation and Its Discontents* (Freud 2002a): 'Lacan's assault on ego psychology can be best justified as a profound fidelity to psychoanalysis itself, as a recognition that a psychology of adaptation to the world is by definition a nonpsychoanalytic psychology. Psychoanalysis gives a persuasive account not of human adjustment but of that which makes us unfit for civilised life; this should at least cast some doubt on the validity of any notion of a psychoanalytic "cure"' (Bersani 2002: xxi).

This rejection tout court of the adaptive version of psychoanalysis, whether of Freud or Lacan, links Bersani clearly to the perspective of the Ljubljana School of Psychoanalysis, and especially to Dolar (although we will see that this situation has changed somewhat). We might also cite here Zupančič's critique of what she terms contemporary 'bio-morality' and the fetishization of 'happiness' in her book on comedy, to which we will return later (Zupančič 2008a). However, we will see that, in their most recent work, both Dolar and Zupančič complicate the binarism between 'desire' and 'drive' or 'eros' and 'thanatos', instigating more of a 'doubling' complicity between these binary concepts. This 'doubling' will also allow for a way out of the impasse of life drives versus death drives. In this breakthrough, we can also see a distancing, in their readings of (Lacanian) psychoanalysis, between Dolar and Zupančič on the one side, and Bersani on the other.

This more 'deconstructive' reading of psychoanalysis links Dolar among others to Derrida, whose own relations to Lacanianism are complex (Hurst 2008). We see especially a strong affinity with Derrida in *A Voice and Nothing More* (Dolar 2006), although there Dolar is keen to stress his differences from the reading of 'phonocentrism' in deconstruction. In Dolar, following the later Lacan, the 'object voice' would foreground what Malcom Bowie has referred to as a 'localisation of strife' (Bowie 1991: 28): 'Thus is the strife of the Presocratics no longer at work ubiquitously in the cosmos but localised in the human species' (Bowie 1991: 28). This would perhaps be the paradox of Dolar's work, delivering a more apocalyptic (and satirical) message than either Žižek or Zupančič, while doing so with the utmost politeness and seeming goodwill (as the interview testifies). Dolar's deep suspicion of theology in philosophy, notable in the interview, and again very much in the spirit of the late Freud, can only look rather askance at some of Žižek's more recent theological affinities (Kotsko 2008; Žižek and Milbank 2009; Pearson 2013), and this would perhaps be a more significant philosophical difference than the interview admits. Here, Dolar and Zupančič would appear to be more congruent in a thoroughgoing psychoanalytical atheism. A paradigmatic example of this eschewal of the God-concept by Dolar is in his analysis of the 'cogito' in Descartes, where he views the latter as ultimately opting for a get-out clause of 'God as big Other' (Dolar 1998). This last move is rejected by Dolar as a residue of traditional (pre-modern) metaphysics, which awaits Kant and especially Hegel's ultimately atheistic phenomenology to be fully exorcized.

Reading Lacan-Hegel-Marx in Dolar

Lacan's work on the enigmatic notion of the 'subject' in the *Écrits* (Lacan 2002a) is also influential on Dolar's extraordinary reading of the 'cogito' in his seminal essay 'Cogito as the Subject of the

Unconscious' (Dolar 1998), which is also noteworthy for its brilliant overall meta-reading of Lacan. In this context, Dolar concludes his essay with an exploration of the whole corpus of Lacan's work. His analysis seems to have shown many different conceptions of the notion of 'subject' as it relates to other key concepts in psychoanalysis such as the 'Real' and this shifting ground is, Dolar admits, one of the oft-quoted reasons for Lacan's supposed 'difficulty' in being read. Dolar sees this as a paradox as he describes simultaneously not only 'the baffling differences of Lacan's system' but also 'the exceptional unity' (Dolar 1998: 37), 'the implacable logic . . . and the stubborn search' (Dolar 1998: 38). Again, we might see this as connected to a more traditional understanding of philosophy, going back to the Greeks, as an endless questing or in Platonic terms a 'dialogue' with truth or even, understood more negatively, a 'refutation' of truth (elenchus) (Plato 1961). We will see Dolar link the psychoanalytic quest with the Platonic once again in his book on 'voice', where he describes both psychoanalysis and the Socratic philosophical project as forms of 'aprotreptic' (Dolar 2006), that is, forms of 'leading away from the truth' rather than towards it. But here, his analysis is focused specifically on the Lacanian trajectory. 'The problem with understanding Lacan stems among other things from the fact that one has to follow the logic of the development of his theory and not to take any of the stages for granted as some definitive shape of truth' (Dolar 1998: 38). And here we get to the nub of his meta-level reading of Lacan – against all appearances to the contrary (his 'dogmatic stance'), Lacan would in no way be a dogmatic thinker: 'Lacan's dogmatic stance goes hand in hand with his most undogmatic demeanour; only a dogmatist "on the level of the task" can never be afraid of putting into question the previous results, turning them upside down without mercy, if the new questions make it necessary' (Dolar 1998; 37). Of course, in an indirect way, this is also Dolar describing his own philosophical (Lacanian) method and, by extension, the method of the Ljubljana School of Psychoanalysis more generally.

Along with his avowed Lacanianism, there is also a markedly strong Hegelian influence in Dolar's work throughout, which can be seen, for example, as early as his PhD work on 'Hegel and Lacan' (Dolar et al. 2014). Arguably, this has itself had an effect on Žižek's more recent Hegelian emphasis (Žižek 2012a). What Dolar also demonstrates very well is the complexity of the relation between Lacan and Hegel, insofar as the former's reading of Hegel 'gets it significantly wrong' (Dolar et al. 2014). This is an enigmatic scene of interpretation which, for example, Bruce Baugh's (2005) work has helped us to understand better. Baugh provides some very helpful historical contextualization of this problematic and begins by complicating 'the notion that Alexandre Kojève's lectures brought Hegel to France' (Baugh 2005: 1). This common argument with regard to Kojève (while undoubtedly an influence in view of Lacan's faithful attendance at his seminar) nonetheless underestimates the alternative influences of surrealism, Marxism and also Jean Wahl, whose book on the 'unhappy consciousness' in Hegel precedes Kojève by a decade, beginning in 1929/1939. We discussed this matter in a different key in Chapter 2, in relation to Macey's controversial reading of Lacan (Macey 1988). Dolar's work is exemplary in the clarity of its exposition of this rather contorted and problematic scene of interpretation, which can also be seen in the light of the significant influence of surrealism on Lacan's work, which is much in evidence (Macey 1988; Lacan 1994).

As Baugh (2005: 5) outlines, the neo-Kierkegaardian Wahl also developed early a penetrating analysis (via a negative reading of Hegel) of 'a self divided against itself, an internally divided and self-alienated subject; a subject that strives vainly for synthesis but instead oscillates between self and non-self, being and nothingness'. We should keep this background in mind when coming to explore, through Dolar's analysis, the relation between Hegelianism and Lacan. The influence of this vision of the 'internally divided self' significantly influences Lacan in his notion of the 'subject', although in Dolar, this notion has more Hegelian resonance. What is also striking about Dolar's reading of Hegel is its critique of the latter's philosophical system as some kind of 'overarching synthesis'. The originality of the interpretation here is that it counters the accusation that somehow, for example in Derrida's view, that 'Hegel neglects dissymmetry': 'It is this dissymmetry which Hegel "misses"'; 'poetry, laughter, ecstasy are nothing; Hegel knows no other aim than knowledge; his immense fatigue is linked to his horror of the blind spot' (Derrida 1978: 256). For Derrida, Hegel cannot seem to philosophically register the absence of meaning or the dissymmetry of meaning. He tries to turn the blind spot into some kind of meaningful vision. For Dolar, to the contrary, the Hegelian system is on the side of 'nonmeaning', that which doesn't make sense. It is in this way that Hegel anticipates the Freudian and Lacanian 'unconscious', which is a 'thought which doesn't make sense' (Dolar 1998). Dolar's critical comments on Lacan's reading of Hegel also give the lie to those who would read Dolar as an 'orthodox Lacanian', in any sterile sense. Again, as his interview makes clear, for Dolar, *orthodoxy is transformation*.

Alongside Hegel, in the thinking of the troika, there is also Marx. Dolar's interview foregrounds the difficulties and significant conflicts between competing versions of Marxism in the history of the politics of the former Yugoslavia (Dolar et al. 2014), for example in relation to Žižek's difficulties in having his master's thesis accepted at Ljubljana, or in the distinction between 'dogmatic' and 'nondogmatic' Marxism which Dolar and Žižek invoke with regard to the reading of 'punk as a symptom' (Žižek 1981; Motoh 2012). The whole reading of Marx vis-à-vis psychoanalysis is at the heart, first of the movement of Praxis in Zagreb and Belgrade and then succeeding that phase, in the disagreements between the Ljubljana School of Psychoanalysis and the Praxis school. But what perhaps at least the Praxis school and Dolar, Žižek and Zupančič can agree on is the contribution of Marx to philosophy, which Balibar has described as another kind of 'Copernican revolution' in philosophy's self-understanding (Balibar 2007). For Balibar, while the early Marx starts out in a very philosophical mode, his mid-to-late work signifies a critique of philosophy's self-understanding as a kind of master discipline. To invoke Frederic Jameson, Marxism is 'unlike any other contemporary mode of thought, what I will call a unity-of-theory-and-practice'. The most obvious instance of this is in Marx's text 'Theses on Feuerbach' (Marx 1992a), where he outlines that, whereas previous philosophy had primarily sought to interpret the world, the point is 'rather to change it' (Marx 1992a: 423).

Dolar, as with both Žižek and Zupančič, thus takes a very modernist view on the nature of philosophical practice or 'praxis'. As with Žižek, philosophy proper is seen as beginning with Kant (or Descartes) (Dolar et al. 2014) and the premodern metaphysical conceptions of philosophy, seem rather for Dolar 'metaphoric approximations' of philosophical conceptuality in a post-Kantian sense. In this way, psychoanalysis is inconceivable for Dolar in a pre-Cartesian world and the notion of the 'unconscious' itself is a significantly radicalized concept in Freud and (further again) in Lacan, and should not be misunderstood in terms of earlier models which might, on a surface level, seem compatible (e.g., we might think here of Plato's conception of the 'tri-partite' psyche in *The Republic* or some of the conceptions of the mind in Aristotle's *De Anima*). In this way, psychoanalysis represents a radical break with previous philosophical thought. But, again, as with Žižek and Zupančič, Dolar does not read this as a rupture with philosophy per se. Each of the three thinkers is unequivocal on the status of their work as philosophy (perhaps even more than as psychoanalysis). Psychoanalysis in this sense *is* nothing but philosophy. Indeed, the urgency of Dolar's work stems precisely from a sense of philosophy's age-old responsibility to speak against the 'doxa' of the times, and here the legacy really does go all the way back to early Greece. Despite Dolar's emphasis on modern thought, his work is excellently grounded in the tradition of philosophy and his employment of, for example, pre-Socratic thought (in the shape of Heraclitus or Empedocles) or of Socrates or Plato is often rich in suggestion and insight.

Socrates and the daemonic voice

One significant example of this reference to the tradition of philosophy is Dolar's in-depth discussion of Socrates and the latter's 'daemonic voice' at a crucial juncture of the argument concerning the 'object voice' in *A Voice and Nothing More* (Dolar 2006). In a beautifully wild reading of Socrates (reminiscent of the brilliance of Derrida's reading of Plato in 'Plato's Pharmacy' [Derrida 1981] but wholly original in its own right), Dolar mesmerizes the reader into an understanding of the 'agent voice' as the connecting link between Plato, Lacan and the absurdity of contemporary existence (Dolar 2006). This section of the text is also noteworthy in that it thematizes what Dolar calls an 'ethics of the voice', foregrounding the concept of the *ethics of psychoanalysis*, which will become so crucial as a theme for Zupančič most especially (Zupančič 2000). But, of course, ethics as understood by psychoanalysis owes very little to traditional concepts of morality. In effect, ethics constitutes a full frontal assault on the *ressentiment* (Nietzsche 1967) of traditional forms of thinking, often linked together in a morality–theology matrix. As Bowie notes apropos Lacan, the superego grounds traditional morality and is an 'infantile solution to infantile problems' (Bowie 1991). Freud is similarly castigating concerning the 'illusions' of religion in, for example, *Civilisation and Its Discontents*, referring to religious belief as a particularly degenerate and persistent form of 'psychic infantilism' (Freud 2002a).

Here, Dolar follows both these examples, but paradoxically in relation to the more seemingly traditional figure of Socrates (Dolar 2006). In a powerful and original reflection on the voice and ethics, Dolar outlines how the 'daemonic voice' in Socrates can be seen as an ultimate authority, moreover an 'infallible authority beyond logos' (Dolar 2006: 85). Dolar connects this back to the very origins of philosophy itself, understood to be in the practice of Pythagoras, who spoke from behind a curtain to maintain the mystique of his philosophical voice. This original example captures, for Dolar, the paradox of the voice, simultaneously transcendent and the most intimate phenomenon, as in the case of Socrates who describes the daemonic voice as, at the same time, 'coming from on high' and a 'most inner voice' (Dolar 2006: 85). It is, Dolar says, 'intimate and extimate', an 'atopical voice' and of course, in these characteristics, the voice seems to resemble the very structure of subjectivity itself, as delineated in its very enigmatic contrariness in Seminar XI (Lacan 1994).

One might imagine, Dolar says, that such a voice would be 'prescriptive' but to the contrary, it tells us nothing positive. It only tells Socrates what he must not do and so in this way it is like the very method of elenchus (refutation) which Socrates uses as his paradigm of philosophical disputation, always pleading ignorance while undermining hubristic assertions of truth. Here, Dolar draws the comparison to philosophy itself, both the daemonic voice and philosophy being forms of 'aprotreptic' (Dolar 2006: 85), forms of leading one away from the truth and not closer to it: 'the voice has a negative aprotreptic function' (Dolar 2006: 85). Of course, by implication, we are also foregrounding here the analogy between psychoanalysis and philosophy. How far we are here from the assertive protreptic of, for example, ego psychology, where the answers to our problems would be clear and concise. Here, the aforementioned logic of Freud's *Civilisation and Its Discontents* converges almost perfectly with Dolar's Lacanian 'object voice'. In itself, perhaps, this is surprising enough. What is perhaps more startling is the connection back to the veritable Platonic tradition of philosophy.

We will also see Plato invoked crucially by Zupančič later in our analysis when she comes to read Plato's dialogue *The Symposium*

(Plato 1961) as the master text of the philosophy of comedy (Zupančič 2008a). Time and again in Freud and Lacan, one reads this avowal of Plato and the Platonic tradition (alongside a simultaneous, and vehement, disavowal of Aristotelianism) (Freud 1977, 2002a; Lacan 1992; Zupančič 2008a). A final point we might note here (although Dolar's important analysis here deserves greater time) is that the Socratic voice very much sets up ethics against legality and the 'political law' or in Greek terms, the *polis* or custom (*nomos*). As Dolar notes: 'The voice pertains to the moral law and not the political laws of the community, as the voice actually dissuaded Socrates from taking part in active political life. The Kantian opposition between morality and legality; morality as a matter of the voice and legality a matter of the letter' (Dolar 2006: 86). Here, we might see the 'voice' as an instrument of the 'critique of ideology', a critique which we have seen Dolar undertake, for example, in relation to his early defence of punk and alternative culture, an issue we will return to in the conclusion to this chapter (Dolar 1982, 2003). Of course, in the case of Žižek's work especially, this critique of ideology (still 'pertinent', despite all appearances: Žižek 1994b) will take centre stage (Žižek 1989, 1992a, 2008b).

Finally, with regard to Dolar's *oeuvre*, the inter-disciplinarity of his work must be mentioned. As he mentions in the interview (Dolar et al. 2014), *Tel Quel* was an early influence with its war cry of 'Lautréamont and Rimbaud for the 19th century, Bataille and Artaud for the 20th century'. Dolar's readings of literature and art (and more recently music and opera in his co-authored work with Žižek, *Opera's Second Death* [Dolar and Žižek 2002]) are always subtle and immensely patient, as befits the work of the son of a great Slovenian literary critic, Jaro Dolar. But it is perhaps Dolar's work on film, evident in all his texts, and especially his work on Hitchcock, extending in translation all the way back to the early 1990s' collection *Everything You Always Wanted to Know About Lacan But Were Afraid to Ask Hitchcock* (Žižek 1992b; Dolar 1992a, 1992b), which constitutes one of his most original contributions, again influencing a significant strand of recent film criticism and theory. But, as with all of Dolar's work, his analysis of film is done less for its own sake and more as part of an overall Lacanian philosophical vision, with a strong emphasis on political intervention. It was this emphasis which, as Močnik (1993) has noted, was one of the most powerful levers in the development of a society-wide critique of the former Yugoslavia and its problematical ideologies, breaking through the impasse. What is clear there is Dolar's leading role in what Močnik (1993) refers to as the emergent Lacanian orientation in Slovenia. It is arguable, in Slovenian philosophical circles, that Dolar may well be the more influential figure over Žižek, perhaps also insofar as his institutional role, in the philosophy department at the university, has led him to have a greater proximity to the next generation of philosophical thinkers. We can also see Dolar's role as paradigmatic in relation to Gantar's key analysis of the conflict between civil society and alternative culture in Slovenia (Gantar 1993; Motoh 2012). As the interview makes clear, the philosophical friendship between Dolar, Zupančič and Žižek remains as significant now as it ever was. Nonetheless, we can also point to significant differences between the approaches taken by the three thinkers in their own right.

'From Structuralism to Lacan' – Interview with Mladen Dolar

Helena Motoh and Jones Irwin: Slovenia has been described (for example, by Alexei Monroe) as having a markedly problematic genealogy in terms of nationhood and cultural independence. Can you say if and how this problematical genealogy might be seen as affecting your own work and how significant it is for you that you are seen as a 'Slovenian' philosopher or part of a 'Slovenian school' of philosophy?

Mladen Dolar: This is indeed a very complex history and let me seek to delineate some of its key aspects, as they are relevant to our problematic. First, one must say that the Yugoslav political and economic system was one of self-management and non-alignment under Tito and this was of course anti-Stalinist and in opposition to the Soviet system in principle. However, whether one takes this issue in a theoretical sense of Marxism or a practical sense of policy, one can argue that there was really only lip service paid to a critique of Stalinism in Yugoslavia. That is, in reality, the theory and practice was quite similar to what it was in the Soviet bloc. This explains the emergence, for example, of the Praxis movement in opposition to the regime, which itself was a Marxist philosophy, but one more consistently guided by an anti-Soviet 'humanism'. While this movement was mostly associated with philosophical figures in Belgrade and Zagreb, it also had a powerful influence in Slovenia and Ljubljana. In the 1970s, however, Praxis would be crushed by the authorities who saw it as a dangerous source of dissent and resistance. As an undergraduate philosophy student at Ljubljana, I can say that there was a mix of Marxism and Heidegger – they were the key early influences for me and for others, including Slavoj, who was just ahead of me in the philosophy degree at Ljubljana. However, while we can state this aspect of the Tito regime, nonetheless one should also be aware of the cosmopolitan nature of Ljubljana especially, with a mix of Germanic, Italian and Slavic influences. The partisan struggle of World War II was a key moment of identification for many, and of course, we see this recurring in some of the motifs of the work of the NSK.

The first opposition journal which was both cultural and philosophical was *Perspektive*, founded in 1957, influenced by existentialism and especially by Heidegger and Sartre. In 1969, *Perspective* was banned by the authorities and the writers joined another journal, *Problemi*, which had already been established. This was a key moment of struggle, the late 1960s and early 1970s which formed me – for example, I can cite the Vietnam War protests and also the evolution of more radical resistance groups. It was a time of tumult. Žižek had enrolled at university in 1967 and I enrolled in 1969. Slavoj and I first met in 1970. For us, the key moment was not 1968 but here in Ljubljana at the Faculty of Arts it was May 1971, when there was an occupation of the Faculty of Arts by protesting students, including ourselves. I became the chief editor of the student newspaper called *Tribuna*, and this involved a crystallizing of French structuralism and an attendant politicization of philosophy. If we want a connection between Lacan and 1968, for example, we can mention that Lacan smuggled Cohn Bendit to safety at the time. But, more importantly, structuralism can be seen as one framework in which to understand first, the May 1968 events and second, the evolution of this original moment later in Ljubljana. Of course, it was not simply a philosophical revolution. We might also mention the Vietnam protests, for example, as well as the occupation of Czechoslovakia, events which radicalized the students and the population. Another key figure here from a political perspective was Che Guevara. I might also mention that our specific situation in Slovenia meant that different and more varied influences were at work, both Austrian and Italian influences as opposed to the rest of Yugoslavia. These influences were more pronounced in Slovenia, as well as the influence of West Germany, of course. Although 1968 is often seen simply as a culturalist phenomenon, this is to miss the significant political issues of equality as well as liberty which were addressed in such a radically original way.

In Ljubljana then in May 1971, there was an occupation of the Faculty of Arts. Due to the wisdom of the Slovenian leadership at the time, and the view that strict punishment of those involved would only make matters more acute, no one was imprisoned. In May 1971, from a philosophical political perspective, we were still trying to evolve a very different kind of Marxism from the official state version. There was dramatic momentum and we looked to structuralism as a vigorous intellectual movement of unity – of course, later we would radically call into question this unity and opt instead for Lacan as the more singular figure within this movement. Later, the conflicts between different versions of structuralism became more apparent. But we should also note that we didn't in any way see Marxism and structuralism as mutually opposed or exclusive, quite the contrary in fact. *Tel Quel* as a journal of the Parisian literary Left was especially important to us at this juncture, as it seemed to unify these great figures of structuralism, whether one is talking about Lévi-Strauss, Lacan, Jacobson, Barthes, Kristeva, Sollers or the more generalized ferment of Maoism. Julia Kristeva was especially important to us, as due to her Bulgarian background we felt a key affinity with her. Again, we look forward here to one of the key thematics of the NSK, and especially IRWIN, their conception of the specificity of the Eastern European identity and culture, despite all the latter's internal differentiation, from the Western bloc. Also, this will recur as a theme especially in Slavoj's work. Translations of these French texts were also a key part of this hermeneutics; we would translate these French texts into Slovenian for the journals we were editing. For example, in 1974, I translated Kristeva for *Problemi*. We can note here the preponderance of this kind of intellectual culture of journals in Slovenia, something which has continued to the present. There is a terrific vibrancy within the Slovenian context in this regard, and all the while through the 1970s and 1980s, myself and Žižek were publishing essays in these journals as well as publishing books. So, again, when people say that *The Sublime Object of Ideology* came out of nowhere in 1989, I would say that this is a very ignorant misunderstanding of the genealogy of this strand of thinking. It significantly underestimates the pre-history of this text.

Helena Motoh and Jones Irwin: So this is how it all got started, as it were, in Ljubljana? What seems particularly striking is first, the fusion from the beginning in Slovenia of structuralist and Marxist elements (elements kept apart elsewhere until significantly later). Second, however, how the attempted fusion of Marxism and structuralism, for example, in the work of the journal *Problemi*, was deemed to be heterodox and bourgeois by the state Marxist ideology. Can you say a little more about this complex of issues and how Slavoj became a paradigmatic figure in this ideological struggle with Yugoslav official policy?

Mladen Dolar: Yes, this, one can say, is how it did all get started in Ljubljana, with regard to a group of people who took up the task of intellectual revolution. The key period in this regard was 1968–72 in Yugoslavia, where there was a terrific political, cultural and philosophical moment, both in a lifestyle sense and also in a more philosophical sense. In the former case, what was going on in Slovenia connected to the radical social movements in the wider world, the student and political movements and the liberalization of sexual mores and behaviour. But there was also a terrific philosophical movement in Ljubljana, connected especially to French structuralism and the Frankfurt school. What became known as the later orthodox Lacanian school thus had its origins in this turn towards structuralism, a move which the Yugoslav authorities had great difficulty with. If we think of the aforementioned *Tel Quel*, we can say that its motto was 'Rimbaud and Lautréamont from the 19th century, Artaud and Bataille from the 20th century'. So what separated us and *Tel Quel* from the Praxis group was, of course, structuralism, but structuralism understood in a broad sense, which included, for example, the surrealist element and some of the dissident poets I have mentioned. It really was at this point a 'unity in difference' and even when we went on to embrace Lacan, one should not forget that Lacan is very linked to this broader framework of the French avant-garde. For example, his doctoral work was on surrealism. Praxis, however, as an intellectual ideology and grouping, couldn't support us in some of these new aspects: they took particular exception to our positive employment of the work of Louis Althusser, as they saw him (correctly) as attacking the very basis of humanism. Insofar as Praxis remained premised on a humanism, the 'early Marx' so to speak, Althusserianism constituted a significant threat. Indeed, Althusser was a very divisive figure in Marxism and beyond, precisely because of his avowed anti-humanism. Lacan was the key figure for us only retrospectively. At this point, all the main figures were being affirmed; Derrida, Althusser, Lévi-Strauss, Foucault, Kristeva, the lifeblood of the journal *Tel Quel*. However, later, this common framework was to break down.

What one should also mention here is that, politically, things had been liberalizing through the 1960s in Yugoslavia. This took place from 1965's so-called 'economic reform' onwards, leading to a more market economy. This period of liberalization was seen as having got out of hand by the authorities in the early 1970s. For example, I have said already how 1971 was a key period of unrest in Ljubljana. So, the economic reform had been accompanied by cultural reform and there was especially the issue of a reactionary nationalism, which was becoming more acute, particularly in Croatia. In 1971, Tito forcibly removed the political leadership of Slovenia, Croatia and Serbia, replacing the left liberals with a more hard-line conservative wing of the regime. The Praxis group was also dissipated at this time, dismantled by the regime as part of the critique of the progressive liberal left wing in Yugoslavia. The 1970s was thus a period of shutting down, of closure after the more recent period of openness and flowering. At this time, we were governed by a bleak and bureaucratic style of organization and politics, but we carried on in Ljubljana trying to keep the spirit of 1968 and 1971 alive. Slavoj, I and others continued to be deeply involved in *Problemi* and other cultural and philosophical journals and movements, throughout the 1970s.

While the younger generation of philosophers and cultural thinkers had embraced the fusion of Marxist and more 'Continentalist' elements, there remained a distinct hostility to French contemporary 'Continental' thought more generally in Slovenia as it was seen as being in revolt (both implicitly and explicitly) with more orthodox versions of Marxism central to the Yugoslav system. This is perhaps best exemplified by Slavoj's difficulties in having his work recognized by the academy and also with his later difficulties in securing a post within the Slovenian academic system in philosophy. Central to the possibility of our intellectual revolution (and I cannot overstate this enough) was the singular story of Slavoj Žižek – I can speak of him unquestionably as a brilliant genius. Slavoj's work took its cue from the French structuralist school (also influenced by Marx and Hegel) but he had already published a book early in the 1970s on Heidegger and Derrida, entitled *The Pain of Difference*. Žižek submitted his MA thesis in 1975, on the topic of structuralism, entitled 'Sign, Signifier and Writing'. It was rejected by the Ljubljana academic authorities not for any issue of competence (it was unquestionably brilliant) but precisely because of what was perceived as its problematic relationship to Marxism, its obvious challenge to the more stilted orthodoxy. The question became where did his thesis stand in relation to Yugoslav Marxism, that particular brand of what Tito termed 'self-management' socialism, based on the principle of 'nonalignment'? Žižek was asked to write an additional chapter which would explain his relation to Marxism more clearly and he did so. His thesis was thus finally passed and he was promised an assistant professorship, but this job never materialized. This was an unusual situation, a philosopher recognized as brilliant was unemployed. I do not speak too strongly when I describe this as a 'scandal': it was certainly seen as such at the time and made Žižek infamous. But what underlied this situation was an issue which would become central to the work of the Slovenian School of Psychoanalysis – what is the relation between Marxism and psychoanalysis? Of course, Žižek being Žižek, he did manage to get a post eventually in the Institute for Sociology and through this post he supported a whole range of work of his contemporaries in philosophy, for example, in his work as editor to the book series *Analecta*.

Helena Motoh and Jones Irwin: As you say, at this point in time, there was a perceived affinity in your work, as in Žižek's, between structuralism and Marxism, and the former was seen as an intellectual movement of 'unity in diversity'. However, this approach was to be superseded in the late 1970s by what has become the more famous method, that of a specific kind of Lacanianism. Can you clarify how and why Lacan became *the* key intellectual influence?

Mladen Dolar: If structuralism was the first influence in a broad and eclectic sense of its meaning, then certainly, as the 1970s progressed, Lacan became the more defining line of interpretation and conceptualization. Again, we can focus this problematic to its most important nodal point – that of the theme of the subject. The theme of the subject is the key for the distinct Lacanian emphasis in our work, although it is far from being the only rationale for this Lacanian turn. Structuralism, of course, can be seen as precisely a critique of the subject, as in Foucault's infamous 'death of man' and 'death of the subject' theses. What was evinced consequently by the structuralist revolution in philosophy was a supposedly 'subjectless structure'. 'The subject is an effect' is the bottom line of structuralism. For Lacan, on the other hand, the subject is always there at the level of the structure itself; the subject is non-ideological. The subject is a short circuit of the structure (Short Circuits became a book series edited by Žižek for MIT Press to which a number of Slovenian authors contributed). Structuralism was based on a fantasy of the pure matrix of the symbolic. But the unconscious is the crack in the structure there because of the malfunctioning of the structure. We are the subjects of the unconscious, which goes against the grain of the Althusserian concept of interpellation which sees all subjectivity as ideological through and through. Because of the unconscious, one cannot recognize oneself in the structure. Thus, a point of non-recognition creates the subject.

The subject is always already there, one has to think the notion of the subject in any philosophy worthy of the name and this is where structuralism falls down ultimately. It also explains the singularity of Lacan from our perspective at the time, and this shouldn't be divorced from the political questions in Slovenia. In a sense, we needed a theory of the subject and Lacan allowed us such a theory in a way which the other structuralist thinkers, including Althusser, did not. At the same time, what Althusser did allow and what linked him to Lacan (as he explicitly demonstrated in his own readings of Lacan) was an anti-humanism, a move away from more traditionalist humanist concerns. Despite the worth of the Praxis school and its links to the Frankfurt school, this was thus the missing element there. The Praxis and Frankfurt schools remained too traditionally humanist from our perspective. They needed to be supplemented with a more radical understanding of the human which was evidenced in Lacan's anti-humanism and in the more radical fringes of the psychoanalytical reading of politics and culture. Despite all our differences with Badiou, for example, this is what links his work to ours.

Here we can trace a lineage which has become important in the work of the school – the line which connects Descartes to Kant to Hegel, the story of the subject, beginning with Cartesian subjectivity. However, this is a philosophical problematic which goes back to the early Greeks. Plato's *Parmenides*, on which I have written recently, for example, foregrounds the two paradigms of the One and the Two, which have dominated philosophy since. Here, the influence of Kojève on Lacan is not insignificant. And what marked Slovenian structuralism out from its compatriots in different sociocultural contexts, was precisely the continuing relation to Hegel. We might argue that our brand of philosophizing was thus more eclectic and more heterodox than most, fusing elements that were usually divided. We were quite a heterogeneous group to begin with in the 1970s, under trying circumstances, but often the laughter kept us going and Slavoj's high comedy spirit.

Helena Motoh and Jones Irwin: This is a fascinating genealogy of the Lacanian emphasis in your work and the work of the Slovenian school more generally. In 1980, you left Slovenia to study at Vincennes in Paris. Can you say something about the detail and significance of this period for your theoretical work?

Mladen Dolar: I went to France by complete coincidence. I met a friend on the street in Ljubljana and he told me that there were two bursaries left for Slovenian postgraduate study in France. It was a late application but I was successful and I went to Paris in 1979, as I received a grant for an academic year. 1980 was a pivotal year for French philosophy and especially the legacy of the French structuralist movement which had originally been such an influence on us in Ljubljana. It was, one could say, 'the last moment' of Lacan and Foucault, whose lectures I followed. Sartre died in 1980 and the figures of Barthes, Deleuze, Derrida, Lévi-Strauss were still highly influential. 1980 was thus, in every sense, a formative year for me, it formed me in great vigour. One could say that it was in effect the last year of the original 'spirit of structuralism'. If we look back to 1970, it is clear that structuralism (as understood in a Slovenian context) was a 'unified heterogeneity'. But in 1980, it was now Lacan who was the key figure of influence. Why? I would say because Lacan is the thinker whose thought can take the impact the most. But I have a great passion for all of these figures, I view them through a non-sectarian lens, although my own orientation is now fundamentally

Lacanian. For example, Deleuze's thought is fundamentally anti-psychoanalytic (especially the work with Guattari) and indeed the same goes for Foucault if we understand that his *History of Sexuality* is primarily a criticism of psychoanalysis, a genealogy of the psychoanalytic paradigm. Nonetheless, I have learnt and continue to learn a lot from these thinkers, despite the opposition.

The history of thought progresses by huge leaps and epochal shifts. For example, one can think of the Greek period and of the modern period of Kant and Schelling. But this period of the 1970s and 1980s was also key; one has to recognize that the period of French structuralism was a time of immense intellectual tumult. In 1980, one had huge intellectual philosopher 'stars' in the sense that the French have a tradition of philosophers as stars, from Voltaire to Sartre, both of whom had what might be termed 'phantasmatic presences' in their own country and indeed worldwide. Vincennes, the university I studied at in Paris, had a very particular relation to this tradition, having been created as a result of the 1968 demonstrations. Vincennes was, in effect, an experiment. The lease had been signed for 10 years and 1980 became the last year of Vincennes, its eleventh year. Its location in the middle of a park in a series of prefabricated buildings in a district of significant ethnic and class diversity already gave a clear sign of the specificity of this institution. Additionally, the lecturers who had been appointed there reinforced this: Foucault, Deleuze, Lyotard, Badiou, Judith Lacan. It was a place where illegal substances were traded openly, a place which was incredibly democratic and where terrorists and freedom fighters from Africa and South America came to learn about political instruction. The French students doing a formal degree there were, ironically, in a significant minority. It was a real social mix, all strata of society were represented there and there was what one might call a universal vision of philosophy at work. One would have to queue for hours beforehand to hear Foucault speak. But despite the universal appeal and commitment to philosophy as a practice, there were also very significant tensions evident. Badiou's presence in the department, as a Maoist, was very divisive for some. For example, Badiou read Deleuze's work, his colleague, as that of an anarcho-capitalist and he vehemently rejected this approach to philosophy and society. It wasn't until just before Deleuze's death that Badiou would seek some reconciliation between the two, in terms of his book on Deleuze, *The Clamour of Being*. Badiou's book is thus a statement which represents both the very real conflict between the two figures but also the respect which nonetheless remained and the eventual rapprochement. I was still in Paris when they 'erased Vincennes', when the lease ran out and they moved the university to St Denis. One can say with all respect that the university was never the same afterwards; what had gone on before was now socially impossible, a last remnant of the 1968 spirit; the spirit was never the same again.

Helena Motoh and Jones Irwin: So you returned to Ljubljana in late 1980. This was also a period of great change in Slovenian society, where we might say the spirit of Vincennes lived on. Can you explain some of these developments leading up to independence for Slovenia in 1991, with special reference to some of the important Slovenian Art movements known as NSK, and also their relation to the philosophical movement which you were a part of?

Mladen Dolar: Yes, I returned to Ljubljana in late 1980 and began a PhD thesis on Hegel and Lacan. This certainly was a period of great tumult in Slovenian society, with things again opening up after the closed approach of the 1970s. Slovene history is complex and people speak of there being no unified military power and no political autonomy in our history. But what kept Slovenia together, what maintained the identity, was the culture and the literature. This again happens in the 1980s. Here, I can mention as an example the punk movements and its developments, especially the issues of the so-called *Punk Problemi* issues which show the intersection of different genres of culture, from 1981. I can talk of the art movements such as NSK, including the internationally known Laibach and IRWIN. Of course, connected to these were the political developments and movements, leading to eventual independence for Slovenia. Here, certainly there is a difference within our intellectual troika between myself and Slavoj on the one side and Alenka Zupančič on the other, insofar as Alenka comes from a later generation and perhaps experiences at least some of these developments in retrospect or from a different angle.

What we also have to recognize is the tension within and between these various movements seemingly going on in tandem. For example, the punk movement especially can be seen as rejecting the notion of traditional Slovene culture and the paradigm of a national poetry or aesthetic. They rejected this paradigm vehemently. Similarly, the artistic movements, although seeming to affirm a sense of Slovenian and indeed Slavic identity in their work (especially

IRWIN) can be seen as also critiquing this very same culture. There is a particular strategy at work here, what some commentators have termed a strategy of *overidentification* with the dominant ideology. This approach, while appearing complicit, is actually subversive of the maintenance of the ideology. Žižek, for example, in several texts, has asked the question 'why were the NSK important?'. He comes to the conclusion that the NSK actually developed a very subtle philosophical framework, which he describes as Lacanian–Althusserian. Again, this demonstrates strong connections between the art movements and philosophical movements in Slovenia, or at least that between NSK and the Lacanian orientation in the Ljubljana School of Psychoanalysis. For my part, the key question here is the topic of fascism. I wrote a book on fascism in 1982 and I have been significantly interested in this topic throughout my philosophical trajectory. It is relevant to why, for example, we were found guilty of publishing pornography with the *Punk Problemi* issues. We can say that at issue here is the question of the interpretation of elements which often overidentify with certain extremist ideologies. But the artistic and philosophical works are often far more complex to understand than the criteria applied by the police and legal procedures would allow. As for NSK, I thought that collectively they were a brilliant manifestation of the critique of fascist ideology, precisely walking the thin blue line. Their quasi-Nazi imagery was profoundly unsettling. One can also mention here the video art of FV, which if anything was more transgressive and direct (and more 'pornographic') than NSK, each contributing to what we might term the Slovenian 'alternative culture'.

There is also the question of nationalism and how the political movements, in seeking independence, partook of a nationalism which was reactive. This is interesting not simply for the difference in view between philosophers and politicians but also for the different perspectives evident in Slovenian philosophy as opposed to that, for example, in France. Badiou, for example, has taken a rather more negative perspective on the Slovenian independence movements than any of us within the Ljubljana troika. Here the question could be framed thus: was 1991 a betrayal of Marx, as Badiou suggests it was?

Helena Motoh and Jones Irwin: What this also raises is the question of the 'civil society' in Slovenia. To what extent did a civil society develop which was independent of the state sector? This is a question which several important Slovenian commentators have taken up in their work, arguing for a very specific relation between civic culture and alternative culture in the Slovenian context. Can you also say something about the relation between Yugoslavia and the West?

Mladen Dolar: Yes, there is a complex relation here, as you describe. Civil society can sometimes be very conservative and reactionary as for example Mastnak has described in his work as a 'totalitarianism from below'. We might cite as a recent example the case of the Tea Party in the USA. This is a grass roots but nonetheless right-wing view of civil society. In Yugoslavia, there was a complicated relation between civil society and alternative culture, and commentators especially associated with the punk movement, such as Gregor Tomc, have seen the alternative social movements as developing in opposition to civil society and the state rather than developing as part of a civil society opposed to the state. In many respects, civil society also looked unfavourably on these alternative movements.

With regard to Yugoslavia, we can say that Yugoslavia represented a kind of 'unconscious' for the West, which can be seen as a condescending attitude. In particular, we can see the attitude of Western Marxism towards this version of self-management socialism as indicative of a sense that this was the way forward, without looking at some of the inner tensions and social lack of freedoms which contradicted the very philosophies, which these leftist ideologies were seeking to espouse. In this way, we can again cite the singular importance of Žižek in our trajectory, in that he is a thinker who cannot be condescended to. From *The Sublime Object of Ideology* onwards, that is from 1989, we can say that Žižek restructures the Western agenda of Marxism (the foreword to that text for example comes from Laclau). Žižek's reading of the Yugoslavian context and of the situation of communism more generally thus has a singular import. It also relates to the whole issue of 'Eastern Europe' and the way that the latter concept is interpreted in the West, where it tends to be viewed in a reactive way, as backward culturally and philosophically. This is also a thematic in the work of Laibach and IRWIN, who as part of the NSK, while critiquing a certain Easternist ideology, nonetheless also defined a certain Slavic or Eastern identity as specific and worthy, both from an artistic and political perspective.

Here, one interesting case of this condescension or problematic relation between East and West can be evidenced in the interpretation of the Slovenian situation by Badiou. Badiou and Rancière came to Ljubljana in 1993, giving ten lectures, five lectures each. We can say that this was a very important moment in the history of the Slovenian School of Psychoanalysis. Since that date, the relation between Badiou and Žižek especially has become increasingly important. Similarly, we can cite the fact that Zupančič has studied with Badiou, at St Denis, the successor to Vincennes (Zupančič cites this as key for her in her interview). With regard to those lectures in Ljubljana, we can cite Badiou's *Theory of the Subject* as a key text.

Helena Motoh and Jones Irwin: The philosophical orientation of the troika of Slovenian thinkers has been described as 'ultraorthodox Lacanianism'. For some, this might be viewed as a rather dogmatic approach to philosophy. Can you articulate first, the relation between psychoanalysis and philosophy in your own work and second, your conception of this issue of supposed 'dogmatism' linked to orthodoxy.

Mladen Dolar: For me, there are no real dialogues in the philosophical tradition, one cannot have dialogues between philosophical opponents, and in this I follow, for example Deleuze's thinking. As Deleuze observes somewhere, 'never has a thought *against* made any difference'. This is an important point for an understanding of the evolution of Slovenian neo-Lacanianism and it can also be said to develop faithfully out of a meta-level understanding of the philosophical and psychoanalytical enterprise in Lacan's own work. For Lacan, a certain grounding of a thinking is constitutive, a certain positivism is key. It is only starting from a well-defined philosophical position that we can be open to other perspectives. This, for example, is a paradigmatic difference between Lacanian psychoanalysis and Derrida's deconstruction, which Žižek especially has made clear. However, one must be careful in the designation of Lacanianism as dogmatic if one takes the latter to mean a refusal to be open to difference. This is not the case with Lacan as it is clear from even a cursory reading of his work that there is an extraordinarily wide range of authors employed and discussed. Lacan's work is truly eclectic and affirmative of difference in precisely this sense. Nonetheless on the other hand, one can say, from a Lacanian perspective that every good philosophy has been dogmatic, that is, having the courage to take the dogmatic decision. Dogma is the expression of the freedom of spirit, a fundamental decision.

Helena Motoh and Jones Irwin: If we locate the decision to develop an orthodox Lacanianism in the late 1970s and early 1980s, with special reference to the Parisian context, can you articulate how this Lacanian philosophy has developed from a conceptual point of view since that time?

Mladen Dolar: A key moment here is obviously Žižek's first main work in English, *The Sublime Object of Ideology*. Žižek had been writing books since the early 1970s in Slovenian and my own work in essay and book form also dates from an earlier period, especially through the 1980s. In the late 1980s, Žižek had published a book in French but (as he himself has acknowledged) this did not really develop an interest in the way he had wished. However, *The Sublime Object of Ideology* precisely marks the moment of the arrival of Slovenian philosophy on a global stage. I have already spoken for example of the foreword by Ernesto Laclau as being symbolic in terms of its reception by the Western Left, which relates back to our earlier discussion of East and West relations. Second, this book represents the beginning of a whole series of texts in English by Slovenian authors, both by Žižek himself, as well as edited anthologies by Žižek which include Slovenian authors such as myself and Alenka (for example, *All You Ever Wanted to Know . . .*), as well as monograph texts in English by Alenka and I. This then is the origin of Slovenian neo-Lacanianism, in English. But what I have been suggesting and what your book demonstrates is that while acknowledging the importance of Slavoj, we must also say that he was not a giant standing alone. Rather, his work is best understood as the culmination of a whole series of intellectual and cultural discussions and conflicts which originate in the Slovenian context, from the late 1960s onwards. My own work and Alenka's are also a significant part of this evolution, as well as a whole series of Slovenian authors, some of whom appear in translation more recently (such as Renata Salecl etc.) but also we must mention the artistic and political movements which were part of this ferment. You asked me, Jones, at one point, 'Mladen, did you know Laibach, personally?' but truly this is only a question which a foreigner could ask. What we need to understand in this context is the intense interaction between these distinct movements in a

Slovenian context, focused on the cultural hubbub of Ljubljana. What Žižek's 1989 work does is to open out this cultural context to the wider world, in a way that goes beyond the usual exoticism of the East etc. What this also allows is for other Slovenian work to be considered in its own right. Thus, while there are strong connections between Lacanian thinking in Slovenian, especially in our own troika of intellectual friendship, that is between my work, Alenka's and Slavoj's, nonetheless there is no homogeneity here. Rather there are distinctions to be made in this context too, between the various ways our work has evolved and developed.

Helena Motoh and Jones Irwin: Let us return to that question of the specifics of the work, especially in a conceptual sense. You have spoken of Lacan's understanding of the theory of the subject as key to an understanding of his specific difference from structuralism. At the same time, his anti-humanism distances him from the more revisionist approaches to Marxism, such as that of the Praxis group. What other conceptual aspects of Lacan's work would you foreground as crucial for a reading of your own work?

Mladen Dolar: Above, I spoke in detail about the importance of the theory of the subject in Lacan and how this differentiated him, for example, from the wider movement of structuralism. However, at the same time, we can speak of the importance of the notion and theme of the object in Lacan. To speak precisely, an object in Lacan's sense is not an object at all, it is not objectively existing in any way, not being something you can lay your hands on, and this is absolutely essential from an ontological viewpoint. Lacan sees his view of the object as his singular contribution to philosophy as it involves the reframing of the very notion of philosophy itself. In the same way, we might argue that the Ljubljana School of Psychoanalysis is also involved in a reframing of what contemporary philosophy means.

This is not a new problematic as such but goes back to the very first meta-level discussions of the role of philosophy in early Greek philosophy, as Plato often articulates in his texts. For example, we can speak here of the dramatization of Parmenides by Plato (in his dialogue of the same name), in which there is a stark contrast between the Way of Being on the one side and the Way of NonBeing on the other. For Parmenides, it seems that the Way of Being is the only way, that this constitutes a dividing line between philosophy and anti-philosophy. Lacan focuses here on Plato's enigmatic text the *Sophist* and I, in a recent text, have analysed in detail Plato's related text the *Parmenides*. In the *Sophist*, the Stranger is presented as killing father Parmenides, of in effect carrying out a parricide against philosophy proper by arguing for an inversion of the Parmenidean thesis. That is, the Stranger argues (*contra* Parmenides) that being is not and only non-being is. This dualism between being and non-being needs to be understood, however, in a modern context philosophically to understand its true import. Here we can cite Hegel's *Logic*, where Hegel, in a discussion of the relation between being and non-being, adds a lengthy footnote on Parmenides. It is a mistake, Hegel tells us, to choose between being and non-being. Being and non-being are one – and Hegelian dialectics starts by getting rid of this very distinction. One can argue that Plato already understood this, both against Parmenides and against the Stranger (the latter whom, among other figures, might be seen as a representation of Heraclitus). Like Hegel, Plato is also, on some accounts, a dialectical thinker. And, again, what I want to claim is that Lacan can be seen precisely in this lineage of thought, in relation to his thinking of the dialectic between subject and object. For Lacan, as for me. The subject's perception of being can only come through the object, which however is not a real object at all, what Lacan calls the *objet petit a*. Here it is precisely *the division between the subject and object* which is indivisible; the division is constitutive, the between. That is, both the subject and object become divisible while the division between them is irreducible in itself. Here the Ljubljana school follows very closely the readings of Lacan's son-in-law, Jacques-Alain Miller. In effect, this then is *the* thematic of psychoanalysis. We can also say here that while there can be reference back to the earlier premodern tradition (here for example that of Greek philosophy), that ultimately psychoanalysis can only truly happen after Descartes, after the modern 'Copernican' revolution in philosophy. Žižek says somewhere that philosophy proper begins with Kant and I would agree with this wholeheartedly, although, as I have suggested, there are metaphoric approximations or suggestions of similar themes and insights in the work of earlier thinkers such as the Presocratics and Plato. Psychoanalysis only makes sense in a Cartesian or Galilean world. It is the subject which emerges with Descartes. The subject is different from the ego or consciousness and in this way, undoubtedly, Descartes does not truly realize the importance or insight of his own discovery. Lacan is thus, we might say, neo-Cartesian or neo-Kantian. For Lacan, the cogito is a crack in the structure of the universe. Lacan also demarcates his own evolution of the Cartesian and Kantian subjects as follows. On the one side, the Kantian subject which is a transcendental subject is said to be 'subjectively objective', that is, the objective structure is mediated subjectively and understood by the subject. The Lacanian subject, on the other hand, is said to be 'objectively subjective'. That is, the structure of the subject as unconscious is not accessible to the subject; it is only accessible 'objectively' as the structure of this very subjectivity, which is in itself hollow or void, without content.

Helena Motoh and Jones Irwin: One question we would have here is in relation to the question of agreement and disagreement among the 'troika'. For example, in relation to the issue of the 'subject', would you say that there is complete agreement? With regard to the other related themes and concepts of Lacanianism, where do the significant agreements and disagreements lie?

Mladen Dolar: I would say that in fundamental terms we are in complete agreement, although of course there are also differences in emphasis and direction of thinking. We agree on the Copernican revolution as irreducible between the modern and premoderns, as I have suggested, and that psychoanalysis is a post-Cartesian development or can only be understood in such a context. However, one significant difference which I could cite here between my own work and that of Slavoj's, for example, is in relation to the question of the premodern question of theology and God. Whereas my own work takes the Nietzschean declaration that 'God is dead' as paradigmatic, and thus consigns premodern metaphysics to a metaphorical status only, Žižek's work has shown increasing signs of a more differentiated and complex relation to theology and the premodern works of metaphysics, for example in his work with John Milbank (the recent text, *The Monstrosity of Christ* and his forthcoming work with a Croatian theologian). This might be seen as a significant distinction, although I wouldn't overplay it in contrast to the more fundamental agreement. One might also mention that Žižek's work has become more and more focused on the Lacanian notion of the Real, in a way that perhaps is more distinctive than in mine or Alenka's works. Similarly, this notion of the Real has undergone a transformation in Slavoj's work and this has become very central in his recent work, especially as the Real is mediated through transgressive moments in cinema. To what extent this is a reading against Lacan, is open to question, as, for Lacan, the Real designated more of an inaccessible notion. Žižek himself (in *The Plague of Fantasies*) speaks of the need (following Paul de Man) for 'reading as disfiguration', which is an interesting way to think about Lacan's own method of reading, and which brings deconstruction and psychoanalysis perhaps closer than one might have thought.

Similarly, Alenka's work perhaps takes up the issue of Nietzsche's declaration slightly differently in her text on Nietzsche and also her emphasis on the relation between desire and drive is somewhat specific, in her work on comedy. Again there are interesting questions here in relation to when the issue of drive becomes foregrounded in Lacan's own work. It really only becomes a key notion in his later work, whereas the notion of desire and the symbolic is prominent in the early Lacan. In the same vein, my own work on the voice as partial object (in *The Voice and Nothing More*) retains a distinctiveness from the work of the other thinkers.

Helena Motoh and Jones Irwin: Your own work also evidences a profound engagement with the work of Hegel, from your PhD onwards. While this is also a distinctive feature of the other two thinkers' work, it is perhaps more pronounced in your own work. Can you conclude by saying something about this specific interpretation of Hegel in your work and how this relates to your own understanding of Lacanianism?

Mladen Dolar: Certainly, my fascination with Hegel goes back a long way, especially as you suggest in his relation to Lacan. I would cite here a key source, the lectures of Kojève, 1934–39, which Lacan (among other key French luminaries) attended diligently. Lacan was profoundly influenced by an understanding of Hegel, but he does not have an independent take on Hegel, and this is crucial to how we understand some of his limitations as a thinker. Like philosophers such as Georges Bataille, Lacan's Hegel comes only through Kojève's lectures, although as with Bataille, this is not to say that he simply repeats the Kojèvian interpretation. Rather, his reading takes its cue from Kojève, while taking it in his own direction. For Kojève, famously, the understanding of Hegel is as an anthropological thinker, whose thinking is framed in relation to the master–slave dialectic from *The Phenomenology of Spirit*. For me, as a reader of Hegel, outside the Kojèvian circle I might say, this is a complete misconception of Hegel's original texts. The master–slave dialectic is not, in my view, key to Hegel and he is not an anthropological or existentialist thinker, as Kojève understood it. But as I have suggested earlier, it is sometimes precisely through misreading, interpretative distortion or by accident, that we get the most extraordinary understandings. We might speak similarly of Sartre's *Being and Nothingness*, which is also powerfully influenced by Kojève, as a great text but, in many ways, similarly mistaken in its reading of Hegel. Kojève thus gets Hegel wrong in my view, badly wrong, but still comes up with a powerful thinking which becomes paradigmatic for a whole generation. Even Deleuze acknowledges this when he says that 'poor is the generation who doesn't have the master', referring to the benefits of Sartre's hegemony for his own generation, a point that Lacan reiterates elsewhere (in relation to May 1968, for example). The figure of the master, in other words, gives one the freedom of thought and for Deleuze's generation, despite all the conflicts, Sartre was still a kind of philosophical master.

In my PhD on Hegel and Lacan, I argue that there is a very different Hegel to Kojève's and Lacan's which, if understood correctly, would come far closer to Lacan's own understanding of psychoanalysis than the Hegel which he presents as a kind of philosophical straw man. Nonetheless, Kojève's misunderstanding of Hegel was key to the evolution of Lacan's own thinking and, we must say, immensely productive. This was an extremely fortuitous philosophical mistake or error, which can also tell us something very important on a meta-level in relation to the progress of philosophy, or the supposed progress of philosophy. So we can say simultaneously that this was a hugely productive misunderstanding which nonetheless limited Lacan's thinking in key respects. Again, this demonstrates that orthodox Lacanianism as we call it should not simply repeat the mistakes of the master, should not be so modest as to not point out the mistakes of the master, to the contrary.

Also, I can cite a related point. 'Not to give up on Hegel' is also a key rallying cry of the Slovenian neo-Lacanians. Any orthodoxy worthy of the name has to come up with a radical innovation which also calls into question what orthodoxy means. It certainly does not constitute sterility as might be suggested for example by deconstructive or neo-Derridean opponents. One might think here of Judith Butler's attack on what she sees as the 'fixity of the

Lacanian conception of the Real', which she speaks of as occluding the possibility of philosophical or political transformation. Rather, I would say that *orthodoxy is transformation* – Žižek takes up this point, for example, in his reading of GK Chesterton. Paradoxically, then, I can mention that despite my holding unequivocally to Nietzsche's declaration that 'God is dead', that I can also see the worth of thinkers in the Christian tradition such as Pascal, Kierkegaard and Augustine. In each of these cases, we can say (albeit for different reasons) that *orthodoxy is transformation*. This is true then, despite the simultaneous truth of the fact that Nietzsche's declaration that 'God is dead' philosophically demonstrates that there is an impossibility in God any longer being the condition of freedom. We might thus say something analogous, in conclusion, of the adherence to an orthodox (even 'ultraorthodox') Lacanianism among our troika. Such an orthodoxy does not designate intellectual stagnation or dogmatism and neither does it designate an uncritical acceptance of all elements of the philosophical inheritance. To the contrary, in essence, our Lacanian emphasis signifies the transformative dimension of orthodoxy and 'positioning' in philosophy. In this case, it has involved no less than a reframing of the very nature of philosophy, from Marx through to structuralism (as 'unity in diversity') through to Lacan and finally, through to the Ljubljana 'moment'. [Interview ends]

Conclusion – Dolar: Breaking through the impasse

Dolar's interview provides us with a rich and varied sense of the trajectory not simply of his own work, but of the work of the Ljubljana School of Psychonanalysis as a whole. He has led us with great dexterity through the early days, the 1968 and 1971 moments in Slovenia and the early critique of state socialism coming through, for example, the 'critique of the red bourgeoisie' in civil society. We know from Gantar's work that this critique was to remain limited (Gantar 1993) and this highlights the very great importance of the emerging discourse of renewed critique which Dolar led (alongside Žižek and others such as Močnik) in the late 1970s and 1980s, especially in relation to two key aspects. First, in terms of the intra-philosophical acute discussion which led initially to an embracing of the wide (and then new) field of French structuralism through the influential Parisian journal *Tel Quel*. Consequently, and crucially, a more singular affirmation of Lacanianism emerged as a specific and particular example of the possibility of 'breakthrough', of transgressing the paralysis of societal and psychic 'impasse' (Močnik 1993).

Dolar's second key contribution can be connected to his relation to alternative culture and particularly, the movements of punk and the NSK. As we have already seen, the bridge between intellectuals and alternative culture in this context was surprising and somewhat unique. Slovenia seems to have been one of the only places where such a dialogue between alternative culture and young intellectuals such as Dolar and Žižek was possible and what it allowed was a supersession of the limitations of the 'civil society' forms of resistance, a breaking through what, for example, Močnik has described as the 'colonisation of the life world' (Močnik 1993).

But as with Močnik, Dolar's own work displays no simple nationalist or (Slovene) culturalist bias and has remained as subversive and critical of ideological issues and problems, post-independence in Slovenia, as before. Here again, we can see the continuity between Dolar's most central work (for example, on the 'voice' [Dolar 2006]) and his earlier and seminal work (with Žižek) on the changing conceptions of the 'symptom' in Lacanianism as it relates to political ideology most especially, from fascism to socialism to contemporary capitalism (Žižek 1981: Dolar 1982). If we think back to the original analysis there, contemporary regime critics of the punk movement had used the term 'symptom' as the meaning of a sign of an underlying disease. We might say that this was in line with a more standard reading of the notion of 'symptom' in Marxism, or as Žižek puts it 'how Marx invented the symptom' (Žižek 1989). This approach to diagnosing an underlying problem with societal (e.g., socio-economic or 'base') structures in Marxism could be connected to an apparently similar strategy in certain versions of 'adaptive' psychoanalysis, supposedly derived faithfully from Freud (e.g., ego psychology or even Marcuse's version of psychoanalysis [referred to as 'psychoanalytic essentialism' in Žižek 1989]). The Yugoslav/Slovene regime's critical reading of the 'punk movement', then, saw punk precisely as a negative symptom in this way (as Motoh [2012] titles her recent essay, 'Punk is a Symptom').

Žižek's editorial for *Problemi* in 1981 (written perhaps in conjunction with Dolar, who was the official editor) is precisely entitled 'Punk is a Symptom' (Žižek 1981). The editorial states: 'Thus, their diagnosis was that punk warns us of an alarming danger of "nihilist", "foreign" or even "anarchist and fascist" tendencies among the young generation, a spreading disease that needs to be "cured", thereby also taking care of the symptom' (Žižek 1981: 26). In a poignant moment, however, of what we might call conceptual (or ideological) reversal, the editorial turns the concept of symptom back against the state system itself: 'The symptom, however, reveals an intrusion of the suppressed "truth" of the most calm, most normal everyday life, of exactly that life that is so shocked and annoyed by it. Symptom returns our suppressed truth in a perverted form. . . . punk literally *enacts* the suppressed aspect of "normality" and thereby "liberates", it introduces a defamiliarizing distance' (Žižek 1981: 27). If punk is a symptom, and it would clearly seem to be, this is not a diagnosis of an underlying problem with punk or the alternative culture itself, but precisely of an underlying problem with the system (which punk can now be seen as 'liberative' from). Some of the ambiguity over the authorship of some of these short pieces in the early 1980s (Žižek 1981; Žižek et al. 1984; Dolar 1982) might precisely have been because of the dangers inherent in the clear articulation of such a critique of ideology in the former Yugoslavia. We will return to the specifics of Žižek's ideology critique in the next chapter. What is also striking in this context is the introduction by Dolar/Žižek of a clear and important distinction between what they here term 'dogmatic' and 'nondogmatic' forms of Marxism (Žižek 1981: 28): 'If the distinction between non-dogmatic and dogmatic Marxism has any meaning, this distinction must (also) mean that – when research of the social phenomena encounters a symptomatic point – "the symptom" is above all allowed to speak, without being "understood" (reduced to what is already known) in advance. Such is the aim of the present issue' (Žižek 1981: 28). Here, it would seem that the regime's attempt to silence or penalize *Problemi* for publishing the punk issues is associated with dogmatic Marxism, while the *Problemi* editorial board claim the 'nondogmatic' Marxist angle. While this claim to being free of dogmatism is not surprising, more startling is the very invocation of Marx, given the pre-history of problems for the group through the 1970s (Dolar et al. 2014) precisely with the relation between French theory and Marx, as outlined in the interview above. Nonetheless, it is clear that the *Problemi* board consider themselves the more authentic Marxists, precisely in their disavowal of dogmatism (a reading of Marx strongly in line, for example with, among others, Balibar [2007]).

But, to conclude our analysis of Dolar's work for now, it is perhaps not coincidental that the later evolution of the counter-culture, in the form of the NSK (Monroe 2005), takes a less 'direct' approach to matters ideological. In an article on the succeeding avant-garde, Dolar clearly notes the origins of the NSK in the punk movement: 'Just like NSK, IRWIN grew out of the punk movements of the late 1970s and early 1980s which enacted a big shock back then' (Dolar 2003: 155). However, he also notes a significant difference in approach to ideology: '[there was] no irony or game when it came to ideology. IRWIN were so hard to classify' (Dolar 2003: 155). This lack (or refusal) of irony or distance when it came to the exploration of the state socialist ideology in the later Yugoslav (and Slovenian) avant-garde marks a significant shift from the unequivocal and vitriolic assault on state ideology by punk (and later FV 112/15) (Motoh 2012). It is an artistic and philosophical strategy of ideology critique which will become known as 'overidentification' or to employ a concept we spoke of in Chapter 1, 'retro-gardism' (Monroe 2005). We will see, in the succeeding chapters, how this more complicated form of ideology critique will also be practiced in more recent texts by the Ljubljana School of Psychoanalysis.

CHAPTER FOUR

'Learn, Learn and Learn' – On Slavoj Žižek

Introduction

Žižek's first text in English translation, *The Sublime Object of Ideology* (Žižek 1989), signalled not simply his arrival on the international philosophical scene, but the arrival of the whole Ljubljana School of Psychoanalysis. This becomes clear in succeeding years with the publication, for example, of several anthologies of Slovenian philosophical (Lacanian) work in translation, such as *Everything You Always Wanted to Know About Lacan But Were Afraid to Ask Hitchcock* and *Cogito and the Unconscious* (Žižek 1992b, 1998a; Dolar 1992a, 1998; Zupančič 1992, 1998). *The Sublime Object of Ideology* (Žižek 1989) is also accompanied by a significant preface by Ernesto Laclau (1989), one of the earliest thinkers (alongside, for example, Chantal Mouffe [1993]) to combine Marx and Lacan in the critique of ideology in political philosophy.

Laclau's (1989) preface is thus an interesting contextualization of some of the issues which we have already discussed in Chapters 1 and 2 and also looks forward to and anticipates some of the issues which will develop over future years in relation to this Lacanian orientation, especially as they bear on the critique of ideology. In the first case, Laclau highlights the different receptions given to Lacanianism, from country to country, foregrounding their context-specific importance (Laclau 1989: ix). He notes the important influence of Lacan's son-in-law Jacques-Alain Miller on the Ljubljana interpretation of Lacan, 'placing an accent on the theoretical importance of the last stage, in which a central role is granted to the notion of the Real as that which resists symbolisation' (Laclau 1989: x). We will see below how this conception of the 'Real' becomes increasingly important for Žižek's analysis of social reality (Žižek and Daly 2003). For Laclau, one of the most 'original features' of the 'Slovenian Lacanian school' is its 'insistent reference to the ideological-political field' as well as its outline of 'the main characteristics of radical democratic struggles in Eastern European societies' (Laclau 1989: x). In the latter case, Laclau also describes how such a Lacanian perspective has been one of the principal reference points of the 'so-called Slovenia Spring, that is to say the democratisation campaigns that have taken place in recent years' (Laclau 1989: xiv). This dovetails with our analysis in Chapter 1 and the commentaries of Močnik (1993) and Gantar (1993), among others. Finally, Laclau foregrounds the crucial importance of this understanding of the Ljubljana school, not simply within Slovenia, but more broadly in terms of the 'democratic socialist project in a post-Marxist age': 'for those interested in the elaboration of a theoretical perspective that seeks to address the problems of constructing a democratic socialist political project in a post-Marxist age, it is essential reading' (Laclau 1989: xv).

At the end of Chapter 2, we discussed how the ideology critique became transformed (and more oblique) as we moved from punk through to the later alternative culture in Slovenia of the Neue Slowenische Kunst (NSK) (Monroe 2005; Dolar 2003). This evolution of the concept also affects the approach of the Ljubljana School of Psychoanalysis and especially the work of Žižek in this respect (Žižek 1989, 1992a, 2008b). Žižek's own analysis of ideology shows some level of transformation as it develops from 1989 onwards. Already in 1989, Žižek was signalling an important move away from the 'false consciousness' notion of ideology: 'ideology is not simply false consciousness as an illusory representation of reality, it is rather this reality itself which is already to be conceived of as ideological; ideology is a social reality whose very existence implies the nonknowledge of its participants as to its sense' (Žižek 1989: 21). In his introduction to his edited volume *Mapping Ideology* (Žižek 1994a), entitled 'The Spectre of Ideology' (Žižek 1994b), Žižek continues to argue for the 'pertinence' of the notion of ideology: 'we are within ideological space proper the moment (whether true or false) a content is functional with regard to some relation of social domination ("power", "exploitation") in an inherently nontransparent way' (Žižek 1994b).

We can also trace Žižek's understanding of the concept of ideology through different versions of the same text, showing significant variations, most especially the paradigmatic Žižekian text *Enjoy Your Symptom: Jacques Lacan in Hollywood and Out* (Žižek 1992a). Originally published in 1992, the successive versions of this text show a transformed and evolving notion of ideology, also as it relates to connecting Lacanian (and Marxist) notions such as 'fetish' and 'symptom' itself (the latter being a particularly 'slippery' concept in Lacan). First, in 2001, the second edition of *Enjoy Your Symptom: Jacques Lacan in Hollywood and Out* (Žižek 2001a) is published, including a new introduction and an additional final chapter. Then, in 2008, another version of the text is published in a different series, this time with a new preface (Žižek 2008b), entitled 'Enjoy your Symptom – or Your Fetish?'. As the title suggests, Žižek is generating a certain ambiguity here between the original concept of 'symptom' and the newer concept of 'fetish'. Can one concept replace the other in the Žižekian analysis? The related notion of 'sinthome' also comes to have significance in the later Lacan's work and in Žižek's own analysis (Bowie 1991; Dolar 1998), complicating matters further.

The crucial move here seems to be away from a conception of ideology which sees the latter as a resolvable problematic to a notion of ideology where a certain 'deadlock' must be borne, both at the subject level and at the societal level. For example, the conception of 'fetish' is described as follows in its difference from the 'symptom', this from the 2008 preface: 'Fetish is effectively the reversal of the symptom; that is to say, symptom is the exception which disturbs the surface of the false appearance; the point at which the repressed other scene erupts. While fetish is the embodiment of the lie which enables us to sustain the unbearable truth' (Žižek 2008a: ix). Here, we might also remember the rereading of the 'symptom' in the *Punk Problemi* situation which Dolar and Žižek put forward in 1981–82 in Ljubljana (Žižek 1981; Žižek et al. 1984; Dolar 1982). Although each of these successive notions can be seen as Lacanian (and indeed Freudian), there is also a strong connection back to the Marxist understanding of these concepts (as Žižek [1989] notes in *The Sublime Object of Ideology*, 'How Marx Invented the Symptom').

In his most recent text, however, Žižek has described some of Lacan's final efforts to resolve the issues around ideology and the 'sinthome' as a 'failure', signalling perhaps a new direction yet again for Žižek and the Ljubljana school on this topic. As Žižek notes there: 'Seminar XX [Encore] stands for his ultimate achievement and deadlock; ... in the years after, he desperately concocted different ways out [the sinthome, knots etc] all of which failed; so where do we stand now?' (Žižek 2012a: 18). We will return to the problematic of a possible 'new direction' in the Epilogue.

The core of the Freudian revolution

This question of conceptual and philosophical inheritance is, of course, always a crucial matter for Žižek. Lacan spoke of a 'return to Freud' and we can see in the respective interviews how the allegiance to an 'orthodox Lacanianism' (Dolar et al. 2014; Žižek et al. 2014) is more than merely polemical posturing. For both Žižek and Dolar, as later for Zupančič, this kind of approach in philosophy allows one a 'positioning', a comportment philosophically in the world towards existence and politics, in a way that for example, it is claimed, Derrida's deconstruction undermines (Žižek et al. 2014). Whether the accusation of an aimless drifting is true of Derrida or not (we should remember that one of Lacan's synonyms for Freud's '*Trieb*' or 'drive' is *dérive* or 'drift' [Lacan 1994]), nonetheless it is clear, on the other side, that the kind of Lacanian orthodoxy described does not signal sterility or philosophical passivity. Quite the contrary, and we have already seen Dolar's far more positive explication of such 'orthodoxy' in the phrase 'orthodoxy is transformation' (Dolar et al. 2014).

Although this is a characteristic of each of the key members of the Ljubljana School of Psychoanalysis in turn, in Žižek's case, the question of a very particular 'style' of writing and exposition has become a trademark. We might again say that this is completely in keeping with the Lacanian inheritance in the measure to which Lacan's texts are infamously 'difficult' and seemingly wilfully obscure, to the chagrin of many commentators. Even Derrida, his own work famous for such abstruseness, points the finger at Lacan for a kind of neglectful or destructive obscurantism (Muller and Richardson 1988; Hurst 2008; Derrida 1987) in his critique of Lacanianism, 'The Purveyor of Truth' (Derrida 1987). Here, we can certainly place Lacan's philosophical-poetic style in a subversive tradition which Charles Taylor has referred to as the 'immanent Counter-Enlightenment' in French literature, the poet *maudits* or damned poets, such as Rimbaud, Baudelaire, Lautréamont and Mallarmé espousing an 'immanent transcendence' (Taylor 2007). We have seen, in the previous chapter, Dolar foreground these 'philosopher-poets' as crucial in the reception of the journal *Tel Quel* and the early influence of 'French Structuralism' in Ljubljana, during the late 1960s and early 1970s. These poets vehemently reject the rationalism of the Enlightenment and instead revive a mystical tradition (at least in aesthetics) with a focus on the irrational, sin and thanatology.

We might see Žižek, without much difficulty, in a similar lineage. For example, in this context, it is not surprising that one of Lacan's more obscure texts 'Kant with Sade', originally a preface for a new edition of Sade's *Philosophy in the Bedroom* (Sade 1980), has come to play such a key role for Žižek's reading of Lacanianism (it will also have a significant impact on Zupančič's reading of a new 'ethics of the Real' [Zupančič 2000]). Susan Sontag's seminal essay 'The Pornographic Imagination' (Sontag 2001) is especially important here for an understanding of the twentieth-century rereading of Sade, coming through the dissident surrealism of Bataille and Klossowski, as we discussed in Chapter 2 (Macey 1988). Again, we can note here the significance of this Bataille reading for Lacan's conception of 'jouissance' or 'enjoyment' (Lacan 1998), as well as on the wider (and radicalized) reading of sexuality in Seminar XX, *On Feminine Sexuality. The Limits of Love and Knowledge, 1972–1973. ENCORE.* (Lacan 1998), perhaps the key Lacanian seminar for Žižek which I will return to in the following section. Clearly, there is a powerful (if underplayed) Bataillean and more generally, surrealistic inheritance in Žižek, via a 'return to Lacan'. Žižek admits as much, for example, in *The Plague of Fantasies* (Žižek 1997) when he says, 'the Surrealists also practiced traversing the fantasy' (Žižek 1997: 84).

But what of Žižek's relation to either Freud or Lacan? Some commentators, for example Kay (2003), have played down the Freudian connection to Žižek. Kay argues that, in many respects, Žižek bypasses Freud and goes directly to influences from Hegel to Lacan. There is some truth in this hypothesis and certainly, one can argue that there is a lesser Freudian emphasis in Žižek's work than in the work of either Dolar or Zupančič. However, one can overstate the case too, to the neglect of specific and important Freudian aspects. After all, Lacan by his own estimation always remained a 'Freudian' (and 'not a Lacanian' [Bowie 1991]). Consequently, there remain important relations of intellectual dependency here. Certainly, as with Dolar et al. (2014), there is a significant debt to be paid to *Civilisation and Its Discontents* (Freud 2002a), which, for example, in the introduction to *The Ethics of Psychoanalysis* (Seminar VII), Lacan cites as the most influential Freudian text on his own work (Lacan 1992). Unsurprisingly, Lacan explicitly mentions the concept of the 'death drive' as the key Freudian concept and this notion has played an increasingly important role for Žižek in terms of his reading of the matrix of ideology, fetish and symptom (Žižek 1989, 1992a, 2008b). We will see how this 'death drive' also relates crucially to perhaps Žižek's most central of concepts, the concept of the Real (Žižek and Daly 2003), an originally Lacanian concept.

At the beginning, for example, of his introductory text on ('How To Read') Lacan from 2006 (Žižek 2006a), Žižek directly addresses this problem of how the 'Freudian picture' might now be seen, in the twenty-first century, as somewhat outdated. As he notes, 'the Freudian picture seems outmoded today when the Freudian image of a society and social norms which repress the individual's sexual drives no longer seems a valid account of today's predominant hedonistic permissiveness' (Žižek 2006: 3). Here, Žižek is keen to argue against such a view of the obsolescence of psychoanalysis and instead precisely claims that 'it is only today that the time of psychoanalysis has come' (Žižek 2006: 2). Crucially, for our purposes, he also connects this defence of psychoanalysis specifically to 'Lacan's return to Freud', which he understands not 'as a return to what Freud said but to the core of the Freudian revolution of which Freud himself was not fully aware' (Žižek 2006: 2).

At a meta-level of interpretation, this again demonstrates the complexity of the concepts of 'return' or 'orthodoxy' for both Žižek and the wider Ljubljana School of Psychoanalysis. In Žižek's important text *The Plague of Fantasies*, he invokes a metaphor of the Derridean critic Paul de Man to explicate this issue, with his notion of 'reading as disfiguration' (Žižek 1997: 95), which he takes from the text *The Rhetoric of Romanticism* (Žižek 1997: 95). In a suitably adept aside, actively rereading one of the great mottos of Marx from 'Theses on Feuerbach' (Marx 1992a), Žižek says 'one is thus tempted to say that the motto of the Lacanian reading of

Hegel is: "philosophers have hitherto only interpreted Hegel; the point is also to change him"' (Žižek 1997: 95). Again, we might see this approach as characteristic of Dolar and Zupančič's mode of Lacanian interpretation. It is also an accurate description of Lacan's hermeneutic relation to the history of philosophy, as well as his interpretative relation (paradigmatically) to Freud and the more orthodox tradition of psychoanalysis (Lacan 2008).

Lacan, then and now

What can we say about the specifics, then, of Žižek's own reading of Lacanianism? As with Dolar and Zupančič, there is a strong influence of three of the main Lacan seminars on Žižek. First, Seminar VII, *The Ethics of Psychoanalysis* (Lacan 1992) constitutes the starting point for much of Žižek's work on the critique of happiness and the break with the Aristotelian understanding of being. Yet, it also allows the foregrounding of a notion of the ethical which must disavow the superego pathologies of the Good (in Freudian terms, a pathological 'infantile solution to infant problems' [Bowie 1991]) and instead ground itself in the 'erotic' (Lacan 1992). De Kesel's (2009) *Eros And Ethics* brilliantly contextualizes this appeal to an erotic ethics as critiquing Aristotelianism through a recourse to Platonic Eros, most notably to the dialogue *The Symposium* (Plato 1961). We will see this dialogue become crucially important also for Zupančič in her most recent work on ethics, comedy and eroticism (Zupančič 2008a). For Žižek, in relation to the discussion of ethics, the aforementioned Lacan essay 'Kant with Sade' (Lacan 2002b) similarly plays a key role. In Žižek's most recent work, however, the monumental *Less Than Nothing: Hegel and the Shadow of Dialectical Materialism* (Žižek 2012a), there is an attempted move away from the ethical towards the 'political'. The extended conclusion is entitled 'The Political Suspension of the Ethical' (Žižek 2012a), and Žižek here draws on the work of the 'Party Troika' (e.g., one of Dolar's most recent texts in Slovenian), to indicate that this move towards the political is a generalized move of the Ljubljana School of Psychoanalysis. I will return to this important problematic in the Epilogue.

In brief, we can also mention two of the other Lacan seminars as especially influential on Žižek's philosophical trajectory, namely, Seminars XI and XX (Lacan 1994, 1998). With regard to Seminar XI, alongside the key notion of 'drive', what Lacan calls the 'encounter with the Real' becomes especially important. In *The Plague of Fantasies*, Žižek defines the 'Real' as follows: 'the hard traumatic reality which resists symbolisation' (Žižek 1997: 157). Žižek, at this point, follows the analysis of the 'Real' in Lacan's Seminar XI (Lacan 1994) on *The Four Fundamental Concepts of Psychoanalysis*. There, Lacan introduces this fundamentally 'elusive' notion (drawing on the Aristotelian concept of 'tuche' or 'luck') in order to redirect psychoanalysis away from a tendency towards misguided 'idealism': 'I wish to stress here that at first sight psychoanalysis seems to lead in the direction of idealism; [rather] . . . no praxis is more orientated towards that which, at the heart of experience, is the kernel of the real than psychoanalysis' (Lacan 1994).

The originality of Žižek's approach is that he develops the notion of the 'Real' as central to his philosophical analysis, not simply in relation to Seminar XI but also, perhaps more importantly in relation to the famously enigmatic Lacan Seminar XX, entitled 'Encore' (Lacan 1998): *On Feminine Sexuality. The Limits of Love and Knowledge, 1972–1973. ENCORE*. This amalgamation of the two perspectives leads Žižek to a notion of the 'Real of sexual difference' (Žižek 2002), developing some of Lacan's most infamous (and least understood) principles from Seminar XX. These include such psychoanalytical principles as 'Woman does not exist', 'There is no such thing as the sexual relationship' and 'Love is giving what one does not have to someone who doesn't want it' (Žižek 2002; Bernard 2002). These conceptions remain some of the most elusive (and also controversial) tenets of Lacan, Žižek and the Ljubljana troika's philosophical approach to psychoanalysis. We might also say that these notions remain some of the least developed of the conceptions under scrutiny. The interviews with Žižek and Zupančič touch on their import (and controversy) to some extent. The important Appendix to Zupančič's text *The Odd One In: On Comedy* (Zupančič 2008a) is the most systematic and interesting attempt to come to terms with these issues, focusing on the concept or phenomenon of 'Eros' or 'love' as it potentially allows for the 'sublimation' of the death drive in a non-repressive way. We will return to this discussion in the next chapter.

We might conclude by returning to the Ljubljana context of Chapter 1, and the various important commentaries in Slovenia on the evolving political and cultural situation as it developed through the 1970s, 1980s and 1990s (Močnik 1993; Gantar 1993). As Močnik argues strongly, the Lacanian orientation makes the 'breakthrough' after the (French structuralist) 'impasse', and we have seen that Žižek was perhaps one of the main figures (alongside Dolar) in the struggles between state socialism, the (dissident) intellectuals and the alternative culture, in what would eventually lead to what Laclau refers to as the 'Slovenia Spring' (Laclau 1989). In the following interview, we discuss the genealogy of these events with Žižek, all the way back to the 1970s. We will see how he foregrounds both the more personal and the more conceptual (Lacanian) strands to this story and how he comes back, in his conclusion, to the abiding importance of this 'troika' of thinkers.

'From Lacan to Hegel' – Interview with Slavoj Žižek

Helena Motoh and Jones Irwin: Slovenia has been described (for example, by Alexei Monroe) as having a markedly problematic genealogy in terms of nationhood and cultural independence. Can you say if and how this problematical genealogy might be seen as affecting your own work and how significant it is for you that you are seen as a 'Slovenian' philosopher or part of a 'Slovenian school' of philosophy?

Slavoj Žižek: Let me say first of all that this is totally unimportant, this Slovenian national identity or context, or at least it is unimportant in at least one significant sense. That is, we never set out to be identified as Slovenian. Perhaps however, as we will see, the Ljubljana connection is more important to us. But what we can say in terms of being Slovenian is that we were lucky, all of us Slovenian thinkers and philosophers, both vis-à-vis the West and vis-à-vis the East. Why? Because it gave us a clear sense of what was going on in Yugoslavia, behind the illusions. We had no illusions about the great project of Tito's Yugoslavia, non-alignment and so on. This differentiated us first of all from those Western intellectuals, including ones we were and are deeply allied to such as Badiou, who precisely did foster and in some ways still do foster illusions shall we say about what was going on. This 'ideology' (it is a kind of Western leftist construct of the 'East') continues to affect their thinking on matters political, more globally. Second, we will also see how it distinguishes our thinking from within Yugoslavia, for example, in contrast to those thinkers in the Praxis school. If you are looking to pinpoint the specifics of the Slovenian situation philosophically, and I agree that there are specific elements such as Lacanianism in its idiosyncratic form here (Močnik 1993), well this may have something to do with the political context. You also see it, the 'Slovene Lacan', in the NSK and Laibach, not simply in philosophy or psychoanalysis. The main thing to note here was that we were far more Westernized (in the hybrid sense), I would say, than the other federal members and certainly than any countries in the Soviet Union. Mladen (Dolar) says somewhere, for example, 'you cannot pretend that we were Czechoslovakia'. We had much more freedom of movement and access to the West, simply. I am talking about the 1960s and 1970s, although there were different periods here, phases of liberalization, phases of repression, and sometimes economic liberalization might be accompanied by sociopolitical repressions, and vice versa. One aspect of this of course, if you are thinking of the Ljubljana school, Dolar and I but also others early on such as Močnik, is that we could study in France without having to go into exile, like many Eastern bloc intellectuals we might mention. So, this notion of the 'East', of 'Eastern Europe' is often used far too reductively in the West, not taking account of the local differentiations. Mladen has an essay 'Yugoslavia was Structured as the Unconscious' which captures this well, the dual sense of the specific and peculiar dynamics but also the 'exoticisation' of the Balkans, in Freud and succeeding thought (Dolar 1989). This was also happening through the 1990s when I kept getting asked to write about this Western perception of 'tribal wars' in the Balkans, as if this Balkan Other was a kind of 'id'. This also applies to the concept of (Eastern) 'state socialism' and this is a big part of our evolution, the Ljubljana School of Psychoanalysis (as it is called), in terms of the problematic of ideology, for example. I wrote an article on this, for example, in *The New Left Review* (this was later developed as Žižek 2007d).

Perhaps, I can say more about this lucky aspect of our history. Here, of course, I am speaking primarily of the generation of myself and Mladen and not so much of the generation after – Alenka (Zupančič) would have to speak to this specificity more. Our generation, studying in Ljubljana in the late 1960s, was the generation on the cusp of the explosion of French structuralism as a form of thinking. We entered university just before this took place which was in effect here in Slovenia in the early 1970s (we had entered university to study philosophy in the late 1960s). Of course, there might be an assumption abroad that, before this, Slovenia would have been simply designated intellectually or philosophically as Marxist in some traditionalist or even positivistic (scientific etc.) sense, but this certainly was not the case. Presaging the later explosion of French structuralism was an earlier version of Marxism which we can describe as a version of the Frankfurt school approach. Here again, what we can also discount is the myth of a unified Yugoslavia, philosophically. Rather, if the Frankfurt school and, for want of a better term, its 'humanist Marxism' (Marcuse etc.), could be seen as central to Slovenian thinking at the time, significantly in Croatia it was rather Heideggerianism which held sway. In Serbia, it was then again analytical philosophy which held sway, in Bosnia something else, consequently here we see the complexity of the internal differentiations to begin with, within the bigger ambit of the Yugoslav project. This is not even mentioning the complex political differentiations, the distinctions of the so-called civil society, and later this notion of 'civil society' will be a contested term with the dynamic with 'alternative culture', the punk movement, NSK etc. (Gantar 1993; Motoh 2012). So, that's the context, the overlying background, but then what? Next comes the explosion of what we can call broadly 'French structuralism' (I'm thinking here, for example of the influence and example of the *Tel Quel* journal but also the wider tradition of Althusser, Foucault, Derrida, Kristeva etc.). This latter became really influential on this younger group of philosophy students in the late 1960s at Ljubljana.

Helena Motoh and Jones Irwin: Can you develop this thematic in a little more detail, as to how exactly this notion of French structuralism came to influence your thinking in the early stages, and the place of the more specific figure of Lacan in this intellectual trajectory?

Slavoj Žižek: Perhaps surprisingly the two hegemonic philosophical schools in Slovenia at the time, previously fierce opponents, that is, the Frankfurt school on the one side and Heideggerianism on the other, start to speak the same language so as to precisely oppose this new birth of French structuralism. So this is where we come in, Mladen and I and a host of other thinkers in the 1970s' era in Ljubljana.

We were defending or following the French explosion of thought in contradistinction to this unholy official alliance of Heideggerianism and the Frankfurt school theorists. In the mid to late 1970s, we get this genesis of a new way of thinking here which of course will evolve and transform and that is in effect your story, the story you want to tell, the story of the so-called Ljubljana School of Psychoanalysis, or as I prefer to see it, our 'party troika' of Mladen, Alenka and I. Our thinking at the time was then preoccupied with the new French thinkers we were translating into Slovenian obsessively and so on, but it was also not myopic to the past. It had a clear genealogical line back to Hegel and Marx, in particular. Even then, this was certainly the case and it is not simply a more recent development, the link of Lacan and Hegelian–Marxism. And it wasn't homogeneous either, certainly not across the broad spectrum of Slovenian thinkers represented, but even in our own group, between Mladen and I at the time (there were differences).

How would I characterize this? In the first instance, Mladen was more Marxist then I at the beginning (and nowadays let me say I think fairly that he is less Marxist than I). Similarly with Alenka, if we are thinking of some internal differentiation within our so-called troika, we can say that Alenka is also less Marxist than my own thought. My own work has certainly become more overtly political, although one can trace all these political battles through the 1970s and the 1980s, the *Problemi* issues, for example, and then later the NSK and the democracy/independence movement etc. This is a theme we can return to later when we explore the more contemporary developments of the thinking and the more recent evolutions of our thought. Just recently, there are changes, perhaps a sense of the limitations of the approaches used. I articulate, for example, some of these contemporary problematics, they are political and philosophical, in my new book on Hegel, *Less Than Nothing: Hegel and the Shadow of Dialectical Materialism* (Žižek 2012a). Within our troika, we have, I think it is fair to say, an internally differentiated politics, although we should not overplay the difference. They, Alenka and Mladen, are not as attracted to the notion, for example, of 'communism' as I am.

But let me return to the genealogy which I was outlining, and which I think is significant for our story. This is not just a story about Slovenia or an intra-Slovenian issue of course, as precisely our mobility, our ability to travel, is part of the story. In 1969, when I was 20/21, I went to France, Mladen went there first in the mid-1970s I think, and we would both have significant relations to the milieu of French thinking, not just from outside but also from within our experience of the French system, not just intellectually but politically also. This of course will also continue with Alenka's trajectory, who like us goes to France, in her case to study with Badiou at St Denis. Mladen and I had studied with (Jacques-Alain) Miller in Paris, and had connections to the earlier department at Vincennes before they moved to St Denis. There is a very particular story attaching to that department at Vincennes (and the difficult relations with the philosophy department, Deleuze and Lyotard etc.). The Department of Psychoanalysis had Judith Lacan alongside Miller so this is a rather protracted history here, in terms of its problematicity.

Originally in the 1970s certainly, as I mentioned earlier, we would have been influenced by the wider gambit of French structuralism, understood broadly and therefore including figures such as Lyotard and Deleuze. Lacan, we might say, was already in the mix then but as one thinker among the many. As with the others, we would have translated Lacan into Slovenian, during this period. Not the least interesting aspect of this history is the way we move from the wider unity of French structuralism to the more specific orthodox Lacanian orientation. But, second, we should also note how there are significant schisms between, for example, Deleuze and Lacan, Derrida and Lacan etc. But Miller certainly was key for us in the early 1980s, especially in our experience of working with him closely on his reading of Lacanian thought. Just as there are clear differentiations to be made within the neo-Freudian schools of thought – I have referred, for example, in *The Sublime Object of Ideology* to 'psychoanalytical essentialism' in relation to Marcuse's thought, not to mention ego psychology (Žižek 1989), so too we can differentiate between different Lacanian readings. One aspect of Miller's reading is his emphasis on the later Lacan (although not in an exclusionary sense) and also his emphasis on the concept of the 'Real'. His close readings of Lacan were formative for us, beyond doubt; this is why we refer to ourselves as orthodox Lacanians. In my case, I would take a class of 4 hours a week with Miller in Paris. I would describe his reading as as close as possible to a 'miracle'. Miller was a magician in my eyes, still is and remains so for us. That said, we have also looked beyond Millerian Lacanianism in our thought, quite obviously. But the original influence remains intact and significant in a perennial way, throughout our thinking and theoretical production.

So there is the issue of the internal reading of Lacan within or from within Lacanian circles, and here I am speaking of Miller. But of course there is also and perhaps more importantly the meta-level question of 'why Lacan at all?'. Or more accurately, why Lacan specifically?. To explicate this, I can say that, in the late 1970s, Lacan was the closest thing one could get to an authentic religious experience! Lacan was the real 'thing', although we flirted also of course with Kristeva, among others. Let's get this straight then. We embraced a certain 'unity in difference' of French structuralism to take us out of the hegemony in those days shared between Heideggerianism and the Frankfurt school or Praxis school in Yugoslavia. But why did we move beyond French structuralism towards a singular Lacanian (orthodox) interpretation? We would say that it was the Lacanian reading of the concept of the 'subject' which was irreducible and key for us, at this time (perhaps later, we can say other concepts became more important). This needs to be emphasized; it was the reading of the 'subject' which was key for us, unequivocally. It was what differentiated Lacan from structuralism proper but also from more obviously post-structuralist thinkers such as Derrida.

Lacan, in this sense, is neither structuralist nor post-structuralist – we here start to jettison those terms, not to mention the overused concept of 'postmodernist'. And, of course, there is a key political dimension to this foregrounding of the concept of the notion of 'subject'. We can see this, for example, in Badiou's taking up of Lacan and in the work of Alenka, as well as in Peter Hallward's work, among others. But it is also key if we want to keep our eyes on the Slovenian specifics of the political mobilization. In many respects, the notion of 'subject' was indispensable here, insofar as it points beyond a simple or completely determining notion of ideology and the impossibility of resistance etc. Here, we can think of all the issues around the Althusserian 'subjectless structure', not so much before but after 1968, as by leaving the 'subject' out of the equation, there could be no explanation or justification for what happened in 1968 (which led to the early 1970 critiques from the ex-Althusserians, for example Badiou, centred on a reintroduction of a concept of 'subject').

Another way into this thematic is to make the distinction between the respective concepts of 'productivity' and 'representation', which divide a generation of French thinkers. Deleuze spoke of productivity and Derrida spoke of the closure of representation, for example, paradigmatically in his *Writing and Difference* texts. To some extent, at least, I think Badiou remains within this problematic. However, Lacan went beyond this distinction and the best way to see this is in terms of Lacan going back to Hegel and Marx. I might even say here that Hegel is more materialist than Marx (Balibar [2007], for example, makes a similar claim in his recent book on Marx). Hegel is undoubtedly closer to Lacan than Marx is on this. Marx remains caught within a more traditional notion of representation, for example, in his notion of 'alienation' (Lacan supersedes the notion of 'alienation' in his earlier texts with his later notion of 'separation'). I take up these issues and problems in *Less Than Nothing: Hegel and the Shadow of Dialectical Materialism*.

But, again, we would need to take stock here a little more. Nothing is simple in this zone of interpretation and we must be patient conceptually at all times. For example, it is clear that when we speak of Lacan being close to Hegel, that we are not talking strictly at all about Lacan's reading of Hegel, that is the reading through the influence of the Kojève seminars on the *Phenomenology of Spirit*. No. This is one of the dilemmas of reading Hegel through a Lacanian lens, that you can't depend on Lacan. We have to take it as an axiom that Lacan's own reading of Hegel is fundamentally misguided. Lacan gets Hegel wrong, perhaps even very wrong. This also isn't just down to Kojève but to some aspects of the internal dynamics of Lacan's own evolution as a thinker (the influence of surrealism, for example, or the surrealist Hegel). What we must say, then, is that Lacan is more authentically Hegelian when he is being (as he sees it) anti-Hegelian. Again, we can trace several different movements in Lacan's own itinerary of thought, early to late, from the 1950s, for example, through the 1960s and right up to his final works. As a troika, I think we tend to agree with Badiou that Lacan's later works are perhaps the strongest conceptually, also however the most enigmatic. In the 1950s and into the early 1960s, for the most part, Lacan is closer to Kant, 'Kant with Sade' etc. And, of course, this line of Lacan and Kant has been taken up very fruitfully (and insightfully) by Alenka in her readings of philosophy (Zupančič 2000). It is really only later Lacan becomes authentically Hegelian.

Helena Motoh and Jones Irwin: In the late 1970s, for both your work and that of Dolar, a specific kind of Lacanianism becomes key. You have spoken of some of the history and personal dimension of this story. Can you clarify how and why Lacan became the key intellectual influence from a more avowedly conceptual perspective. What in other words for you are the key Lacanian concepts of importance?

Slavoj Žižek: I have spoken of structuralism as the initial influence understood in the broad sense and how that very structuralism acted as a midway point between, on the one hand, Heideggerianism and on the other, a leftist Praxis school influenced by the Frankfurt school more generally of course. But, as we developed our thinking through the 1970s and especially the Parisian influence of Miller's readings, we came to see the Lacanian perspective as quite singular in relation to the influence of the wider structuralism. It is this distinctiveness, as we saw it, of Lacan within the structuralist movement which led us to emphasize his work specifically and to seek to develop a Lacanian orthodoxy of our own. With regard to the question of structuralism, it is clear, for example, that this was no unified group, apart from Lacan. There were significant and important differences between Althusser, Foucault, Lévi-Strauss and between the *Tel Quel* group, for example, between Derrida and Kristeva.

Perhaps I can tell an old Soviet joke here to exemplify why Lacan became important. The key to the joke is that in the Soviet times, Lenin's famous phrase was 'learn, learn and learn' and this was the motto in all the schools, and so on. But the joke goes that Lenin, Marx and Engels were once asked would they prefer a wife or a mistress? Marx, being a traditionalist in private matters, said he would opt for a wife. Engels being the dandy said he would opt for the mistress. Lenin said he would opt for the wife and mistress combination. Why? Because, Lenin said, he could tell the wife he was with the mistress and tell the mistress he was with the wife, and then he could go alone to the library or wherever, and of course there he could 'learn, learn and learn'. It was like this with us and Lacan. We told the Althusserians we were with the Derrideans and the Derrideans we were with the Althusserians, but we went with Lacan, alone as it were. Why? Because he allowed us the wife and the mistress, the both/and, not just the either/or. And with him, we could 'learn, learn and learn'!

Lacan alone, a singular Lacanianism, allowed us to develop a particular set of concepts. The concepts which were key here were myriad. But first, for me at least, was the concept of the 'Real' certainly. Here, we had the chance of a certain reference to a notion of the 'Real' but obviously avoiding the simplifications of a more traditional philosophical or even metaphysical realism. Lacan speaks to this strongly in Seminar XI, *The Four Fundamental Concepts of Psychoanalysis* (Lacan 1994), with reference surprisingly for some to Aristotle's notion of 'tuche'. We should also note here the significance of Lacan's transfiguration of the traditional 'object' in philosophy or 'object relations' in psychoanalysis. Lacan's 'Real' represents an 'object' which is not an object in any ontological sense; there is an ontological impasse here, which is one of the key claims of psychoanalysis.

Here, Hegel was closer to Lacan than Marx in that Lacan's materialism was less 'realist' in a universal sense. Here, as Lacanians, and as a troika, we sought to repeat but also go beyond Hegel. We might say as our motto, the Ljubljana School of Psychoanalysis: 'Philosophers up to now have only interpreted Hegel. The point however is to change him'. So what was it about Hegel's philosophical reading of reality and the relation to Lacan that was so important for us? As I've clarified before, Lacan's actual reading of Hegel was a misinterpretation but what we are saying here is that Lacan's own philosophy was closer to Hegel's philosophy than Lacan actually realized. So, in this sense, we are also going against a certain Lacanian reading of Hegel. We are authentic Lacanians on this question, *contra* Lacan who was an inauthentic Lacanian on the question of Hegel. Although just to complicate matters further, Lacan, in fact, always said he was a Freudian and never a Lacanian. This is not some simple abstract (or academicized) use of Hegel or Hegelianism for its own sake but it is an inherently politicized reading of Hegel which contrasts Hegel with Marx most especially, where we view Hegel as more productive politically in his reading of capitalism (and the critique of ideology) than in effect Marx ultimately was. Why and how can Hegel speak to the crisis of contemporary capitalism, this crisis being another thematic of our work?

There is, we can say, a radical Left impotence in the current moment. Here, also of course, the concept of ideology is key and we know how this notion has evolved in the Marxist tradition most especially. Our reading of ideology is also somewhat distinctive.

We assert a Lacanian pessimism of the obstacle as a positive condition of possibility. Marx in this sense was too utopian. The second main difference which we can delineate here between Hegel and Marx is the issue of necessity versus contingency. Briefly put, we can say that Marx is far too determinist. Even in his least determinist moments, of a more subtle notion of the progressive movement of history and the sense of historical agency, there is it seems to me, from a certain Hegelian perspective, too much of an idealist position being maintained in Marx. With Hegel instead, on my reading, and more broadly the reading of the troika, we have a concept of radical (political-economic) contingency. Again, this reading is central to Lacan and the importance for us of Lacan vis-à-vis the other thinkers in the structuralist tradition. We could trace this through a more complex reading of Hegel which we get in French philosophy in the twentieth century, beginning with Kojève and the way that Lacan takes up a perspective rooted in Kojève on Hegel and is misguided by that, misdirected by it. But of course in the Kojèvian reading of Hegel there is also something true, that is the tragic dimension, a step further into despair. This concept of despair or its equivalent will be important for both Hegel and Lacan.

Helena Motoh and Jones Irwin: Beyond the clear Hegelian influence which you delineate here, can you say something about the other key concepts and thinkers which contribute to your Lacanianism? Additionally, can you contextualize these conceptual influences in relation to the troika of thinkers in Ljubljana as a whole, drawing out their similarities and difference?

Slavoj Žižek: The range of influences on my own thought are complex and on the troika as a whole more complex again and more differentiated. That said, what draws our project and indeed the project of your book together is precisely this sense of a 'unity in difference'. Let me say something first about the nature of philosophical influence on my own thinking. In no particular order, I might first mention here the figure of Pascal. In recent times, the theological dimension has become important in my work, not to defend the tradition but as a tradition which one must go through to understand concepts such as belief etc., which in today's culture have such a superficial and over-hasty understanding. There is a notion of subjectivity in Pascal (alongside his important conception of belief per se) which becomes important for my own thinking in relation to Lacan's notion of the subject. This conception of the subject is also linked to radical thought and political struggle, for example, in the twentieth century and also in our more recent developments. In another recent short text *On the Year of Dreaming Dangerously* (Žižek 2012b), I explore some of these recent developments of resistance movements, through, for example, the 'Arab Spring' and the 'Occupy Wall Street' movement. Thus, the notion of ideology critique remains pertinent here although it needs to move away from such vulgarized versions of false consciousness or related notions which can still be present on the Left. This is where Lacanianism can make a contribution with its more nuanced critique of ideology.

Certainly, the critique of ideology becomes more and more oblique and we see this, for example, in Slovenia before independence in the shape of the NSK, and especially Laibach, who really did succeed in becoming 'unbearable' (as many commentators claimed at the time) with their 'strategies of dissidence'. I followed their trajectory in several texts, moving on from the original defence of their work as not amenable to the ridiculous accusation of 'fascism' or 'neo-Nazism' thrown at them by the state (in 'Why Laibach and the Neue Slowenische Kunst Are Not Fascists' [Žižek 2007c]). Of course, all of this 'neo-Nazi' witch-hunt was really just a repetition of the earlier accusations of 'fascism' made against punk in Ljubljana in 1981–83 and the so-called *Punk Problemi* affair, and so on (Žižek 1981; Dolar 1982). In another text, I relate what the NSK did to what Freud calls 'acheronta movebo', or precisely 'moving the underground' (which he uses in *The Interpretation of Dreams* text). This shows the connectivity between NSK and Freud, and how the ideology critique that was adopted in Slovenia against the state socialism needed the psychoanalytical perspective. Yes, as I make clear in *The Sublime Object of Ideology*, 'Marx invented the symptom'. But 'dogmatic' Marxism, as we used to call it, was using this conception in a very repressive way. We need to read the Marxist symptom in the context of Freud and Lacan, and this is what I have done successively in my texts. With the NSK, one also sees that this Lacanianism is something perhaps 'peculiar' in Slovenia. It emerged as a precise delineation not just for Mladen and I but for a whole grouping of thinkers, activists and artists like NSK. Močnik, also a Lacanian in his own right, and one of our grouping through the years, has written about this as a Lacanian 'breakthrough' (Močnik 1993). I have spoken about it already as emerging from within an allegiance to a more generalized French structuralist orientation. But I have also indicated the struggles (the philosophical ones too) which we had to come through, at the Department of Philosophy in Ljubljana, for example (this continues until today). I was unemployed for many years as the state socialism did not want me to teach, did not want me in a position of influence. Why? Again, you can trace this back to my Master's thesis and having to write an extra chapter on the 'relation to Marxism'. In effect, this is exactly the instantiation of the distinction between dogmatic and non-dogmatic Marxism which we foregrounded in the 1980s (Žižek 1981). Here, the notion of symptom which the system was using (i.e., 'punk is a symptom', 'Lacan is a symptom' etc.), this had to be turned back against the system itself so that the very diagnostic the system put forward was a symptom of its own malaise. But how to say this in the language of, for example, dogmatic Marxism? It was impossible in this sense to articulate. We can compare it to the way the philosophical and political journals of the time in Slovenia, were constantly having to negotiate censorship, what couldn't be said, or how to say what couldn't be said in a different way. Anyway, some of us ended up in court, Mladen as the editor was charged and fined. But here as well you have another sense to the 'moving the underground' idea from NSK. NSK, coming after and emerging from the embers of punk, they couldn't approach it directly, therefore they went after the 'obscene underlying supplement' of the system. And they did this, of course, by taking the ideology of the system more seriously than the system ever did itself, more than they were meant to. They overidentified with the very notion of state socialism (its ideal moment) and that is what made them 'unbearable'.

We might contrast this with Badiou's perspective on the subject and ideology for example, which I remained unconvinced by. Politically, and remember Badiou was quite critical back in the early 1990s of some of what happened (in some ways rightly so) but also you had here the kind of Western Left perspective on the 'East'. There is also (for all our alliances) more of a notion of determinism in Badiou, his political perspective still connecting with Maoism and so on. I would say that the political perspective being outlined here and he is not alone in this but it is more of an index of a certain thinking on the Left, is overly utopian, overly idealist as opposed to genuinely materialist and one indicative element of this is the complete lack of a critique of political economy. The perspectives on former Yugoslavia also show, I think, that ideology critique needs to be context-specific. There were incredible peculiarities at work here, as elsewhere in Yugoslavia or in the former Soviet bloc. Here, we had Tito, we had the very different and individualized federal republics, the 'rabid' emergence of nationalisms of all sorts, we had a strange mix of liberal and repressive, we had a complex philosophical trajectory going from Heidegger to Praxis to Lacan, and last but not least, we had the punks, FV and NSK, the 'alternative culture'. The attempted colonization of the life world (Gantar 1993) by state socialism is key to all this, but it would be different elsewhere. This was ideology, Yugoslav style.

Helena Motoh and Jones Irwin: You have spoken about this wider context and also about your own formation as a philosopher, as a Lacanian. Can you say something more in-depth about the philosophical relations at the heart of the so-called troika: you, Dolar and Zupančič and the relations between your respective works?

Slavoj Žižek: You ask me, then, about the internal similarities and disaffinities within our troika of thinkers, myself, Mladen and Alenka. Of course, let me say first of all, we are friends, we are great friends, the three of us and we meet up if and when we can to talk about philosophy, when we are all in Ljubljana at the same time, not as often as we would like. Philosophy, by definition (let us not forget) is forged in friendship, in the 'philo-' and also there is 'eros' here too, love, and we know how central this is for us, from Plato's *Symposium* to Lacan's (1998) Seminar XX (*On Feminine Sexuality. The Limits of Love and Knowledge*).

Politically first of all, I think that it is fair to say that, from an ideological perspective, Alenka and I are the hardliners. Mladen is shall we say politically softer than either of us. I've already mentioned this, for example, in terms of the take-up of the notion of communism. In terms of the reading of Hegel which I have cited as key, absolutely key, to the evolution of our group of thinkers, I would actually say that the difference in reading is negligible if even non-existent. Mladen, as we know, is an especially strong reader of Hegel and Dolar's work has been important in making the Hegel–Lacan affinities crucial for us as a troika, more and more. And I have already said something about the counter-intuitive aspects of all this. Lacan explicitly critiques Hegel but gets Hegel very wrong, so what he posits as his own alternative to Hegel is really Hegelianism, and so on. Certainly, the understanding of our troika as being focused on the Lacan–Hegel relation has been long in coming, but perhaps this is also as some of the earlier texts in Slovenian were not translated. In his preface to *The Sublime Object of Ideology*, Laclau was already clear on the question of the Hegel interpretation being constitutive, one of our 'original features' as he referred to it then (Laclau 1989).

There is also significant confusion over the question of our orthodox Lacanianism. The question goes like this – 'how can you be an orthodox Lacanian and a philosopher at the same time?'. Here, the conviction is that philosophy must always be questioning its presuppositions endlessly and therefore having a position amounts to dogmatism, is unphilosophical etc. This issue also bears on the supposedly problematic relation between psychoanalysis and philosophy. Again, the question goes something like – 'are you a philosopher or a psychoanalyst?'. And further, there is the assertion that it must be 'either Hegel or Lacan, never both at the same time' as one would be a philosopher and the other from psychoanalysis, and so on. How do we respond to this? This is obviously a question for the troika of thinkers, rather than simply for me, as we are referred to as the Ljubljana School of Psychoanalysis. On this reckoning, we could not be philosophers, any one of the three of us, as according to the title we subscribe to psychoanalysis. You can see how contorted the scene of interpretation becomes. But not one of us in the troika sees it like this.

I don't like answering for Mladen and Alenka on this, but let me just make two points. The concept of the cogito is an interesting example here, a revealing example. Back in 1998, I edited a text that we all collaborated on, *Cogito and the Unconscious* (Žižek 1998a). Dolar wrote an essay there, a very good one, on the relation between the cogito and the Lacanian 'subject'. Certainly, there are key differences (Lacan is not a Cartesian, doesn't use the 'big Other' as a get-out clause from doubt etc.). Nevertheless, as Dolar (1998) shows very well, the 'subject' of psychoanalysis is nothing other than the 'cogito', albeit as I put it at the time, 'with a (Lacanian) twist'. So, my key point here is that psychoanalysis as understood by Dolar does not involve some extraneous site to philosophy (as Derrida keeps talking about; a 'nonphilosophical site'). No, the psychoanalytical conceptuality derives from (and is very much an extension of) this very philosophical tradition. One could mention so many examples, 'Kant with Sade' being another one. Badiou writes an interesting essay (Badiou 2006) on 'Lacan and the Presocratics'. Aside from the individual examples, the crucial point is that psychoanalysis, while distinct from philosophy, is still very much (in our eyes at least) to be seen as a philosophical practice of thought.

I have mentioned Dolar on this and it becomes also one of Zupančič's key themes in her recent work, for example, *Why Psychoanalysis? Three Interventions* (Zupančič 2008b). There, she takes several psychoanalytical concepts (cause etc.) but especially the concept of 'sexuality' and demonstrates that far from this being some extra site to philosophy (as it is often claimed to be) what, for example, Freud is seeking to achieve with this conception is a claim about an 'ontological impasse' (Zupančič 2008b). Thus, psychoanalysis, whether Freudian or Lacanian, is a thoroughgoing form of philosophical, ontological critique. And these two concepts, 'cogito'/subject and 'sexuality' would be just two examples of the many concepts one could make the same case for.

But what of the 'orthodoxy' issue? How can one be an orthodox Lacanian? In *The Plague of Fantasies*, I refer this question to a metaphor from Paul de Man, of reading as a certain kind of 'disfigurement' or distortion (Žižek 1997). If we are, and yes we can say that authentically we are, orthodox Lacanians, this does not mean above all agreeing with everything which Lacan said, or seemed to say, or thought himself that he said. Rather, to be orthodox Lacanians, we must in effect read *Lacan against Lacan*. 'Philosophers up to now have only interpreted Lacan. The point, however, is to change him'.

In terms of the troika of thinkers, you also asked what differentiates us, where do we disagree philosophically? A topic which certainly does differentiate us as more individual thinkers within the troika is Christianity and the relation to religion. Here, there is a key distinction in the readings of my own work and that of either Mladen or Alenka on religion and Christianity. It is clear that there are different phases of the relation to Christianity in my own work and it develops more fully later on, especially, for example, more recently in terms of some of my debates with John Milbank and the Radical Orthodoxy movement in theology. We don't see such a substantive relation to the theological tradition in either Dolar or Zupančič.

Certainly, in her Nietzsche book, Alenka addresses some of these topics, but in a different way from mine. Mladen takes up a position which is seemingly indifferent to some of the theological issues I deal with, and his philosophy is a more thoroughgoing atheism than mine. My claim here is not merely that I am a materialist through and through and that the surviving kernel of Christianity is accessible also to a materialist approach. My thesis is much stronger; this kernel is available only to materialist approaches and vice versa. To become a true dialectical materialist, one should go through the Christian experience.

That said, of course, I have argued strongly in my books on theology (for example, in *The Monstrosity of Christ. Paradox or Dialectic* [Žižek and Milbank 2009]), that although one 'must go through the Christian tradition' philosophically (e.g., Augustine, Pascal etc.), that one nonetheless emerges as what I call a 'Christian atheist'. Atheism is the truth of Christianity, therefore I am of course far closer to either Dolar or Zupančič than I am to Milbank or Radical Orthodoxy on this question.

Helena Motoh and Jones Irwin: To return to a more biographical trajectory for a moment, you returned to Ljubljana in the late 1980s. This was also a period of great change in Slovenian society, where we might say the spirit of Vincennes lived on. Can you explain some of these developments leading up to independence for Slovenia in 1991, with special reference to some of the important Slovenian Art movements known as NSK, and also their relation to the philosophical movement which you were a part of?

Slavoj Žižek: My sense of these groups under the ambit of NSK including of course Laibach as perhaps the most infamous among them (also IRWIN) is that the kind of critique of ideology they developed was very acute and insightful at a particular moment of our history. Ljubljana being a relatively small city meant that all of these 'alternative culture' moments were interdependent with the intellectual culture, the philosophers etc. So, for example, I have written extensively on NSK and Laibach and earlier punk, and we know the histories of these successive conflicts in relation to the various accusations of neo-Nazism first against the punks, then against Laibach and the NSK. Also, we can trace the development of the critique of ideology from its more explicit rendering in the punk movement to the kind of implicit or more nuanced approaches later on. Two things are clear in relation to the NSK and Laibach. First, that there was no way that they were fascistic in the sense in which they were accused by the state socialist ideology. These were the 'decaying years' of socialism and obviously, this whole period was a kind of desperate period for the ideological maintenance. The second thing is that the NSK exploited this 'state decay' to its utmost, they took the ideology seriously which of course was fatal to the ideology. They enacted the truth of what the ideology claimed itself to be and in so doing demonstrated that it was empty, hollow, a mere hypocrisy. But as events evolved and developed, with 1991 and independence, the situation completely changed. Now, you had this whole opposition of nationalism on the one side and left liberalism on the other, and then the residues of communism and state socialism and their adherents. In this scenario, perhaps one can say that NSK were not as effective any more. Their contribution had been made but it was a contextual moment, or perhaps they became overly self-conscious of their role. They ceased to be an underground, an alternative culture.

On the identity question more related to me personally, my own sense of being a Slovenian is very ambiguous. I would say that I do not feel very strongly about being a Slovenian, although of course I was swept up a little in the independence movement and that moment of Slovenian independence. Still, three minutes of a movie means more to me than Slovenian independence, no two minutes (I'm serious here!). Part of the problem with independence and the break-up of Yugoslavia was the way in which everything was split (from, for example, a Western left-liberal perspective) into 'you are either proto-Fascist nationalist sympathisers or you are left-liberal democrats'. But this refuses to question the 'normality' or universality of liberal democratic capitalism. There was a missed political opportunity then, in what we might call the 'vanishing mediators' between state socialism and (capitalist) Slovenia. This is also part of the discussion on the civil society constraints that, for example, we hear from Gantar (1993) and Močnik (1993). Still, on a more general level, let me put it more starkly regarding Yugoslavia. I would say that Mladen, Alenka and I have no nostalgia for Yugoslavia: I would say that Yugoslavia was dead for us from Milošević.

Helena Motoh and Jones Irwin: You have clarified the position of orthodox Lacanianism to a great extent. How important is the relation between psychoanalysis and philosophy for your work specifically and for the troika as a whole? Put simply, would you describe your writings as philosophy? Do you consider yourself a philosopher?

Slavoj Žižek: Am I a philosopher? Yes, absolutely. But again, we have to be careful here. I am on the record as saying that I am an orthodox Lacanian and commentators then interpret your relation to philosophy in terms of Lacan's explicit pronouncements on the topic of psychoanalysis and philosophy and their relation. But this to me is a misunderstanding of the sense of what orthodox Lacanianism means or indeed what orthodoxy means. When I say this I am understood 'definitively' by philosophers, but such orthodoxy for me does not entail literalism which I think is more the hermeneutic misunderstanding. I think that when people see the concept of orthodoxy they understand a blind literalism. However, nothing could be further from the truth.

Perhaps the situation can best be understood in terms of the relation between Hegel and psychoanalysis or Lacan which I described earlier. Commentators think that when you say that Lacan is close to Hegel that we understand that means proximate to Lacan's literal pronouncements on Hegel. But quite the contrary – I might invoke again de Man's important concept of 'reading as disfigurement', which I foreground in *The Plague of Fantasies* (Žižek 1997). Lacan in his literal readings totally misunderstands the nature of philosophy. I would draw attention here for example to Lacan's paradigmatic reading of Socrates as the founding gesture of philosophy. However, as a troika, I can say that we are opposed to Lacan's conception of what Badiou calls 'anti-philosophy'. We are also wary of Badiou's own co-option of this notion of anti-philosophy in that we might say in contradistinction that he, Badiou, doesn't realize to what extent he remains a philosopher. We thus also reject Badiou's limitation of psychoanalysis. His notion that you can go through psychoanalysis and specifically Lacan's thought and then somehow leave it all behind, supersede it, as it were. Philosophically, we can say that Badiou misses an entire dimension of the concept of death drive. There is thus a critique in the troika of Badiou on what we might call this meta-philosophical level of thought. I might refer specifically to Chapter 13 of my recent text, *Less than Nothing* (Žižek 2012a). We try to be precise: philosophy is not homogeneous.

Helena Motoh and Jones Irwin: How does this affect for example the relation between philosophy and literature which is so paradigmatic for many of your contemporaries?

Slavoj Žižek: In this context, the troika and I are with Badiou wholeheartedly in his reading of the relation between philosophy and literature, or philosophy and the artist poet. Here, additionally, we are with a whole tradition of thinking that goes back to Plato's Republic Book X, if not before. That is, literature and poetry are far more terrifying than philosophy. How can I put this? – Plato was right; poets should be sent out of the city. Why? Let me say provocatively that there was no ethnic cleansing without poetry, poetry is always more important in totalitarian regimes and societies. This is no doubt because of the mythic dimension to poetry, mythos rather than logos, mythos against logos. In this, I am a militant philosopher no doubt. I can also say that this is something we need to think about in terms of some of the things we said earlier about the relation between Hegel and Marx. Now this relation is far from being any one relation, among others. Rather, let us think of Thesis 1 of the 'Theses on Feuerbach', Marx's famous intervention in the paradigm shift of philosophy. 'Philosophers up to now have interpreted the world; the point however is to change it'. I would say with the troika and this is a Hegelian moment contra Marx; 'philosophers up to now have changed the world; the point however is to interpret it'.

Helena Motoh and Jones Irwin: Regarding such interpretation, it is clear that there are significant difficulties in interpreting Lacan. There are different phases of his thought, with some commentators positing an early and late phase, others an overarching unity. There is the question of how we might make sense of the 'return to Freud'. Also, what do these interpretive issues mean for psychoanalysis as such?

Slavoj Žižek: Yes, of course, the interpretive issues are clearly there. Dolar for example in the 'Cogito' essay delineates this hermeneutics of Lacan carefully, arguing against this hard and fast early/late distinction and against the notion that one notion might jettison another, earlier notion. I agree with this meta-level reading, which continuously brings the earlier concepts and texts back into the equation and seeks to reassess them in the light of the later work.

This is exactly what Lacan meant by the 'return to Freud', it was never a literalist or originary orthodoxy. Rather, Lacan saw the open-ended aspect of the 'Freudian field' and he reworked it in different contexts, according to different challenges. The Ljubljana School of Psychoanalysis does the same, reworking the Lacanian texts and philosophy, in relation to the challenges being faced. We see this in relation for example to the notion of ideology as it has developed in my work through *The Sublime Object of Ideology* and through various texts, including several versions of *Enjoy Your Symptom*. Or the theological emphasis (making use of Lacan's 'God is unconscious') and the defence of a certain kind of 'Christian atheism'.

While the early/late Lacan distinction is not hard and fast, there is a certain pertinence to it that we must take note of, as it affects particular thematics in Lacan's work, whether for example we are talking of the move beyond the early emphasis on the symbolic or the so-called move from 'desire to drive'. Another key concept for the late Lacan (appearing systematically first in Seminar XI) is, of course, the 'Real'. This was the key revision of the notion of the object as it had been traditionally defined, by so-called 'realism'. Therefore, here we have the two pronged attack of Lacanianism: the notion of the 'subject' which is indeed often foregrounded and seen as constitutive of our approach but just as strongly (and far more underestimated) the notion of the object (which is not an object). Certainly, in terms of the wider influence of Lacan, it is clear that this understanding of the 'object' first emerged as influential in the area of cinema studies. One can see it in the work of Laura Mulvey for example, and the development of specific aspects of feminist thought and queer theory later. Within the Ljubljana troika, the emphasis on cinema has always been strong, for example in one of our early anthologies in English on Hitchcock, *Everything You Always Wanted to Know About Lacan But Were Afraid to Ask Hitchcock* (Žižek 1992b).

Although the triadic register of 'Real, Imaginary and Symbolic' was there earlier, in the late 1950s for example Lacan was almost exclusively focused on the tension between the symbolic and the imaginary. But, by the 1960s and *The Ethics of Psychoanalysis* text, the Lacanian axis and emphasis had changed to the relation between the symbolic and the 'Real'. Briefly, for Lacan, the 'symbolic' sphere is the field of language, of symbolic structure and communication, the 'imaginary' is the domain of images with which we identify and the 'Real' stands for the trauma or 'hard traumatic reality' which resists symbolization. Earlier, Lacan sees symbolization as less of a problem but a whole shift takes place here in terms of the symbolic order itself. From this point onwards, the focus shifts to the symbolic order being 'inconsistent' and the encounter between the symbolic order and the newly emergent 'Real' is the locus for the inconsistency. This for Lacan (and psychoanalysis more generally) is not simply a theoretical inconsistency but rather an 'ontological impasse'. I explore this ontological problem in *The Plague of Fantasies* (Žižek 1997), for example, and Alenka looks at it more recently in relation to the question of psychoanalysis vis-à-vis philosophy in *Why Psychoanalysis: Three Interventions* (Zupančič 2008b). This later theoretical development also casts doubt on the whole notion of 'traversing the fantasy', insofar as the antagonism of the 'Real' is a deadlock which cannot be traversed. We can see something similar in terms of the early Lacan principle 'don't give up on one's desire' which is outlined in *The Ethics of Psychoanalysis*. With the renewed emphasis in the later work on the 'Real' and (death) 'drive', there is also a silence around this earlier dictum, which Lacan seemed to put at the centre of his ethics in Seminar VII. Alenka explores this issue very carefully and insightfully in *The Ethics of the Real: Kant, Lacan* (Zupančič 2000) and Mladen speaks of it as the 'demotion of desire' in his *A Voice and Nothing More* (Dolar 2006), devoting a whole section to the 'ethics of the voice'. The conception of ethics is maintained but now it is an 'ethics' which must reckon with a traumatic encounter with the 'Real' and the death drive. This move between early and later Lacan is also a move away from a more Kantian perspective to a more Hegelian framework.

One concept which is dismissed as pathological in the early Lacan is 'love' but this is reinterpreted in later Lacan and explored in relation to some possibilities of sublimation, for example. Speaking quickly, sublimation is here understood as a 'nonrepressive satisfaction' of the drive, although this is a notion which requires further critical analysis. There is the infamous discussion of courtly love for example but Seminar XX, *On Feminine Sexuality. The Limits of Love and Knowledge* is among other things, concerned with the concept (and the experience) of love and a desire which is not focused on 'lack'. Alenka has taken up this problematic in a very interesting way in her *Odd One In: On Comedy* (Zupančič 2008a), especially in the Appendix of that text, which grapples with the complexity of Plato's *Symposium* and how Aristophanes' speech on eros redirects the whole conception of the relation between sex and love, desire and drive in a way that Lacan takes up (the Aristophanic/Platonic complication of the notions of 'split' and 'lack' are also paradigmatic here). This is an important discussion for all three of us as thinkers, insofar as it also bears on some of Lacan's late (and grossly misinterpreted) pronouncements concerning 'there is no sexual relationship', 'woman does not exist' and 'love is giving something one does not have to someone who doesn't want it'. These principles are still in need of significant critical analysis and consideration. Also at issue here is Freud's whole juxtaposition of Eros and Thanatos, and the sense (for example in *Civilisation and Its Discontents*) that 'Eros' may have some remaining resources to combat the more aggressive or fatalist drives.

Finally, more recently, the troika has begun to come up against the limits of the Hegelian approach and the later Lacanian approach. As I say in *Less Than Nothing*, Seminar XX represents Lacan's ultimate achievement but also a 'deadlock' and a philosophical failure (if we think of some of his attempted conceptual solutions after Seminar XX; sinthome, knots etc.). On another level, there is also an important need to shift the emphasis from ethics to politics, to explore new possibilities for a psychoanalytical politics. Developing a Kierkegaardian logic here, I have referred to the 'political suspension of the ethical'. From the question 'which ethics fits psychoanalysis?' we should therefore pass to the question 'which politics fits psychoanalysis?' [Interview ends]

Conclusion – 'Moving the Underground' with the NSK

The above interview brings out both the highly powerful and unique philosophical trajectory of Žižek alongside his very genuine attachment to a troika of Ljubljana thinkers who have developed a group-level Lacanian analysis with a very significant worldwide philosophical influence. We saw the clear Lacanian position of 'orthodoxy' stated, the 'break' which such a view entails with traditional philosophical notions while, at the same time, the strong affinities to German idealism (especially Hegel) and the Cartesian tradition of 'cogito'. As Žižek says in his introduction to the original *Cogito and the Unconscious* collection of essays which he edits (Žižek 1998a), with contributions from both Dolar and Zupančič, 'Lacanianism represents the common sense view of subjectivity . . . but with a twist'.

In his preface to *The Sublime Object of Ideology*, Laclau (1989) drew attention to the context-specific importance of the Ljubljana interpretation of Lacan, noting how interpretations of Lacanianism 'differed from country to country'. We have noted the warning which Dolar and Žižek give us in their introduction to their jointly authored book *Opera's Second Death* (Dolar and Žižek 2002), where they tell the astute philosophical reader to be wary of simply reducing philosophical approaches to their spatio-temporal coordinates or historical specifics. While there may be a certain truth in this, we should also be attuned to the more universalist dimension of the philosophy. As Žižek and Dolar note here, 'if we reduce a great work of art or science to its historical context, we miss its universal dimension; apropos of Freud, it is also easy to describe his roots in fin-de-siècle Vienna – much more difficult is demonstrating how this very specific situation enabled him to formulate universal theoretical insights' (Dolar and Žižek 2002: vii).

Nonetheless, in this chapter, we have stressed this universal conceptuality alongside the Slovenian particularity, this psychoanalytic (and philosophical) framework deriving from Freud originally and his 'invention' of psychoanalysis and developing through Lacan's 'return to Freud' especially. We have focused on the importance of Seminars VII (*The Ethics of Psychoanalysis*), XI (*The Four Fundamental Concepts of Psychoanalysis*) and XX (*On Feminine Sexuality. The Limits of Love and Knowledge*) for Žižek in their different ways, allowing the latter to foreground notions such as ethics, drive, the Real and finally, sexual difference and the notion of the 'Real of sexual difference'. But, to conclude this chapter, we would like to foreground a brief analysis of the more specific Ljubljana context, especially as it relates to the question of the alternative culture and the relation between the alternative culture and the younger intellectuals. We have looked at other aspects of this problematic in Chapters 1 and 2, especially in the context of Dolar and Žižek's work on punk and the NSK (Monroe 2005).

Žižek devotes several important essays to alternative culture movements in Slovenia (Žižek 2003b, 2003c, 2005, 2007c). The most important of these for our purposes is the 2005 essay, included as a preface to Alexei Monroe's seminal study of the NSK and Laibach, *Interrogation Machine* (Monroe 2005). This preface is entitled 'They Moved the Underground' (Žižek 2005), a reference to the Freudian concept of 'acheronta movebo', or precisely 'moving the underground', which Freud employs in the exergue to his text *The Interpretation of Dreams* (Žižek 2005: xiii). Žižek's question is simple: 'Why did the Slovene post-punk band Laibach have such a traumatic impact in Yugoslavia during the 1980s; the decaying years of really existing socialism?' (Žižek 2005: xii). As Žižek mentions in *Enjoy Your Symptom: Jacques Lacan in Hollywood and Out*, we can distinguish between ideology in Western Europe and Eastern Europe, for example, in one major inversion with regard to hegemonic behaviours and system beliefs. Whereas the citizens of the Western democracies pretend to be 'free' while secretly 'obeying', the citizens of the East under variants of state socialism pretend to 'obey' while secretly disobeying. Here, Žižek uses this insight to explicate Laibach and the wider NSK's strategy of highlighting this contradiction at the heart of the communist states, in the context of the former Yugoslavia. As Žižek notes, 'in really existing socialism, the explicit ideology for socialist democracy was sustained by a set of implicit (unspoken) obscene injunctions and prohibitions, teaching the subject not to take some explicit norms seriously, and how to implement a set of publicly unacknowledged prohibitions' (Žižek 2005: xii).

How can a critique of ideology work in such a context, if at all? How can we frame a dissident strategy in such a complex and self-contradictory political context? Here, Žižek credits Laibach and the NSK with a subtle but nonetheless explosive 'strategy of dissidence': 'one of the strategies of dissidence in the last years of socialism was to precisely to take the ruling ideology more seriously/literally than it took itself; by ignoring its virtual unwritten shadow, . . . [articulating] desperate hints of how this was not the way things functioned' (Žižek 2005: xii). Of course, we can see the strong connections here back to the *Punk Problemi* issues and the problematic of the symptom and accusations of fascism (Žižek 1981; Dolar 1982; Motoh 2012). As Dolar has noted, the NSK emerged as a development of the original punk logic. However, we can also see here how the critique of ideology has evolved from punk to the NSK, much as we have also seen Žižek's own 'strategy of dissidence' evolve from the early years through *The Sublime Object of Ideology* (Žižek 1989) to more recent texts.

This, then, shows how a critique of ideology can operate in such a context of complex ideological manipulation by the state, what Močnik referred to as the 'colonisation of the life world' and this is what 'moving the underground' as a practice of the critique of ideology means: 'not directly changing the explicit text of the law but rather intervening in its obscene virtual supplement' (Žižek 2005: xiii). It was this strategy, a very useful one for Žižek, which made Laibach so 'unbearable' through the 1980s. The crucial question then becomes one of whether such a strategy is possible today? 'the problem however is how to find a similar procedure today; is there, in our cynical "postmodern" ideological universe, still a place for a Laibach type intervention, or is such an intervention immediately co-opted and/or neutralised?' (Žižek 2005: xiii). Žižek is clear here that he still sees real possibilities in the Laibach and wider NSK strategy, in relation to an ongoing critique of ideology: 'And here it is that a Laibach style intervention is needed again, a direct staging of this obscene supplement, of the spectacle of barbarism that sustains our civilisation. Today, the lesson of Laibach is more pertinent than ever. Only such a direct confrontation with the obscene fantasmatic core can actually liberate us from its grip' (Žižek 2005: xv).

In this context, then, Žižek demonstrates the important allegiance between the NSK, Laibach and the Ljubljana School of Psychoanalysis. We can see Žižek's own work as a continuous effort to enact such a critique of ideology, while changing with the changing circumstances. As already noted, the Western and Eastern contexts were different in the 1980s. Post-communism, the situation for the newly independent states of the former Yugoslavia has changed significantly in terms of politics and ideology. In this chapter and through the interview, we have explored how Žižek's own work has developed in relation to the varied possibilities (and limits) of the contemporary critique of ideology. In his more recent work, for example *Less Than Nothing: Hegel and the Shadow of Dialectical Materialism,* Žižek has famously called time on a certain 'failure' of the late Lacan. There, he describes Lacan's Seminar XX, *On Feminine Sexuality. The Limits of Love and Knowledge* (Lacan 1998), as Lacan's 'ultimate achievement' but also as a work which seems to create an unsurpassable deadlock: 'in the years after he desperately concocted different ways out [the sinthome, knots etc] all of which failed; so where do we stand now?' (Žižek 2012a: 18). We await the next direction of the Ljubljana School of Psychoanalysis with great interest. In the next chapter, we will explore how Alenka Zupančič's work has brought a specific originality to bear on these problems, in a way which both continues and also transforms the intellectual trajectory (both psychoanalytic and philosophic) of Dolar and Žižek.

CHAPTER FIVE

'From Haso to Mujo': On Alenka Zupančič

Introduction

Zupančič's philosophical and psychoanalytical work inhabits a clearly different space to our other two main interlocutors. A student originally mentored by both Dolar and Žižek (Žižek et al. 2014), Zupančič arrives on the philosophical scene when Lacanianism properly understood is fully formed. She doesn't come through the period of interrogation of the wider French structuralism that we have seen as so important for both Dolar and Žižek (Dolar et al. 2014). Similarly, her relation to the various alternative cultures in Slovenia, from punk through to FV 112/15 and Neue Slowenische Kunst (NSK) (Motoh 2012) is not so pronounced. Again, this is perhaps a more chronological than ideological issue but it nonetheless leads to a rather different framework for her own philosophical analysis.

That said, Zupančič is also clear in her interview that she considers herself as part of the 'party troika' of the Ljubljana School of Psychoanalysis and while, as we shall see, her work introduces very distinct elements, there are also clear affinities. In the Introduction, we introduced Zupančič through one of her jokes from *The Odd One In: On Comedy* (Zupančič 2008a). Her employment of jokes (and indeed the thematic of comedy itself) is itself part of the troika affinities, deriving from the Freudian emphasis on humour as a key to the unconscious. The narrative about the man who thinks he is a seed (Zupančič 2008a), who is cured by the psychoanalyst but who still wonders if the chickens in the outside world have the same understanding, foregrounds the strong political emphasis in Zupančič's work. 'Dear fellow', says the doctor, 'you know very well that you are not a grain of seed but a man'. 'Of course I know that', replies the patient, 'but does the chicken?' (Zupančič 2008a: 15).

Much has been made, rightly, of Zupančič's emphasis on the ethics of psychoanalysis, her so-called 'ethics of the Real'. Her first monograph in English, *Ethics of the Real: Kant, Lacan* (Zupančič 2000) is a very significant and original contribution to the work of the Ljubljana School of Psychoanalysis, to which Dolar and Žižek often refer. For example, the chapter on the 'ethics of the voice' in Dolar's *A Voice and Nothing More* (Dolar 2006) depends crucially on Zupančič's earlier analysis, which Dolar readily acknowledges. We will discuss the intricate analysis of ethics in the sections that follow, but we should not lose sight of the strong connections between ethics and political critique in Zupančič. As she states, 'what is at stake in psychoanalysis is not simply becoming conscious of the unconscious, and all that often painfully determines [our] actions and experiences. . . . This is insufficient: the main problem is how to shift and change the very symbolic and imaginary structures in which this unconscious is embodied outside [ourselves]' (Zupančič 2008a: 16). From the perspective of Lacan's philosophy, one can link this emphasis on the 'outside' to his critique of idealism in Seminar XI on *The Four Fundamental Concepts of Psychoanalysis* (Lacan 1994) and his understanding (here strongly affirmed by Zupančič) of psychoanalysis as contributing to an 'encounter with the Real' (Lacan 1994).

We have discussed, in previous chapters, the important phases of Lacan's work (as indeed of Freud's). There are earlier and later perspectives in the case of both thinkers and much depends on which texts or concepts one chooses to emphasize. For example, in the case of Freud, it is clearly the case that whereas the earlier texts seem more affirmative and focused on the life-enhancing aspects of Eros, the later texts seem to become more inclined towards an emphasis on Thanatos, with all the necessary qualifications. Similarly, in the case of Lacan, there are significant changes across the texts, for example, in relation to an earlier emphasis on desire and ethics (Seminar VII) to a later emphasis on 'drive' and the 'Real' (e.g., Seminar XI).

However, it is a serious mistake of interpretation to view these conceptual and textual changes on some kind of progressive model of hermeneutics, where the earlier approaches would be completely superseded by the later ones.

Zupančič's work is a singular testimony to the wrongheadedness of this approach as her work is a constant dialogue across the different phases and concepts of Lacanianism. Her work also calls into question the very distinction between life and death drives, or Eros and Thanatos, seeing these different dimensions of drive as inextricably connected. For example, she describes in this context Lacan's debt to Heraclitus (in Seminar XI) when he seeks to introduce the conception of the 'death drive' but what is clear in relation to this Heracliteanism is the interconnectedness of death and life. As she notes, 'Lacan chose to introduce the notion of death drive with reference to Heraclitus' fragment; "to the bow is given the name of life and its work is death". The drive is not being towards death, it is indifferent to death and does not fail to be; it is what animates life, the death which drives life' (Zupančič 2000: 250). We might also note in passing the surrealist connotations of the drive as it is introduced by Lacan in this seminar, which we described in the last chapter (Bataille 2001).

With regard to the meta-level problem of Lacanianism, Dolar's discussion of Lacan's theoretical development in his 'Cogito and the Unconscious' (Dolar 1998) essay is exemplary, a very nuanced interpretation of Lacan which can serve as a key to Zupančič's successive works, developing through her earlier work on ethics (Zupančič 2000) through to her work on Nietzsche (Zupančič 2003) and finally to her two crucial monographs from 2008, *Why Psychoanalysis? Three Interventions* (Zupančič 2008b) and *The Odd One In: On Comedy* (Zupančič 2008a). As Dolar notes, 'The problem with understanding Lacan stems among other things from the fact that one has to follow the logic of the development of his theory and not to take any of the stages for granted as some definitive shape of truth' (Dolar 1998: 38).

The ethics of the real

We can get a hold on Zupančič's methodology here (following Dolar's explication) by foregrounding the title of her first book, *Ethics of the Real* (Zupančič 2000). The title juxtaposes concepts from alternate phases of Lacan's conceptual development. The notion of a Lacanian ethics stems from Seminar VII, *The Ethics of Psychoanalysis* (Lacan 1992), where Lacan breaks with the Aristotelian heritage of being and the notion of virtue (or what Lacan disparagingly refers to as 'the Good'). In his introduction to the seminar, Lacan acknowledges the difficulty some readers may have in understanding what Lacan might mean by 'ethics', if he is breaking with the latter's traditional understanding in a radical way: 'I announced the title of my seminar this year was the "Ethics of Psychoanalysis". I do not think that this is a subject whose choice is in any way surprising, although it does leave open for some of you the question of what I might have in mind' (Lacan 1992: 1). For example, Lacan here makes a clear division between the notions of 'ethics' and of 'morality' (Lacan 1992: 3) and this is also clear in Zupančič's work, for example, in the book on comedy which critiques strongly what she there terms eudaimonistic 'bio-morality' (Zupančič 2008a). Again, the target philosophically is Aristotelianism (although many of the contemporary examples she uses are more populist versions than the latter).

But the second concept in Zupančič's ethics, the notion of the 'Real', is a conception which Lacan introduces more fully in his later work, initially in Seminar XI, *The Four Fundamental Concepts of Psychoanalysis* (Lacan 1994). Moreover, post-Seminar VII, Lacan never returns explicitly to the problematic of the ethics of psychoanalysis he outlines there. This is referred to, for example, by Dolar and Žižek, as the Lacanian move 'from desire to drive' (e.g., in Žižek 2001a). Indeed, Dolar's analysis of the 'ethics of the voice' in *A Voice and Nothing More* (Dolar 2006) also speaks of this ethics in relation to the concept of 'drive' rather than 'desire', and justifies this in relation to what Dolar calls the 'demotion of desire' in Lacan's later work (Dolar 2006).

Thus, there is a certain paradoxical quality to Zupančič's methodology in this context, apparently mixing or fusing Lacanian 'desire' and 'drive'. As we have mentioned, this fusion of early and later Lacanian concepts is justifiable on a meta-level, in terms, for example, of Dolar's argument regarding a more concentric system in Lacan or a 'not taking any particular stage as definitive' (Dolar 1998: 38). We might also helpfully think of this issue in a Freudian rather than Lacanian key. On a surface level, it seems that Freud's oeuvre also can be demarcated into either 'early' or 'later' Freudian phases and texts, but, on closer inspection, matters become more ambiguous. Some commentators (Bersani 2002) point to the later texts such as *Civilisation and Its Discontents* (Freud 2002a) as operating in complete opposition to the earlier phases, and posit this opposition as one of Eros versus Thanatos, or even desire versus drive. While this latter Freudian text does indeed assert drive (and more specifically, 'death drive') more than the earlier work, this remains a qualified emphasis. To return to the famous ending of that text, 'And now it is to be expected that the other of the two "heavenly powers", immortal Eros, will try to assert himself in the struggle with his equally immortal adversary. And who can forsee the outcome?' (Freud 2002a: 81).

Freud inherits this problematic (as he acknowledges explicitly here) from Plato and particularly the Platonic dialogue, *The Symposium* (also an important dialogue for Lacan). Thus, it is not surprising to see Plato and the detail of *The Symposium* (Plato 1961) play an increasingly important role in Zupančič's work. Here, we can focus on the Appendix of her book *The Odd One In: On Comedy* (Zupančič 2008a), which seems to draw the early and later Lacanian emphases into dialogue with one another. We will see Zupančič refer to this as an important moment for her thinking in the interview below. For her, in realizing that the Aristotle book of the *Poetics* on comedy is missing, we can nonetheless cite a Platonic text as the very text we are looking for here: 'There is a fundamental text which deals with comedy. It is Plato's *Symposium*' (Zupančič 2008a: 187).

Sexuality from Plato to psychoanalysis

As Zupančič's analysis shows quite brilliantly, we have a matrix of concepts represented here in *The Symposium* (Plato 1961), that is, comedy, love, sexuality and also (with a twenty-first-century hindsight) the topic of psychoanalysis as it relates to philosophy. Here, we can bring Zupančič's two later texts into dialogue with one another in a way which helps us foreground this problematic of the relation between psychoanalysis and philosophy, a key thematic for the Ljubljana School of Psychoanalysis since its inception. Already in 1984, Žižek had edited an important collection (in Slovenian) entitled *Filozofija skozi psihoanalizo* or *Philosophy through Psychoanalysis* (Žižek et al. 1984). We have discussed in previous chapters the key transition made in the late 1970s between the wider remit of French structuralism (Dolar et al. 2014) and the more singular emergence of 'orthodox' Lacanianism and psychoanalysis in Ljubljana. Zupančič didn't go through this transition but rather, as we have suggested, adopted Lacanianism as a fully formed philosophical 'position' (formulated by her teachers Dolar and Žižek). Nonetheless, Zupančič is clear in the interview on two related points. First, that the conception of a positioning in philosophy is as important to her as it is to Dolar or Žižek, and here the philosophical influence is especially Marxist and the 'Theses on Feuerbach' (Marx 1992a) as we have discussed. Moreover, this orthodoxy, far from being sterile or closed, is, for Zupančič, the condition of philosophical movement or pluralism. Here, we might remember something Derrida says about Lacan's version of psychoanalysis: 'to say that psychoanalysis does not have the concept of what it is in its auto-identification . . . is certainly not to describe a paralysis of psychoanalysis, at least not a banal and negative paralysis. It gives movement, it gives one to think and to move' (quoted Hurst 2008: 182). Second, if anything, her work is even stronger on the intricate relation between psychoanalysis and philosophy than either of the other two members of the troika. Her second text from 2008, *Why Psychoanalysis?: Three Interventions* (Zupančič 2008b), is primarily concerned with the ways in which Freud and Lacan, respectively, negotiate the relation between philosophy and psychoanalysis. Despite significant disavowals of philosophy by both thinkers, Zupančič makes a strong argument for understanding psychoanalysis as exactly a form of radical philosophy. Here, and this links very much with *The Odd One In: On Comedy* (Zupančič 2008a), the debate hinges on the respective psychoanalytical and philosophical interpretations of the Freudian/Lacanian conceptions of 'sexuality'.

It is helpful then to think about the understanding of sexuality, from Plato to psychoanalysis, from philosophy to psychoanalysis. Here, *The Symposium* (Plato 1961) is key for Zupančič. As De Kesel notes in his book on *Eros And Ethics: Reading Jacques Lacan's Seminar VII* (De Kesel 2009), 'ethical self-understanding must not be thought through the paradigm of Christian "agape" but through ancient "eros". The latter does not stem from an all-powerful heavenly love that makes everything turn out all right, but from a frivolous playful "eros" that throws everything incessantly into confusion' (De Kesel 2009: 299). Here, the speech from Aristophanes on the subject of sex in *The Symposium* (Plato 1961) is crucial although, for Zupančič, often misunderstood. Commentators focus on the first part the story of a punished humanity, split in half, and these humans end up dying in each other's arms, yearning to be reunited. We might see this as some kind of (comic) Platonic critique of de-eroticized love (agape) and death (Zupančič 2008a). In contrast, the second part of the myth focuses on the gods intervening to 'move the sex organs to the front', to allow these humans to at least have some satisfaction alongside the drive to reproduction. Whereas the original notion of the split self was based on a lack, a yearning for unity, the second intervention favours more what Zupančič calls a 'surplus excess', sexual enjoyment or *jouissance*.

Lacan also sees this as a crucial reading by Plato of 'eros' or 'love' where the sublimation, which the latter involves, still involves an irreducible sexual element. As Lacan forcefully observes: 'this is unique and stunning in Plato's writing; the possibility of love appeasement is handed over to something that has an indisputable relationship, to say the least, with an operation performed on the subject of the genitals' (quoted Zupančič 2008a: 190). For Zupančič, then, crucially, 'eros' or 'love' itself emerges from inside this specific erotic and relational incongruity and this is precisely what the 'fantasists' of 'humanist-romanticism' seek to deny (Zupančič 2008a: 190).

If the first kind of love is, in psychoanalytical terms, 'desire' as based on a 'constitutive lack', the second concept is more of a 'love' as emergent from the complexity of what Lacan calls the 'impossibility of the sexual relationship' (Lacan 1998). This is a relation that can never give us complete union or satisfaction but instead the sexual encounter is, by definition, a temporary union, which also however crucially (with regard to the Aristophanes myth) interrupts the obsessive yearning of the original lovers. It is thus for Zupančič a perfect example of what Lacan calls 'plus de jouir', which can be translated as either 'more enjoyment' or 'no more enjoyment' (Zupančič 2008a). She describes the situation of the lovers as follows: 'we could also say that the fixing of the genitals is not only that which enables some kind of relationship between the two but also at the same time that which "comes between" the two and the logic of which is – most literally – at odds with the logic of fusions and unification' (Zupančič 2008a: 190).

This second 'eros' is a much more appropriate description for what Lacan calls the 'drive', which is intimately connected to Lacan's conception of the 'Real' (Lacan 1994). So, we see for Zupančič a connection between *The Symposium* and the later Lacan seminars, XI and XX (Lacan 1994, 1998). But in line with Dolar's meta-level interpretation (Dolar 1998), we don't have to subscribe to an 'either/or' logic here. This 'drive' as connected to 'love' is a long way from the kind of pure 'death drive' interpretation that we have seen in some readings of the later Freud and the later Lacan (Bersani 2002). Indeed, in her interview, Zupančič suggests that, at times, the Ljubljana School of Psychoanalysis have flirted with this more apocalyptic or fatalist interpretation. However, her own most recent work especially points in a different direction. Through a more complicating and 'doubling' methodology, as we saw above in her reading of *The Symposium* (Zupančič 2008a), Zupančič manages to relink desire and drive, Eros and Thanatos, not in a synthesis but more through the image that Lacan uses in Seminar XI, and that Zupančič reintroduces, of a Heraclitean bow in tension, between life and death, as the original image of the drive. In the interview which follows, Zupančič draws out her own individual genealogy in terms of the Ljubljana School of Psychoanalysis and explores some of the key issues in relation to early and later Lacan, and the ethics and erotics of psychoanalysis, that we have just described.

'Encountering Lacan in the Next Generation' – Interview with Alenka Zupančič

Helena Motoh and Jones Irwin: As a Slovenian thinker from the next generation to Dolar and Žižek, so to speak, can you pinpoint what were the key moments in your own formation in philosophy and Lacanian psychoanalysis and also from a Slovenian cultural and political perspective?

Alenka Zupančič: I started in high school in Ljubljana in 1981, and started my university studies in 1985; this period of 1981–89 was an amazing time. By the autumn 1980, the punk movement had become a very significant social phenomenon. Laibach were also around with the wider NSK in the early 1980s. The intellectual presence of the 'School for Theoretical Psychoanalysis' was growing in strength and influence. Lectures were organized on different subjects, interacting with other social movements, and these lectures were serious public events, by no means restricted only to a philosophical audience. So, already in high school, I attended some of these lectures. And although I was of course a complete novice then in terms of philosophical background, the conceptual energy, passion and wit involved in these events was arguably the best initiation to philosophy that one could ever get. Also, philosophy very much appeared back then as something that was actively 'changing the world', being involved in its transformation – not by doing something else than interpreting it, but precisely by interpreting it in a new and incredibly powerful manner. This was a time when interpretation actually had the power to move and change things. And this was related, of course, to the fact that the very practice of interpretation was being revolutionized, no longer conceived in terms of a hermeneutics of meaning, but in very different terms. This was perhaps one of the key and most productive influences of the Lacanian orientation in Slovenia. It did not turn people away from philosophical thinking, but rather changed some crucial parameters of philosophical thinking, and made it incredibly attractive. Which is why I already knew very early what I wanted to study: philosophy, of course.

Žižek's book *History and Unconsciousness* from 1982 was a significant work for those of my generation. Already, I can say that 'we knew something was going on'. There was a clear perception that something significant was taking place here, philosophically, culturally and politically. Lacan's *The Four Fundamental Concepts of Psychoanalysis* was an early translation into Slovenian and this was also a noteworthy event, as were many other books published by that circle then (many of them also on art, cinema and so on). With regard to the NSK, I was especially interested (at this initial stage) in their theatre work.

So I was led to study philosophy at the university in Ljubljana. In all his career, Žižek only taught there for one single semester, and I was lucky to study at precisely that moment. But he was a very powerful presence outside academia as well. Mladen Dolar was the key figure of this new orientation in the philosophy department. Although his official courses were one on Marxism and the other on Hegel, he introduced in them more and more of Lacan and French structuralism, as he noticed a vivid interest in this among the students.

Helena Motoh and Jones Irwin: Obviously, the situation you encountered in philosophy was quite different from both Žižek and Dolar. In their case, the Lacanian tendency developed initially from a wider structuralist emphasis which became more singular. With your generation, the Lacanian emphasis in Dolar and Žižek was already there, 'fully formed' (although there were significant other influences in the air, as you have noted). Can you say something about this 'conviction' from a philosophical perspective? Is there not a danger of reductionism or dogmatism in such a context?

Alenka Zupančič: Paradoxically, it was rather the contrary: the singularity of the Lacanian perspective opened up a vast number of different veins along which one could pursue philosophy. They were very unorthodox, from a traditional perspective. For me 'Lacanian dogmatism' was above all a way of thinking, asking questions, a way of not falling into the traps of institutional academia. Lacanian dogmatism is more a question of 'method' in doing theory, then simply about sticking dogmatically to certain notions and their definitions. Lacanian concepts themselves are the subject of intense investigation, we are not applying them to philosophy, but are also using philosophy to develop them and to be able to say, for example, 'this is what the Lacanian notion of the drive is all about'. I would perhaps say that there are two kinds of dogmatisms. One is a way of protecting, shielding a supposedly sacred ground, keeping away all possible foreign elements. This is a reductionist approach, and it often goes hand in hand with insecurity, and with not really believing in, having faith in the thing one protects, in its own convincing capacities. But when you are really convinced, the movement is quite different – it is that of expansion, of trying to convince other people as well, trying to relate what you find convincing to many different topics. Not locking yourself inside a supposed dogma, but affirming it by constantly reviving its effective powers in different contexts.

At stake here was also an understanding of what it means to be a philosopher – how does one become a philosopher? It was this understanding, this meta-level, which attracted me to this philosophical (and psychoanalytical) orientation. Indeed, this latter question of the relation between philosophy and psychoanalysis has been a central theme of my work to which we can return.

From the Lacanian perspective, what we have developed is a very rigorous and close elaboration of the conceptual basis of texts from the tradition. There is also a strong emphasis on the question of the critique of ideology and this has both general (Lacanian and Marxist) features but also some specifics which derive from the particular genealogy of the Ljubljana context, especially for Mladen and Slavoj, as I was their student. They came through a lot of ideological struggles in the 1970s and 1980s with state socialism in the former Yugoslavia (which I encountered later) and then of course there was the whole evolution of the critique of ideology as it led to so-called 'democracy' and independence in Slovenia and the break-up of the former Yugoslavia.

Alongside this dimension of our work (and these references to the political situation are more common in Slavoj's work throughout), there is the aspect of using Lacanianism as a 'privileged instrument' to reread the history of philosophy and psychoanalysis, to 'short circuit' the traditional readings. The emphases of our group, as a troika of thinkers, differ in some cases and are common in others. For example, my work on ethics (*The Ethics of the Real: Kant, Sade* [Zupančič 2000]) relates to the others but is also specific in its close elaboration of Kant. Similarly, my interest in, and work on Nietzsche is quite singular (Zupančič 2003). But there is an affinity in the fundamental principles of thinking, as well as on many chosen topics. We also have had collaborations on different anthologies, for example, on the 'Cogito' (Žižek 1998a; Dolar 1998; Zupančič 1998) or the Hitchcock/Lacan (Žižek 1992b; Dolar 1992a; Zupančič 1992). Therefore, in terms of the 'so-called' Ljubljana School of Psychoanalysis, our themes mostly converge, but with particular diversifications.

Helena Motoh and Jones Irwin: How did your own work develop from this initial point, after your undergraduate study in Ljubljana?

Alenka Zupančič: In a way which mirrors both Dolar and Žižek, the dual influences of Ljubljana and Paris were present in my studies. From 1991 onwards, I continued to work in both cities, doing a PhD with Žižek in Ljubljana and with Badiou in Paris. Badiou was then teaching at the university Paris VIII (St Denis), as well as lecturing at the *Collège International de Philosophie*. What struck me most about this situation was that although for us, as students, Badiou was already a worldwide name, in France he remained a somewhat marginal figure (this has changed a lot in more recent years). This wasn't just the case for Badiou but was the case with many internationally well-known

French thinkers (who were well known and influential outside France, whether we are speaking of Deleuze, Lyotard, Derrida, Rancière etc.), but whose – at least institutional – recognition or position in France have been quite marginal for a long time.

In Ljubljana, I was very lucky as I received very early a research post at the Institute of Philosophy (led by Rado Riha), which – among other things – also provided me with solid material conditions and made it possible for me to study abroad as well. In my first years at the Institute, I was thus able to focus entirely on my masters and PhD studies, with Žižek as supervisor in Ljubljana (he no longer taught at that time, but it was possible to have him as supervisor).

As a student, it was also a wonderful as well as a crucial experience to work with Badiou. Here it was again: a contagious, expanding kind of conviction (he is well known for his 'militant' stances) combined with utmost generosity and respect for the work of others. Badiou's seminars were very powerful experiences, both in terms of content and in terms of form – he is a most charismatic speaker, in the best sense of the term. To some extent I found in Badiou the same kind of winning combination of 'dogmatism' (conviction) and of ability to surprise and produce utterly unpredictable things and stances, that won me over in the Ljubljana context. And it is clear that, when later on, Badiou and Žižek have become friends, it is this feature that guaranteed their bond, beyond this or that particular stance in which they could sometimes very much diverge.

My PhD thesis with Badiou was the 'Ethics of the Real: Kant, Lacan', which was published in English in 2000.

Helena Motoh and Jones Irwin: This was a fascinating period of formation, both at undergraduate and postgraduate levels of the study of philosophy. When you understand the 'Lacan in Slovenia' paradigm, what sense does it have for you in terms of the overall relationship between philosophy and psychoanalysis? Are these two paradigms compatible and/or reconcilable? Are you, for example, more psychoanalyst than philosopher or vice versa?

Alenka Zupančič: The approach which the Slovenian or, more particularly the Ljubljana School of Psychoanalysis, takes is obviously quite specific in its understanding of this question. Lacanianism, we can say, is appropriated as a 'conceptual edifice'. This conceptual edifice is intrinsically related to philosophy, it is not something completely external or non-philosophical (as for example in Derrida's supposed 'nonphilosophical site from which to question philosophy'). Thus, Lacanian psychoanalysis has consequences, we might say, for philosophy, it is not something simply extrinsic to philosophy. To use an analogy, Galilean science had consequences for philosophy, philosophy could not simply continue as if nothing has happened here. Similarly with psychoanalysis, although the repercussions in this case are obviously quite different.

We might say that the importance of psychoanalysis for an understanding of the overall role of philosophy is quite revolutionary. But what is this revolution, what does it involve? I would say, in the first instance, that psychoanalysis is revolutionary because it introduces a genuinely new concept of the Real (at least in its Lacanian version). What this allows is an overcoming, or supersession, of the paralysis induced by the more traditional realism versus nominalism debate in philosophy. The Lacanian concept of the Real allows for a problematization of this opposition which had become paralysing and unproductive philosophically. We must of course be wary of the tendency to see in this Lacanian move a simple affirmation of a naive realism – the Real understood in this objectivist fashion. The 'Real' for Lacan is not reducible to the discursive but neither is it simply an advocation of an ontological realism, understood unproblematically. Especially since Lacan introduces a key difference between the notion of the Real and that of being. They are related via a 'third dimension', that of the 'signifier', but they do not coincide.

What Lacan wants to tell us is that the signifier has ontological significance, the signifier tells us about ontology in a way that the notion of the signified is unable to (this latter being the usual realist referent; the object as the signified). The signifier is interesting not because we could reduce everything to it and to different signifying operations (this reductionist question is completely false), but because there is something in the signifier and its operations that cannot be reduced back to the signifier and its operations. This is the crucial point, and not some mythical or original outside of the signifier, irreducible to it. This is also what the 'materialism of the signifier' amounts to. Not simply to the fact that the signifier can have material consequences, but rather that the materialist position needs to do more than to pronounce matter the original principle. It has to account for a split or contradiction that *is* the matter. It has to grasp the concept of the matter beyond that imaginary notion of 'something thick and hard'. I'm not saying: 'For Lacan, the signifier is the real matter', not at all. I'm saying that, for Lacan, the signifier is what enables us to perceive the non-coincidence between being and the Real, and that this is what eventually leads to a new kind of materialism. From this point of view, we can say that Lacan develops the modern moment in philosophy, but as Žižek says, 'he develops it with a twist'.

Then there is the new concept of the subject – another Lacanian 'revolution' in philosophy, retroactively relating the subject of the unconscious to the Cartesian cogito. This is often one of the great misunderstandings of Lacan (and psychoanalysis), that it jettisons the cogito, that it is anti-Cartesian pure and simple. This is a significant misunderstanding of the psychoanalytical concept of the 'subject' which was one of the main concepts for the delineation of a specific Lacanian orientation in the first place. This concept of 'subject' distinguished Lacan from the wider structuralist movement and their notion of a 'subjectless structure'. But somehow this conception of 'subject' is interpreted as anti-cogito, as the 'subject' is the unconscious subject. Therefore, it was important to clarify the connection between cogito and the unconscious and for example, there is an important anthology from the Ljubljana School of Psychoanalysis, where we explore this problematic in detail (*Cogito and the Unconscious* edited by Žižek [1998a] and including essays by all three thinkers as well as others in the Slovenian wider group of theorists). There is also the question of the radical break with premodern metaphysics involved in the Cartesian gesture, which Lacan judges crucial for the emergence of the subject of the unconscious.

This theme is crucial also for his understanding of ethics. In his important early seminar, Seminar VII, *The Ethics of Psychoanalysis* (Lacan 1992), he is discussing the history of ethical thought as it related for example to the metaphysical tradition. His specific example is Aristotle and there is obviously a debt here on one level to Aristotle's *Ethics* as a text and conceptual scheme. However, there is also a clear and radical parting of the ways.

In my own work on ethics, in *The Ethics of the Real: Kant, Lacan* (Zupančič 2000), I draw out some of these themes. For example, I put forward a critique of what I term 'bio-morality' and which, in its contemporary developments, represents an allegiance (albeit in rather reduced ways) to Aristotle's eudaimonistic ethics and metaphysics of being. This is not simply a criticism of Aristotle, but rather of what a revival of his conceptual paradigm today amounts to.

In relationship to the theme of ethics, I want to stress that what I develop out of Kant's ethics must not be opposed or seen as completely distinct from politics. As Žižek very rightly pointed out, the contemporary fashion of playing ('good') ethics against ('bad') politics is more often than not a direct pendant of the ideology of late capitalism and its conception of democracy. Any rigorous political thought is conceived as potentially dangerous and leading to a possible 'disaster' (that is to say to a more fundamental change in how the present order functions), whereas ethics seems to be much safer, and centred mostly on our individual responsibility, rather than any kind of collective engagement. My own work on Kant and ethics already went against this tendency, pointing both at an unsettling dimension of Kantian ethics, as well as at its emphasis on the universal, rather than simply individual.

It is similar with psychoanalysis which supposedly also focuses on individual destinies and problems. Here, am I allowed to tell my joke about the grain of seed, or the man who thinks he is one? He gets cured by the psychoanalysts and then he comes running back, crying that he has just been chased by a chicken. Don't you know you are a human being, they say? Yes, I am cured. I know that I am a human being, and not a grain of seed. But, please, does the chicken know this? This is the crux of the politics (which is also an ethics) in the Ljubljana School of Psychoanalysis. It is not enough simply to deal with the plight of the 'subject' and fantasy, through psychoanalysis. Rather, we must seek to transform the structures of the symbolic which sustain a given order, determine the Impossible-Real that they grapple with.

Helena Motoh and Jones Irwin: The notion of 'sexuality' is also important here in relation to psychoanalysis, a theme you have taken up for example in your recent text on *Why Psychoanalysis? Three Interventions* (Zupančič 2008b).

Alenka Zupančič: Yes, when we understand the question 'why Freud and Lacan?', or the question 'why psychoanalysis?', we come close to an understanding of the paradigmatic role which a revised notion of 'sexuality' must play in this discussion. Joan Copjec succinctly pointed out how, for example, in the term 'sexual difference' the term 'sex' has been replaced by the more neutered category of 'genre'. As Joan – an allied member of the 'Ljubljana School' – put it: Gender theory performed one major feat: it removed the sex from sex. For a while, gender theorists continued to speak of sexual *practices*, they ceased to question what sex or sexuality is; sex was no longer the subject of an ontological inquiry and reverted instead to being what it was in common parlance: some vague sort of distinction, but basically a secondary characteristic (when applied to the subject), a qualifier added to others, or (when applied to an act) something a bit naughty. This is very far from what both Freud (from his early, 1905 text *Three Essays on the Theory of Sexuality* [Freud 1977]) and Lacan have been saying. For Freud, the notion of the 'sexual' is significantly broader than contemporary notions of sex. It is not a substance to be properly described and understood (by psychoanalysis), but more like an impasse that generates and structures different discursive edifices trying to respond to it. It is linked to a notion of a fundamental ontological impasse; this impasse is irreducible for Freud. But we also see here all the accusations against psychoanalysis, that 'Freud reduces everything to sex'. In one sense, this accusation is true but what it misses is the complexification and radicalization of what we mean by 'sexuality'. Freud discovered human sexuality as a problem (in need of explanation), and not as something with which one could eventually explain every (other) problem. He 'discovered' sexuality as intrinsically meaningless, and not as the ultimate horizon of all humanly produced meaning. A clarification of this point is one of my 'interventions' in *Why Psychoanalysis? Three Interventions* (Zupančič 2008b). Lately, I dedicated a whole book to these questions – it came out in 2011 in Slovenia, but I'm still working on its English version.

Helena Motoh and Jones Irwin: How does this notion of sexuality as connected to the thematics of Freudian psychoanalysis and, as developed by Lacan, relate to the problematic of the body?

Alenka Zupančič: The notion of embodiment is central to psychoanalysis but not in any traditional sense and also not in the senses which supposedly radicalized the body in, for example, phenomenology. We could say, for example, that in psychoanalysis, the body is always more than the body or the organic body (there is a debt to Nietzsche's thematic in this context). Subjectivity or the 'subject' is the concept which comes to designate this something in, or of the body more than body; its non-coincidence with itself. What must be avoided here is the fetishization of the body, casting the latter as the authentic and ultimate Real. This last move has more to do with an 'imaginarisation' of the Real (say in the form of a palpitating flesh) than with understanding of the body in its paradoxical, 'partes extra partes' reality.

Related to the question of the body is also and often the question of materialism, as if the reference to the body as the ultimate reality would be enough to found and guarantee a materialist stance. The materialism of psychoanalysis is not simply materialism of the body; and Lacan has learnt the philosophical lesson that is essential in this respect: in order to be 'materialist' it is not enough to refer to the matter as the first principle from which everything develops. For, in this, we easily succumb to a rather idealistic notion of a somehow always-already spirited ('vibrant') matter. In recent debates, psychoanalysis – in the same package with all of the so-called post-structuralist thought – is often accused of relying on the formula 'always-already' as its magical formula. But this accusation misses the whole point: for psychoanalysis, 'always-already' is a retroactive effect of some radical contingency that changes given symbolic coordinates. What a materialism worthy of this name has to do today is to propose a conceptualization of contingency (a break that comes from nowhere, 'ex-nihilo' so to say) in its complex relation to the structuring of the world. Also, thinking is not simply opposed to things (and to matter), it is part of the thing it thinks, without being fully reducible to it. To advocate materialism and the 'Real' is not to advocate anti-thought. Quite the contrary, we might say – it calls for more and more thinking. And this is a problem that I sometimes detect in the recent flourishing of 'new materialisms' – a kind of abdication of thinking when it comes to more complex structures and arguments, as if common sense simplicities were inherently more 'materialist' than something which is more complex and perhaps paradox ridden.

Helena Motoh and Jones Irwin: You have mentioned Nietzsche as one of the key influences on your work, and this is especially evident in your text *The Shortest Shadow: Nietzsche's Philosophy of the Two* (Zupančič 2003). Can you develop your sense of Nietzsche's significance, for example in relation to the thematic of sexuality which you have cited in relation to Freud? Or what of Heidegger's critique of Nietzsche as a nihilist? How did this critique of Nietzsche operate in Slovenia?

Alenka Zupančič: A key part of the Nietzschean legacy is I think working against the 'moralisation' of the symbolic, which Nietzsche describes so well in *The Genealogy of Morals*, for example, and which for example is also a key theme in relation to the thematic of the 'moralisation of politics', which I mentioned earlier. Concerning nihilism and to quote Ray Brassier, from his text *Nihil Unbound*, there are things to be said for nihilism. It depends, of course, on what we mean by nihilism. If we mean by it a certain materialist position which recognizes contingency of, for example, our being in the world, and which points to a limit of 'making sense of (all) things', then we must say that to a great extent we cannot go beyond nihilism. Yet this does not imply for Nietzsche that we sink in the depressive feelings of 'worthlessness of all things'. On the contrary, it rather implies what he calls 'gay science'. But, we must simultaneously avoid what Nietzsche calls 'reactive nihilism' and this is, of course, bound up with his whole critique of *ressentiment* (or 'acting against', reactiveness). To say that there is no ultimate cause of things is not to say that nothing itself is the ultimate cause of things, which amounts to putting the Nothing in the office of the Absolute.

Describing the difference between active and passive nihilism, Nietzsche famously says that man would 'rather will nothingness than not will' (*On the Genealogy of Morals*). And we could say that what defines (contemporary) passive nihilism is precisely that man would rather not will than will anything too strongly (because the latter supposedly inevitably leads to some kind of 'nihilist' catastrophe). And this seems to become synonymous with what 'ethics' now is in contemporary culture and society and the wider 'moralisation of politics', 'biomorality' etc. (to which I strongly oppose an 'ethics of the Real'). There is a 'deactivation' of the will, which is also a deactivation of the 'political will', of the political as such as a paradigmatic space and temporality of antagonism, of the 'Real'.

In my view, the genuinely new Nietzschean notion of nothing or negativity is not simply that of 'active nihilism' as opposed to 'passive nihilism', but rather a transfiguration of nothing. Nothing/negativity is not a kind of ultimate absolute, but rather the smallest yet irreducible difference that is inscribed in being qua being. This is what I argue in my book. I use Nietzsche's own metaphor of 'the shortest shadow'. When speaking of going beyond the opposition real world/apparent world, Nietzsche describes this moment as 'Midday; moment of the shortest shadow' (*Twilight of Idols*). Midday is thus not for him the moment when the sun embraces everything, makes all shadows and all negativity disappear, and constitutes an undivided Unity of the world; it is the moment of the shortest shadow. And, what is the shortest shadow of a thing, if not this thing itself? Yet, for Nietzsche, this does not mean that the two becomes one, but, rather, that one becomes two. Why? The thing (as one) no longer throws its shadow upon another thing; instead, it throws its shadow upon itself, thus becoming, at the same time, the thing and its shadow, the real and its appearance. When the sun is at its zenith, things are not simply exposed ('naked', as it were); they are, so to speak, dressed in their own shadows. In other words: it is not simply that our representations do not coincide with things, it is rather that things do not simply coincide with themselves.

There is thus an imperative to 'think through' this negativity. We need to philosophize, as Žižek has said, *philosophy is now more important than ever*. It is not a game of textualism as some postmodernists would like to suggest perhaps.

Helena Motoh and Jones Irwin: You have spoken about 'the body more than body' as being the subject. This notion of the subject is key to Lacan's theory of psychoanalysis and it has been commented on, for example by Mladen Dolar, as key to the distinctiveness of Lacan's philosophy vis-à-vis the whole edifice of French structuralism. Can you develop your own understanding of the significance of the concept of the subject in psychoanalysis?

Alenka Zupančič: We can say that subject is 'the answer of the Real', as Lacan puts it somewhere, or that it is the effect of the rift/inconsistency of the structure. And we can indeed contrast this with the structuralist notion that there is a 'structure without a subject', a subjectless structure. But what is at stake is above all a profound reconfiguration of what both 'structure' and 'subject' mean, refer to. We can begin with the notion of the structure which differs in Lacan from the classical structuralist notion. Very simply put: for Lacan, structure is 'not-all' (or 'not whole'), which is what he articulates with the concept of the 'barred Other'. This implies a lack, a contradiction as – so to say – 'structuring principle of the structure'. Structure is always and at the same time more and less than structure. And this is where the new notion of the subject comes in. Subject is not the opposite of the structure, it is not some intentionality which uses structure to express itself, or which tries to get its more or less authentic voice heard through it. Subject is a singular torsion produced by the inconsistency of the structure. Take the simple example of the slips of the tongue: for Freud and Lacan, they do not bear witness to a hidden (unconscious) force repressed by the structure, which nevertheless betrays its presence by these slips. Rather, they are singular existences of structure's own inherent negativity.

This is also the argument that I want to make in the context of the contemporary debates concerning realism, which often disqualify thought or thinking as something merely subjective (facing external reality). Put in a couple of formulas: Instead of taking it as something situated vis-à-vis being, we should conceive of thought as an objectivized (and necessarily dislocated) instance of the non-relation (contradiction, inconsistency) and rift inherent in being (in 'objective reality'). Thinking is a necessarily displaced objectification ('objective existence') of this rift, that is, of the relation of being to its own 'non-', to its own negativity. Although being is indeed independent of thinking, the rift that structures it only objectively exists as thought, and this perspective opens a new way of conceiving realism and/or materialism. This is precisely how I would also read the Lacanian subject. And this is why if we remove subject from the structure, we do not get closer to objective reality, but rather further away from it.

We can also say that the subject for Lacan is 'objectively subjective', there is an asymmetry in the subject, something in the subject which is not just subjective but which is also inaccessible to the subject. We can see the connection back to Kant. The Kantian subject I would endorse is that 'pure something, X, which thinks', the transcendental unity of apperception. The point where subjectivity is not fully assumable and the point where the object is not reducible to or is 'not yet' objectivity (this is Lacan's notion of *objet petit a*). Here, we see also that the Lacanian subject radicalizes the traditional 'object'. The concept of the 'object a' is perhaps the most significant Lacanian conceptual invention.

Helena Motoh and Jones Irwin: In one of your major works, on *The Ethics of the Real: Kant, Lacan* (Zupančič 2000), you develop Lacan's claim in his *The Ethics of Psychoanalysis* (Lacan 1992) and elsewhere that there is a groundbreaking 'ethics' to be developed from the Lacanian approach to psychoanalysis. Can you develop your complex interpretation of the Kantian ethics as evidenced in this work and say something about how it influences your more recent work? Have we left behind the notions of good or evil completely, as Nietzsche would suggest?

Alenka Zupančič: No, the notions of good and evil are not simply irrelevant to ethics, I would say, although they are indiscernible in advance. The responsibility we have is to decide what is good. It is difficult to overstate Kant's significance in this respect. He did two things which may look incompatible: first, he founded ethics exclusively in human reason: no God or any other pre-established Good can serve as basis of morality. But instead of this leading to a kind of 'relativised', finitude-bound morality, it led to the birth of the modern thought of the absolute, the unconditional, and of the infinite as the possible, even imperative dimension of the finite. Whatever objections we may raise to the Kantian ethics – for example, and already, from Hegel's perspective – it was with Kant that the standing oppositions like absolute/contingent, lawful/unconditional, finite/infinite broke down, and the path was opened for a truly modern reconfiguration of these terms. In the twentieth century, Kantian ethics has been largely domesticated to serve as an important ideological foundation of the contemporary democratic liberalism and of the gradual replacement of an emancipatory politics with the discourse of human rights or simply ethics. I've always been astonished by the fact that a really radical, uncompromising and excess-ridden writing like Kant's could be referred to in order to pacify the excess (of the political or something else). When the Nazi criminal Eichmann infamously defended himself by saying that in his doing he has been simply following the Kantian categorical imperative, this was of course an obscene perversion of Kant's thought. As Žižek succinctly formulated: what follows from Kant is not that we can use moral law as an *excuse* for our actions ('oh, I wouldn't do it, but the moral law commanded so'), we are absolutely responsible for the very law we are 'executing'. But Eichmann's perverse defence did point at the unsettling core of ethics exposed by Kant: the unconditional law is one with (the excess of) freedom.

Lacan was probably the first to properly recognize this unsettling, excessive moment that Kant discovered at the very core of ethics. When he wrote his famous essay 'Kant with Sade' (Lacan 2002b), the point was not that Kant is in truth as excessive as Sade, but rather that Sade is already a 'taming', a pacification – in terms of perversion – of the impossible/real circumscribed by Kant. This is the thread I tried to follow in my book: Kant's discovery of this unsettling, excessive negativity at the very core of Reason. I was not interested so much in ethics as ethics, as in this thing that Kant has formulated through his considerations of ethics.

Helena Motoh and Jones Irwin: Does this mean that the 'ethics of psychoanalysis' simply pits the Real against the symbolic or is there something else going on here? Also, how does the concept of 'drive' and especially the concept of 'death drive', which Žižek emphasizes, relate to an ethical dimension? Finally, what does the Lacanian concept of 'desire' (as he describes it in *The Ethics of Psychoanalysis*) have to do with this? Is 'desire' simply jettisoned in the later work?

Alenka Zupančič: In respect to the relation between symbolic and the Real, there are certainly oscillations and shifts at work already in Lacan, as well as in the work of the three of us (together and separately). The idea that the Real is a kind of unbearable, repulsive thickness beyond the symbolic, left out of it and inaccessible to it, may have had some presence in our work at some point. But I think it is fair to say that for many years now we are all struggling precisely with the problem of a different way of relating them as absolutely crucial. There are some differences in the way we go about it, but the main and shared shift of perspective that orientates our work could be perhaps summed up as follows: the Real is not any kind of substance or being. It pertains to being (and to the symbolic) as its inherent contradiction/antagonism. I started working on this issue first by getting a bit more into Nietzsche (the first, Slovene version of the Nietzsche book was published in 2001). Borrowing from Badiou his notion of the 'minimal difference' and relating it to Nietzsche's notion of the 'shortest shadow', I tried to develop the notion of the Real as not that of some Thing, but of the fundamental non-coincidence of things with themselves. This non-coincidence is not caused by the symbolic; rather, the symbolic is already a response to it: it is discursivity as necessarily biased by the constraints of the contradiction in being. Parallel to this work on Nietzsche was also my working on the theme of love, and later on comedy as possible ways of articulating what is at stake in the relation between the symbolic and the real. Lately, and for some time now, I have been working on this through the question of the ontological implications of the psychoanalytic notion of the sexual. I could perhaps put it in one formula: *The real is part of being which is not being (or which is not qua being), but which as such dictates the (symbolic) logic of its appearance.*

Helena Motoh and Jones Irwin: Can you say a bit more about the two key Lacanian concepts (not without political ramifications of course) of 'desire' and 'drive'. You have already explicated these, to some extent, but can you develop some of the tensions between them? Also, how do these concepts develop in your work, as they seem to have a paradigmatic status while undergoing some transformation for example from the 'Ethics of the Real' book to the book on 'comedy'. Finally, are there philosophical tensions between your work and the other members of the troika on this fraught relationship between 'desire' and 'drive'?

Alenka Zupančič: Certainly, you are right to point to these concepts as paradigmatic, and they are also crucial when it comes to the articulation of the relationship of the symbolic, the imaginary and the Real. You are also correct that there are some differences here – one would expect nothing less in a philosophical movement worth its salt. In my own work, I take up the themes of desire and drive throughout. In *Ethics of the Real* I focused mostly, although not exclusively, on Lacan from *The Ethics of Psychoanalysis* and *The Transference* (Seminars VII and VIII). The concept of desire is in the foreground in both, but there is also a shift that starts taking place there, a conceptual move from *das Ding* as the impossible/Real as the focal point of desire, to the introduction of the object *a*. This shift then gets a further and very complex elaboration in Lacan's subsequent seminars. But to formulate what is at stake very briefly and simply, we could say that what is involved here is a move from the Real as the abyssal beyond of the symbolic, to a concept (of the object *a*) which undermines the very logic and nature of the difference on which the previous conception of the Real was based. Object *a* is neither symbolic nor Real (in the previous sense of the term). It refers to the very impossibility to sustain this kind of difference between the symbolic and the Real, and it is this impossibility that is now the Real. This also opens the door for a more systematic introduction of the concept of the drive. The notion of the object *a* is crucial both for desire and drive, they are different ways of relating this impossible non-ontological dimension (*a*) to what is, to being. In the Seminar X (*Anxiety*) Lacan provides a formula that I think is absolutely crucial and which I also took as the guiding line of my work after *Ethics*: he says that love is a sublimation, and then defines sublimation in a very surprising way, namely that sublimation is what makes it possible for *jouissance* to condescend to desire. If one remembers the famous definition of sublimation from Lacan's seminar on *The Ethics of Psychoanalysis* ('sublimation is what elevates an object to the dignity of the Thing') then the shift is indeed dramatic and surprising. This new notion of sublimation becomes directly associated with the question of the drive, for sublimation is also defined as a 'nonrepressive satisfaction of the drive'.

Now, in Lacan, as well as in our reading of him, there is indeed perceptible a turn from the logic of desire to that of the drive as somehow truer. But this is not simply a turn (of interest) from the symbolic to the Real, as it sometimes seems. What is at stake is rather the recognition of the fact that the status of the Real as the impossible Beyond of the symbolic is actually an effect of desire and its logic. Desire casts the internal contradiction that drives it in terms of the inaccessible Beyond to which it can only approach asymptomatically. With drive, the contradiction remains internal, and the impossible remains *accessible as the impossible*. This, I think, is absolutely crucial, and this is what I tried to formulate with the formula the 'Real happens': the point of Lacan's identification of the Real with the impossible is not simply that the Real is some Thing that is impossible to happen. On the contrary, and in this reading, the whole point of the Lacanian concept of the Real is that *the impossible happens*. This is what is so surprising, traumatic, disturbing, shattering – or *funny* – about the Real. The Real happens precisely as the impossible. It is not something that happens when we want it, or try to make it happen, or expect it, or are ready for it. It is always something that doesn't fit the (established or the anticipated) picture, or fits it all too well. The Real as impossible means that there is no 'right' time or place for it, and not that it is impossible for it to happen ('On love as comedy', Zupančič 2000).

So what is important to stress in this whole 'turn' to the logic of the drive is the following: this is not simply a turn to the drive on account of its supposedly being closer, truer to the Real (as established independently), but rather a turn toward a different conception of the Real as such. With drive, the Real is no longer a relational notion (sustaining questions like 'what is our attitude toward the Real?'). It rather suggests something like: our relation to the Real is already in the Real. This is why questions like 'How to get outside to the Real?' seem to be the wrong kind of questions.

This is because there is no outside of the Real from which one would approach the Real.

Helena Motoh and Jones Irwin: Is this why in your more recent work, for example in the book on comedy, *The Odd One In: On Comedy* (Zupančič 2008a) and *Why Psychoanalysis?: Three Interventions* (Zupančič 2008b), you seem to move away from perhaps a more simplified notion of this conception of 'drive versus desire' which was still there in *The Ethics of the Real: Kant, Lacan* (Zupančič 2000). Later, with the notion of 'comedy', you seem to be arguing for a more contestable notion of drive, with desire and drive more co-mingled. We are thinking here for example of your discussion of Aristophanes in the Appendix to the book on comedy. Is this a return to the early Lacan? What are the implications of this reading for the possibility of, for example, 'love'? How would such a concept of love relate to Lacan's discussion in Seminar XX (Lacan 1998) of 'sexual difference'?

Alenka Zupančič: The question of love – as related to sublimation and drive – was the pivotal point already in what you describe in the first part of your question. The first version of my paper 'On Love as Comedy' was published in 2002, and I see this paper (which has also been published as an appendix to the English version of my book on Nietzsche) as establishing the basic outlines for the configuration within which I have been moving, conceptually, ever since. The Impossible-Real as something that happens; as the internal contradiction/non-coincidence of the same; as not referring to any substance; as implying accessibility at the point of the impossible. . . . And you are right in pointing out that also the relationship between desire and drive becomes more complex in this shift: it becomes less that of an opposition and more that of a different topological configuration, desire *and* drive both being crucial in this context.

And I don't think one should read Lacan simply in terms of a progression from 'desire to drive' from the earlier 'ethical' Lacan, for example of Seminar VII, and the moving away to a notion of 'drive' in Seminar XI and later. Instead of this 'progressive' reading of Lacan, I think with Mladen and Slavoj we all three opt for a reading where the various 'phases' and the various concepts of Lacanianism are constantly in dialogue or confrontation with one another. One of the errors of the chronological interpretation of

Lacan is that it all too easily passes over the most interesting, even if complicating factors in each and every of Lacan's 'positions'.

As Monty Python knew very well, one should be wary of the logic: 'And now for something completely different!' This is important to stress because my interest in comedy after the book on *Ethics*, which was very much focused on tragedy, is sometimes understood in this way. That is as something that can be described as shifting of my interest from tragedy to comedy, or even from 'negative' to 'positive' feelings. I would say that, on the contrary, my interest has never shifted but has remained pretty much the same all along. It is not that I became interested in comedy, rather, I started suspecting that a serious consideration of comedy can bring me further along the lines of articulating what I have always been interested in. And this is: elaborating a concept of the Real that neither opposes nor fuses 'objective' and 'subjective' reality.

You mentioned the Appendix to my book on comedy (the Appendix in *The Odd One In: On Comedy* [Zupančič 2008a]), where I discuss, among other things, the famous Aristophanes' speech from Plato's *The Symposium* (Plato 1961), which is often presented as transmitting Plato's view on love as longing for our lost other half. But what is actually said there (through the mouth of the famous comedy writer), is something much more interesting and funny, and belying the very notion of satisfaction as a kind of rounded fullness based on complementarity.

Aristophanes' speech actually consists of two narratives. The first narrative tells the story of the rounded hubristic humans who were punished for their hubris by the gods, by having themselves split in half. Thus, love becomes a yearning by each half for the reconciliation of the original unified self and Aristophanes (in great drama) describes these lovers as dying in each other's arms, as they cannot bear to be separated or to live as independent entities. This is then love as desexualized, and as premised on the impossible complementariness of relationship, as such.

But there is a second moment to this story. The gods then decide to intervene for a second time to resolve this romanticized carnage. Here, the gods 'move the sexual organs around to the front', thus instigating the possibility of sexual intercourse and pleasure between lovers and bodies. What can we say of this second divine intervention? We can say that the fixing of the genitals is not only that which enables some kind of relationship between the two but also at the same time that which 'comes between' the two and the logic of which is – most literally – at odds with the logic of fusion and unification. This second 'split' introduced by Plato is much more akin to the Lacanian 'split' or 'gap'. It is the split between 'myself' and my jouissance. This split – implying the objective or object-like status of my own enjoyment – is at the same time the very embodiment of non-relation, and that which eventually makes any relation possible.

This is crucial in the understanding of the late Lacan and his adagio 'there is no sexual relation', which is often understood as a kind of almost cynical wisdom about how love never really works. Lacan's claim is understood as implying that non-relation is the *cause* of oddities and difficulties of the concrete relationships. The ontologically stated non-relationship is seen in this perspective as the obstacle to the formation of any 'successful' concrete, empirical relationship. Lacan's point, however, is paradoxically almost the opposite: it is the inexistence of the relation that *only opens up the space for relations* and ties as we know them.

This is also why love is only thinkable outside of parameters of complementariness and of 'filling up' what is missing (in us). If love carries a real, it is because of the element of surprise that inaugurates and sustains it. Love does not come from complementarity, the loved one is not an answer to our (pre-existing) demand, rather it comes as an unexpected surplus that only inaugurates the demand to which it answers. Love can be inaugurated in a fantasy scenario, where the other comes to occupy a certain pre-established place, but then – if we are lucky – it imposes its own dialectic which is independent of and different from that of the logic of fantasy. In short, love is only possible against the background of 'there is no sexual relation'. It is the non-relation that opens up the possible space of love, because it allows for that contingency which, in love, becomes the absolute.

Helena Motoh and Jones Irwin: What can we say might be the future of philosophy from the point of view of the Ljubljana School of Psychoanalysis? Where do you see the future direction of the work going?

Alenka Zupančič: What started to take shape in the 1980s was this practical and theoretical friendship between us and this very much remains the motor behind my work, a 'party' which meets, a Ljubljana troika. It is a real exchange of philosophical ideas, frank and honest, a sound friendship which is sustained. The future direction of our thinking is too big a question for a short answer in conclusion, but let me just point to two strands of it in brief.

First, the political context, not only in Slovenia, but broader. Second, the context of the changing framework of philosophical interpretation and/or intervention. The two are not unrelated. There seems to be a – however vague – connection between the growing political demand addressed to philosophy to do more than just *think* in 'abstract' terms, and the equally growing demand for it to conceptually connect with the world in a way that would amount to some sort of (new) realism. In both these demands, there is a certain danger of casting thought and thinking on the side of subjectivism and idealism. Contrary to this, I think we all want to resist the temptation that often arises in times of crises, which is to stop thinking (and 'kidding') and to embrace some kind of more direct, urgent challenge. 'This is not time to philosophise' – or so we are told from left and right. It is absolutely crucial not to give in to this temptation. Slavoj already started saying this some time ago: if ever there was the time for philosophy, it is now. This does not mean that we should just forget about the reality and go about our highly speculative work. It rather means that sometimes it takes a lot of thinking so as not to forget about the reality, and to be able to see its key antagonisms, instead of being swallowed by its dense complexity. Philosophical analysis is needed more than ever. Both in terms of the 'critique of ideology' and in terms of ontological investigation, including its most 'wild' or speculative level. In this sense, the 'future of philosophy' *is* – philosophy. [Interview ends]

Conclusion – 'From Haso to Mujo'

At the end of her book on comedy, *The Odd One In: On Comedy* (Zupančič 2008a), Zupančič appropriately enough tells a joke. This joke, she claims, in line with the original Freudian claim that jokes link us to the unconscious, points towards the 'logic of the Real of human desire . . . [and] the illogic of comedy' (Zupančič 2008a: 190). This illogic is at the heart of the psychoanalytic enterprise. The story is an old Yugoslav Bosnian joke about two characters, Mujo and Haso. Mujo is describing to Haso his adventures in the Sahara. He tells Haso that 'I'm walking through the desert. Nothing but sand around, not a living soul, absolutely nothing, . . . the sun bright in the sky and my throat burning with thirst. Suddenly a lion appears on front of me. What to do? Where to hide? I climb a tree' (Zupančič 2008a: 190). But Haso is not convinced: 'Wait a minute, Mujo, you've just told me that there was nothing around but sand, so where did the tree come from? My dear Haso; you don't ask such questions when a lion appears. You run away and climb the first tree' (Zupančič 2008a: 190). For Zupančič, we are once again back in this context not with some esotericism but rather precisely with what Lacan has referred to as the 'encounter with the Real' (Lacan 1994). As she notes: 'At stake here is by no means a disavowal of human reality and its limitations but rather a full recognition of the real of human desire' (Zupančič 2008a: 190). We have seen in the interview how important it is for Zupančič to bring the early and later Lacan into dialogue and especially his concepts of desire and drive, with some kind of interlocution being provided by the related concepts of 'love' and 'sexuality'. In her second text from 2008, *Why Psychoanalysis? Three Interventions* (Zupančič 2008b), Zupančič foregrounds precisely these issues again, but especially as they concern the relationship between philosophy and psychoanalysis. Here, in conclusion to this chapter, we will explore some of these issues from Zupančič's perspective. We will also see this issue return in the Epilogue, in relation to the Žižek–Malabou encounter. That encounter is crucially important for the Ljubljana School of Psychoanalysis as it foregrounds some of the most contested concepts in the psychoanalytical register. Malabou (while broadly sympathetic to psychoanalysis) nonetheless sees the conceptuality of 'Freudian–Lacanianism' as ultimately inadequate to deal with some of the contemporary developments in neuroscience. Malabou has articulated these dilemmas in her seminal *The New Wounded* (Malabou 2012). Žižek responds in his text, *Living in the End Times* (in the important Afterword of that book) (Žižek 2010), arguing that while he respects many of the criticisms Malabou makes of psychoanalysis that nonetheless, on Žižek's terms, 'Freudian–Lacanianism' remains a defensible approach.

Let us return here to the approach which Zupančič argues for, in her own right, on precisely this problematic of the relation between psychoanalysis and philosophy. Her early work situates the radical critique of traditional philosophical notions undertaken by psychoanalysis. Reading Zupančič, one is reminded of Badiou's phrase in his obituary of Lacan, 'Lacan from the very beginning was on the warpath' (Badiou 2009). Oftentimes, this Lacanian 'warpath' is not recognized, its power of subversion lost. But in Zupančič's work, once again we experience the crisis-inducing import of psychoanalysis, the 'plague' that Freud described his work as, 'bringing the plague to America' (Bowie 1991). This is particularly the case with her first monograph where the world of traditional philosophical ethics is turned upside down and made to see its affinities with, of all people, Sade's discourse (Zupančič 2000), precisely following Lacan's 'Kant with Sade' (Lacan 2002b). As Zupančič notes here, 'the concept of ethics, as it is developed throughout the history of philosophy, suffers a double "blow of disillusionment" at the hands of psychoanalysis' (Zupančič 2000). How so? Zupančič goes on: 'the Freudian blow to philosophical ethics can be summarised as follows: what philosophy calls the moral law – and more precisely what Kant calls the "categorical imperative" – is in fact nothing other than the superego' (Zupančič 2000: 1). The second blow follows from Lacan's extension of the Freudian moment to make Kant complicit with Sade: 'the thesis of "Kant with Sade" is not simply that Kantian ethics has a merely "perverse" value. It is also the claim that Sade's discourse has an ethical value; that it can be properly understood only as an ethical project' (Zupančič 2000: 2). Sade as an ethicist – this was certainly Lacan 'on the warpath' against conventional morality, society and the repressive psychic register. This is a very complex issue in itself but, in our earlier analysis and in the interview with Zupančič, we have traced how, for Lacanianism, despite this radical critique, there remains a crucial part for ethics to play in existential life.

But what, in conclusion, on Zupančič's terms, does this imply for the relation between philosophy and psychoanalysis? Does Lacanian radicalism destroy this relation, as for example Badiou might suggest in referring to Lacan as an 'anti-philosopher'? (Badiou 2009). For Zupančič, quite the contrary. Despite all the problematic encounters with philosophy that Lacan undergoes, nonetheless his psychoanalysis, on her terms, remains philosophical through and through. Similarly, in terms of the self-identification of the Ljubljana School of Psychoanalysis, it is clear from the interviews that each of our troika, Dolar, Žižek and Zupančič, consider his and her work as philosophy. Zupančič, at the same time, is clear that for Lacan at least (perhaps more so than for the troika), there are tensions in this relation between philosophy and psychoanalysis (Freud's relation to philosophy was even more problematical [Lear 2005]). As Zupančič notes of Lacan, 'despite his persistent claim that "psychoanalysis is not philosophy", Lacan was constantly developing his theory through a dialogue with philosophy' (Zupančič 2008b: 9). This dialogical encounter also represents the framework of her own analysis of the relation between psychoanalysis and philosophy. Here, in *Why Psychoanalysis? Three Interventions* (Zupančič 2008b), Zupančič foregrounds the original psychoanalytical (Freudian) conceptions of 'sexuality' (connected to both Eros and Thanatos) and 'love', just as she emphasizes 'love' and 'sexuality' in her analysis of *The Symposium* in *The Odd One In: On Comedy* (Zupančič 2008a).

Why is this significant? In his recent text *Less Than Nothing: Hegel and the Shadow of Dialectical Materialism* (Žižek 2012a), Žižek emphasizes some of the difficulties associated with the later Lacan's thinking, precisely in relation to some of the later thematics on 'love' ('Eros'), sexuality and the 'death drive' in Seminar XX, *On Feminine Sexuality. The Limits of Love and Knowledge* (Lacan 1998). As Žižek notes there, 'Seminar XX [Encore] stands for his ultimate achievement and deadlock' (Žižek 2012a: 18). Žižek suggests that perhaps a new approach might need to be taken by the Ljubljana School of Psychoanalysis, going beyond the limitations of Hegel and Lacan, respectively. What is perhaps most striking about Zupančič's thought, in conclusion, is that she has always subverted such a linear approach to Lacan (early/late) in her works, bringing concepts such as 'desire' and 'drive', and 'ethics' and the 'Real', into challenging dialogue and encounter. In this way, Zupančič's work testifies to the ongoing ability of Lacanianism to make a theoretical (and political) intervention in this way, much as Močnik originally described it in terms of the movement of Slovenian Lacanianism as a whole (Močnik 1993): Lacanianism allows the breakthrough from the impasse. Even in relation to the highly problematic notion of death drive, for example, Zupančič points to the affirmative possibilities in this regard: 'contrary to Bergson, the psychoanalytical experience ultimately leads to the following point; by objectifying the dead letter itself, by producing it as an object (as comedy does), we do not mortify it even further or glorify this mortification. Instead, we get a chance to break out of the mortifying spell of the latter' (Zupančič 2008a: 126). In this sense, we can say that in terms of Zupančič's joke concerning Haso and Mujo, she is definitively on the side of Mujo: 'My dear Haso; you don't ask such questions when a lion appears. You run away and climb the first tree' (Zupančič 2008a: 190).

Epilogue – 'We Don't Know What Will Become of This Psychoanalysis'

We don't know what will become of this psychoanalysis

(LACAN 2008: 3)

Introduction

In this book, we have explored the complex dynamics of the Ljubljana School of Psychoanalysis, beginning with the narrative of Žižek and Dolar in the late 1960s as students of philosophy in Slovenia, experiencing the social and political tumult of those years. Through their 1970s encounter with French structuralism (often against the norms of the authorities in the former Yugoslavia), we began to see a specific Lacanianism emerge. Through the 1980s, this Lacanianism was put to the sociopolitical test in a number of relations with aspects of the alternative culture from punk through to FV 112/15 through to the Neue Slowenische Kunst (NSK) (Motoh 2012). Here, we see the truth of Močnik's thesis about the Slovenian figure of Lacan constituting a kind of breakthrough against the 'impasse' (Močnik 1993) – an impasse which can be understood philosophically in relation to the wider movement of French structuralism or, more politically, in terms of the system of the former Yugoslavia. In Chapter 1, we traced, in brief, some of the main contours of the political struggle which saw the breakup of the former Yugoslavia into its national constituent parts. However, this 'outcome' of an emergent nationalism should not be seen as some kind of teleology on behalf of the Lacanian school. Močnik, for example, was famously opposed to the dissolution of Yugoslavia. The Ljubljana School of Psychoanalysis, although critical of the state socialism in the way we have seen, have remained wary of some of the new political developments. In his essay 'Eastern European Liberalism and Its Discontents', for example, Žižek describes how the situation after independence is not just problematic because of supposed rogue nationalist elements but because of the tensions within the model of democracy itself: 'the only way to prevent the emergence of proto-Fascist nationalist hegemony is to call into question the very standard of "normality", the universal framework of liberal-democratic capitalism, as was done, for a brief moment, by the "vanishing mediators" in the passage from socialism into capitalism' (Žižek 2007b: 28).

There has been much dissatisfaction with this supposed 'democracy' in Eastern Europe, but this dissatisfaction is not unique to the former Soviet or ex-Yugoslav new nation states. As we write now, for example, the 2012–13 Slovenian protests are an ongoing series of protests against the Slovenian political class, including the mayor Franc Kangler and the leaders of government, some of whom have been officially accused of corruption. In his recent text *The Year of Dreaming Dangerously* (Žižek 2012b), Žižek explores these movements of protest on a more international level, focusing on the Arab Spring and the Occupy Movement. Again, for Žižek, what is at stake here is a 'critique of ideology', the notion of ideological mystification remaining as pertinent as ever. We have seen Žižek trace this important thematic through his work from the 1980s, with the critiques in *Problemi* and *The Sublime Object of Ideology* (Žižek 1989) and the respective versions, for example, of *Enjoy Your Symptom: Jacques Lacan in Hollywood and Out* (Žižek 1992a, 2002, 2008a). We have also discussed how important, for both Dolar and Žižek, the NSK and Laibach have been in developing a critique of ideology through music and art, which avoids overt critique of content and instead demonstrates how the frame of ideology constitutes itself. As Žižek puts it, in a Freudian phrase, 'they moved the underground'. We have seen Dolar's acute analysis of Lacanianism (and its complex 'theory of development' [Dolar 1998]), and similarly, his localization of the problematic simultaneously in the Slovenian context. Here, his essay for *Mladina*, 'The Unconscious is Structured as Yugoslavia' (Dolar 1989), as well as his connections between, for example, certain reifying uses of the 'voice' and the Milošević ascent to power (Dolar 2006), are significant examples. In the case of Zupančič, we have seen her significant stress on the strictures of the 'symbolic', the 'yes, but does the chicken know about my not being a seed any more?' predicament of her psychoanalytical joke (Zupančič 2008a). Zupančič, with all her emphasis on the subversive potential of 'comedy', also demonstrates the strong political commitment of the Ljubljana School of Psychoanalysis. From a Lacanian perspective, we see here the important reference to the notion of the 'Real', which Lacan foregrounds in his Seminar XI, *The Four Fundamental Concepts of Psychoanalysis* (Lacan 1994). Although often misunderstood by opponents of Lacan as precisely an example of esoteric idealism, this concept (understood as the trauma or the 'fissure' in the symbolic [Žižek and Daly 2003]) becomes the lever for philosophical and political intervention in the symbolic sphere.

Here, however, it is not just an inheritance of Lacan and Kant (Zupančič 2000) but also of Marx. Zupančič's most recent text *Why Psychoanalysis?: Three Interventions*, demonstrates this political commitment clearly, and of course, here we also see the dovetailing of psychoanalysis and philosophy, psychoanalysis as a kind of acutely engaged political thought and activism. But where to from here? How might we map out the future directions of the Ljubljana School of Psychoanalysis? In the next sections, I want to explore some of these possibilities, beginning with some suggestions from one of Žižek's most recent texts, *Less Than Nothing: Hegel and the Shadow of Dialectical Materialism* (Žižek 2012a).

Lacan 'On a Warpath from the Beginning'

In the aforementioned obituary of Lacan, Badiou delineates some of the most searching aspects of Lacan's philosophy which will come to have such an influence both on Badiou's own work and on the Ljubljana School of Psychoanalysis (Badiou 2009). The analysis here is helpful in contextualizing some of the most recent developments in the Lacanian analysis of Žižek, Dolar and Zupančič. Badiou starts by focusing on the full frontal assault of Lacan's thought, often missed by commentators: 'it is a fact that Lacan was on the warpath right from the start, denouncing the illusory consistency of the ego, rejecting the American psychoanalysis of the 1950s which proposed to "reinforce the ego" and thereby adapt people to the social consensus' (Badiou 2009: 1). Badiou captures here Lacan's own militancy and also the radicalizing sociopolitical import of his work 'right from the start'. This radicalism was to have its implications for Lacan, who Badiou describes as having been 'excommunicated' from the psychoanalytical establishment. Tellingly, the first chapter of Lacan's Seminar XI, on *The Four Fundamental Concepts of Psychoanalysis* (Lacan 1994), is entitled precisely 'Excommunication'. Alongside this militancy comes a certain 'bleakness' in the philosophical vision: 'desire has no substance and no nature; it has only a truth; his particularly bleak vision of psychoanalysis in which it is the truth and not happiness which is in play . . . the severe position he promoted to the end' (Badiou 2009: 2). But one of the great paradoxes of that 'particularly bleak vision' is that it has had such a powerful impact on militant (and progressive) politics in the last 40 years. We have seen in the analysis of the Slovenian context that it was specifically Lacan who came to exert the greatest influence as the 'lever' which could engender theoretical and political transformation under state socialism. Faced with what Močnik describes as this 'impasse' (Močnik 1993), the Lacanian perspective allowed for movement. In the case of Žižek, Dolar and Zupančič, this came through philosophical works of cultural and psychic critical analysis. In the case of the NSK, it came through music, theatre and art, but they too (in a Freudian–Lacanian mode) 'moved the underground'.

What Badiou highlights here as important in Lacan's later work also has resonance with the Ljubljana School of Psychoanalysis. He states that 'It has become good form to state that the ageing Lacan was no longer transmitting anything worthwhile from the 1970s onwards; in my view it is quite the opposite' (Badiou 2009: 2). This later Lacanianism, famously difficult and esoteric, is also as we have seen the major focal point of the work of Žižek, Dolar and Zupančič. Although we have seen Dolar's meta-level analysis to move away from simple chronological linearity (Dolar 1998), positing a movement to and fro between phases, nonetheless the key concepts of all three thinkers are rooted in Lacan's later more radical thinking and conceptuality. Certainly, this later thought can then be employed to reinterpret some of the earlier work in a more radical light. One example here is in terms of the supposed move from the earlier concept of desire to the later concept of drive (Žižek et al. 2014; Zupančič et al. 2014). While it is undoubtedly true that Lacan instigates what Dolar refers to as a 'demotion of desire' (Dolar 2006) in his later work, nonetheless the more radical invocation of 'drive' is not a simple advocation of 'death drive' as some commentators might suggest (Bersani 2002). Bersani's preface to Freud's *Civilisation and Its Discontents*, then, while we might say it is polemically effective in presenting Freudian–Lacanianism as a virulent nihilism, is nonetheless badly one-sided. The later emphasis on 'drive' also takes account of the enigmatic quality of drive (e.g., its 'partial' aspect) and its complicity with desire, the possibility of sublimation of drive, and so on. It seems no coincidence that when Lacan tries best to explicate the notion of 'drive' (for example in Seminar XI), that the two sources he refers to are Heraclitus and the surrealists (Lacan 1994: 168): '"la pulsion fait le tour"; the drive moves around the object . . . the drive tricks the object . . . the montage of the drive is a montage which first is presented as having neither head nor tail – in the sense in which one speaks of montage in a surrealist collage' (Lacan 1994: 168–9). Lacan struggles to develop an image worthy of this surrealism of the drive, and eventually seems to opt for an image developed from one of the darkest but also most comical surrealists, Lautréamont: 'I think that the resulting image would show the working of a dynamo connected up to a gas tap; a peacock's feather emerges and tickles the belly of a pretty woman who is just lying there, looking beautiful' (Lacan 1994: 169). This image of the drive seems a long way from Bersani's dominance of the primordial aggressive drives. Instead, it would seem (as Freud himself suggests in the last lines of *Civilisation and Its Discontents*) that Eros must also have its say.

In his final analysis of Lacan, Badiou profers a scathing critique of contemporary academic culture and academic philosophy, in its absolute failure to connect with political and cultural life. This seems difficult to refute. How many philosophers in philosophy departments, for example, produce work that is read by non-professional philosophers? Unfortunately, the answer is shockingly few and while there can be valid justifications for philosophical work done on its own terms, often the lack of any connectivity with anything outside the academic culture betokens a sterility and a complacency. Ironically, Lacan is often lambasted in philosophy departments for the supposed 'esotericism' of his approach to thinking. Badiou describes this academic or professional philosophical malaise as a 'trite situation... marked by the platitudes and relative self-abasement of our intellectuals' (Badiou 2009: 5). But he also marks the affirmative Lacanian alternative, with Lacan's work having a significant influence on 'Marxism in crisis' as well as developing a 'highly unusual ethics... the almost incalculable import of that ethics', to which we should, Badiou suggests, 'pay tribute' (Badiou 2009: 5).

Badiou's approach to Lacan has much in common with the approach of the Ljubljana School of Psychoanalysis. In his recent text, *Less Than Nothing: Hegel and the Shadow of Dialectical Materialism* (Žižek 2012a), Žižek takes up several of the issues foregrounded by Badiou and again, we can see how these thematics are significant for the troika as a whole. We can also relate them back to Dolar and Zupančič's most recent work.

The deadlocks of Lacanianism

The notion of an orthodox Lacanianism has been complexified, for example, through our interviews with the Ljubljana troika (Dolar et al. 2014), as less a sterile literalism and more of a transformative rereading. This is in keeping with the sense that Lacan's own philosophy is hardly a closed system in itself. In the significant debates between Derrida and Lacan, for example, Derrida foregrounds a certain pathos for truth in Lacan's work ('the truth of truth'). Nonetheless, Derrida also foregrounds the irreducibly enigmatic quality of Lacan's philosophy. Derrida observes that 'The general question of the text is at work unceasingly in his writings where the logic of the signifier disrupts naive semanticism and Lacan's style was constructed so as to check permanently any access to an isolatable content, to an unequivocal, determinable meaning beyond writing' (Derrida 1988: 176). Lacan had also spoken of this enigma in relation to his own reinterpretation of Freud. If Lacan was a Freudian, he was one who could see that the Freudian system was open-ended. As Hurst notes, comparing Derrida and Lacan's approaches here, 'Lacanian psychoanalysis is an inventive appropriation that in much the same spirit as Derrida's deconstructive reading, uncovers the auto-deconstructing tensions in Freud's text as a warrant for his radicalisations' (Hurst 2008: 207).

It is in this spirit of reinvention and radicalization that we can then best understand the approach of the Ljubljana School of Psychoanalysis. Močnik describes the 'breakthrough' which Lacanianism performed in Slovenia, but there remain significant 'deadlocks' also in the Lacanian approach. In *Less Than Nothing: Hegel and the Shadow of Dialectical Materialism* (Žižek 2012a), Žižek takes up some of these issues so as to point to a future direction for the work of the troika. 'Over the last decade, the theoretical work of the party troika to which I belong (along with Mladen Dolar and Alenka Zupančič) had the axis of Hegel–Lacan as its "undeconstructible" point of reference. Whatever we were doing, the underlying axiom was that reading Hegel through Lacan (and vice versa) was our unsurpassable horizon' (Žižek 2012a: 18). But now Žižek notes a change, a sense of limitation in the theoretical analyses and what they are capable of, first in relation to Hegel. 'Recently, however, limitations of this horizon have appeared. With Hegel, his ability to think pure repetition and to render thematic the singularity of what Lacan called the object a' (Žižek 2012a: 18). As we have seen, the reading of Hegel in the Ljubljana group already goes against a more dominant reading of Hegel as a thinker of 'synthesis', the thinker whom, for example, Bataille and Derrida castigate for his 'terror of nonmeaning' (Derrida 1972), his apparent inability to recognize the limits of epistemology. In contrast, the Ljubljana group read Hegel as a thinker (who perhaps more than any other) allows for the encounter with 'nonmeaning' or the extra-symbolic experience of what Lacan calls the 'Real' (Lacan 1994). But here, Žižek seems to be calling that Hegelian resource into question and precisely in terms of the latter's inability to 'render thematic the singularity of the object a', this 'object a' being another Lacanian term for the 'Real', the absence of an ontological closure (Zupančič 2008b).

Similarly, limitations are described by Žižek in terms of Lacan's own approach: 'With Lacan the fact that his work ended in an inconsistent opening. Seminar XX [Encore] stands for his ultimate achievement and deadlock ... in the years after, he desperately concocted different ways out (the sinthome; knots etc) all of which failed; so where do we stand now?' (Žižek 2012a: 18). The appearance of Kierkegaard, one of Hegel's most vehement critics, as a significant thinker in this new text by Žižek, points towards a different direction in terms of the thematics of the Ljubljana School of Psychoanalysis. Here, while there are internalist critiques going on, there is also the example of criticism from other aspects of philosophy towards Lacan and psychoanalysis. We will see this in detail below in terms of the philosophical approach of Catherine Malabou (2012) more influenced by Derrida, but also by revolutionary developments in the philosophy of mind and contemporary neuroscience. We will see how, for Malabou, such developments show clearly the limits of some of the Freudian–Lacanian approaches to the 'unconscious' and their relation to 'trauma'. At issue here, also, is the very epistemological status of psychoanalysis, that is, the relationship between psychoanalysis and philosophy as such. We have seen that this has also been a key issue for Dolar and Zupančič (Zupančič 2008b). At issue then in the Malabou–Žižek encounter is not simply the specific debate but also its implications for how we see the future work of the troika of thinkers more generally.

'The New Wounded' – Žižek for and against Malabou

In *Less Than Nothing: Hegel and the Shadow of Dialectical Materialism* (Žižek 2012a), Žižek takes up the challenge of psychoanalysis from within the ambit of the troika, the Ljubljana School of Psychoanalysis. As we have seen, he is keen there to point to new directions in the relation between Hegel and Lacan. However, the challenge to Lacanianism also comes from outside its parameters, from critiques which call into question its very terms of reference. One such recent encounter between the Ljubljana mode of psychoanalysis and an alternative approach (which still shows significant affinities on both sides) is the debate between Catherine Malabou and Žižek. Žižek foregrounds his debate with Catherine Malabou in relation to the distinction or the conflict between what he terms, following Malabou, the 'Freudian unconscious' and the 'cerebral unconscious' (Žižek 2010). But the specifics of this debate are significantly contextualized by several more meta-level problematics, whether these are, for example, the theoretical relations between

Lacan and Derrida, or more generally the affinities or otherwise of psychoanalysis and deconstruction. Indeed, one can go further and argue that at issue in the microcosmic critique of Malabou in *Living In The End Times* is the very definition or understanding of what constitutes philosophy itself, or to use a recent Žižekian phrase, what constitutes 'philosophy in the present' (Badiou and Žižek 2009). While there are significant tensions elaborated in the Žižekian reading of Malabou's text *The New Wounded* (Malabou 2012), what is perhaps more striking is the level of agreement between the two philosophers exemplified in the discussion. Again, we can say that this has implications significantly beyond the Žižek/Malabou debate itself, in relation to the future understanding of the boundaries between psychoanalysis and deconstruction, bringing into relief, for example, the underestimated affinities which exist in relation to the two latter disciplines, an argument which Andrea Hurst has recently defended strongly (Hurst 2008). The significant question for our purposes, then, is how this future relationship between psychoanalysis and deconstruction might have significance for the work of the Ljubljana School of Psychoanalysis as a whole.

In *Living in the End Times* (Žižek 2010), Žižek addresses the specifics of Malabou's reading of the brain and mind relation in *The New Wounded* (Malabou 2012), while also exploring some of the meta-issues at stake in the disagreements between deconstruction and psychoanalysis. Additionally at issue here, as Žižek makes clear, is the very status of philosophy as a discipline in its own right. This perennial question of philosophy, in effect, 'what is philosophy?' and its related question, 'what is psychoanalysis?' (or as Zupančič puts it 'why psychoanalysis?') has been a paradigmatic theme for the Ljubljana School of Psychoanalysis as a whole (Dolar 1998, 2006; Zupančič 2008b).

It draws on the very same epistemological issues which preoccupied Lacan and Derrida, in their original theoretical conflicts (Hurst 2008). Žižek thematizes Malabou's contribution to the discussion in terms of a conflict between 'the Freudian unconscious versus the cerebral unconscious' (Žižek 2010: 291). At issue is the complex question of 'abstract violence' and its effects on what Žižek refers to as 'the reality of human lives' (Žižek 2010: 291). This problematic for Žižek is at the heart of Malabou's concerns in *The New Wounded*, specifically as it relates to the 'psychological consequences of this rise in new forms of "abstract" violence"' (Žižek 2010: 292).

Central for Žižek, in this context, is nothing less than the question of the very priority or hierarchy of concepts in psychoanalysis, with regard to the valuation of the concept of the 'unconscious' vis-à-vis the concept of 'trauma'. Žižek elaborates the original Freudian priority as being given to the concept of the 'unconscious' which he explicates as an 'unknown known' on Freudian terms, or in the Lacanian phrase, 'there is a knowledge that is not known, knowledge that is based on the signifier as such' (Žižek 2010: 292). However, we must distinguish this from the lesser-valued notion of 'trauma' in Freud, which is designated as an 'unknown unknown'; 'the violent intrusion of something radically unexpected, something the subject was absolutely not ready for; and which it cannot integrate in any way' (Žižek 2010: 292). Not the least interesting question here is to what extent can the original Freudian priority given to the concept of the 'unconscious' over 'trauma' be seen as being faithfully maintained by Lacan, or indeed by Žižek?

But, at this juncture, this meta-level issue is not Žižek's primary concern. He is rather interested in the exact direction of Malabou's own critique of psychoanalysis, or what he refers to as her 'critical reformulation of psychoanalysis' (Žižek 2010: 292). Malabou's critique here has implications for Žižek, Dolar and Zupančič. The priority given to the concept of 'unconscious' in Freud, for Žižek, amounts to a valuation of the 'inner' over the 'outer' (or the 'internal' over the 'external'). This valuation and hierarchy is fundamental to the very epistemology which underlies psychoanalysis. Outer shocks or events with a traumatic impact on the self derive their meaning not in and from themselves, but from their relation to a prioritized inner psychic life. This, according to Žižek, is a priority which is shared by both Freud and Lacan: 'for Freud and Lacan, external shocks, unexpected brutal encounters or intrusions owe their properly traumatic impact to the way they touch on a pre-existing traumatic "psychic reality"' (Žižek 2010: 292).

On Malabou's terms, there has been an intensification of the outer shocks in our contemporary society, notwithstanding the fact that these latter traumas 'have of course been known for centuries' (Žižek 2010: 292). This intensification leads to a need for a deconstruction of psychoanalytical categories, especially in the context of an era which can be described as post-religious or 'disenchanted', with the attendant effects in terms of metaphysical frameworks of meaning: 'since we live in a disenchanted, post-religious era, they are much more likely to be directly experienced as meaningless intrusions of the real' (Žižek 2010: 292). This latter phrase is especially important in this context: 'meaningless intrusions of the real'. On Malabou's terms, at issue is a supposed misunderstanding of the latter emptiness of meaning, which Freud and psychoanalysis (including, it would seem, Lacan's evolution of the latter), on her terms, misdiagnose. These events are 'brutal but meaningless' and they 'destroy', on Malabou's interpretation, rather than simply reform the 'symbolic texture of the subject's identity' (Žižek 2010: 292). This represents the key node of disagreement between Malabou and Freudian–Lacanianism (assuming, as she does, the unity of the latter theoretical designation). That is, there is disagreement over the exact status of such external shocks to the psyche and the level of their destructiveness with regard to symbolic meaning and the status of the subject per se.

What focuses Žižek's attention, in the first instance, is how this description of meaningless events by Malabou constitutes a fundamental challenge to the very self-understanding of psychoanalysis. Žižek reads Malabou's work as calling for a complete 'critical reformulation' of the very premises of psychoanalysis as a science. This constitutes, on Žižek's terms, her 'basic reproach to Freud' (Žižek 2010: 293), and indeed, it would seem, an equally strong reproach to Lacanian psychoanalysis. Understood in this manner, this would also constitute a fundamental disagreement between Malabou and Žižek, which we might then broaden out to involve a whole disagreement between psychoanalysis and deconstruction as such. As Žižek notes, 'Malabou's basic reproach to Freud is that when confronted with such cases, he succumbs to the temptation to look for meaning. He is not ready to accept the direct destructive power of external shocks; they can destroy the psyche of the victim (or at least wound it in an irremediable way) without resonating with any inner traumatic truth' (Žižek 2010: 293). Žižek reinforces his point here with reference to the example of the 'muselmann', the supposedly resigned and defeated-in-advance concentration camp victim, simply waiting around to die with no fight left. If the 'muselmann' can be said to constitute some kind of human condition, shared by 'victims of multiple rape, torture and so on' (Žižek 2010: 293), this condition again can be said, on Malabou's terms, to transgress the epistemological boundaries of psychoanalytical thought. The 'muselmann' condition is misunderstood on the Freudian terms of the unconscious: '[the muselmann] is not devastated by unconscious anxieties, but by a "meaningless" external shock which can in no way be hermeneutically appropriated or integrated' (Žižek 2010: 293).

Žižek is alert to the ramifications of this Malabouian intervention for the very status of Freudian (and indeed Lacanian) psychoanalysis. Malabou reads her own work as pointing towards the possibility of a 'new self' as opposed to the old, psychoanalytical self: 'The brain in no way anticipates the possibility of its own damage. When this damage occurs, it is another self which is affected, a "new" self founded in misrecognition. What Freud cannot envisage is that the victim, as it were, survives its own death; . . . a new subject emerges which survives its own death, the death or erasure of its own symbolic identity' (quoted Žižek 2010: 293–4). It is clear, on these terms, that Malabou is offering a strong critique of Freudian–Lacanian psychoanalysis, or on Žižek's terms, 'a critical reformulation'. Žižek's own analysis follows that of Malabou quite carefully and, at times, he appears to be wholly in agreement with her analysis. For example, he describes the move from a 'Freudian twentieth century' to a 'twenty first century . . . of the post-traumatic disengaged subject' (Žižek 2010: 295) where 'today, the enemy is hermeneutics; all hermeneutics is impossible' (Žižek 2010: 295). Read in this way, Žižek would seem to be interpreting Malabou's critique of psychoanalysis as persuasive.

But, while admitting the persuasiveness of some aspects of Malabou's critique at a micro-level, crucially Žižek still seeks to defend the more meta-level Freudian–Lacanian framework, as a framework with some limitations but one still capable of addressing philosophically the plight of such a 'twenty first century . . . of the post-traumatic disengaged subject' (Žižek 2010: 295). The works of Zupančič and Dolar would also stand as crucial in this debate.

Conclusion – Enjoy your future!

In 1989, Laclau (in his preface to Žižek's *The Sublime Object of Ideology*) indicated the arrival of the Ljubljana School of Psychoanalysis as an entity in translation as a key moment, due to this being a group of theoreticians whose 'original features' were indispensable to a critique of ideology in the West, which had come up against something of an impasse (Laclau 1989). In this book, we have traced the extraordinary evolution of this group of thinkers since 1989, while also looking back to the complex (and often neglected) genealogy of the pre-1989 narrative which created the context for this group's existence and its very urgency. As we have seen, in *Living in the End Times* (Žižek 2010), we find Žižek (both for and against Malabou's subtle critique) continuing to defend the relevance of this group's Freudian–Lacanian analysis, more than 20 years after Laclau's preface (Laclau 1989). In the later text, as well as in his more recent (and monumental) *Less Than Nothing: Hegel and the Shadow of Dialectical Materialism* (Žižek 2012a), we have seen Žižek seek to resituate the work of the Ljubljana troika.

This resituation of concepts and themes is nothing new in the context of the Ljubljana School of Psychoanalysis. One of the advantages of the longer-term genealogical view of the group that we have taken is that it allows us to pinpoint key moments of transition or transformation. As Dolar noted in the interview, 'orthodoxy is transformation' (Dolar et al. 2014). We have thus witnessed significant shifts in emphasis across the development of the group. First, the space allowed for critique in former Yugoslavia was still subject to what Gantar referred to as the 'colonisation of the life world' (Gantar 1993). Thus, the emergence of a genuinely alternative (Slovene) culture in the shape successively of punk, FV and the NSK (Motoh 2012) allowed for new concepts and emphases to emerge, from the original symptom to the symptom as a critique of the state system itself. Here, we saw a growing sophistication in the critique of ideology, whether through the analysis of Lacan and Hegel in works such as *The Sublime Object of Ideology* (Žižek 1989) and *A Voice and Nothing More* (Dolar 2006) or in the complex works of the NSK, Laibach and IRWIN (Žižek 2007c). This also allowed us to see the specific contextual element at work here, what Dolar brilliantly referred to as 'Yugoslavia is structured as the Unconscious' (Dolar 1989). We have seen Žižek's view of the critique of ideology change significantly through the various texts we have explored, for example paradigmatically in the various editions of *Enjoy Your Symptom: Jacques Lacan in Hollywood and Out* (Žižek 1992a, 2001a, 2008b). Zupančič, as the former student of Dolar and Žižek, has also brought something powerfully original to bear on the recent problematics of the group. Her first monograph *Ethics of the Real: Kant, Lacan* (Zupančič 2000) foregrounded the crucial seminar of *The Ethics of Psychoanalysis* (Lacan 1992) while also demonstrating how the notion of 'ethics' remained a key feature of Lacan's later work, although undergoing transformation there, 'from desire to drive' (Zupančič 2000). Her later work has brilliantly sought a reconciliation between these two terms, desire and drive, with especial emphasis on the concepts of 'love' (reinvoking the connections between psychoanalysis and Plato) and 'comedy' (reintroducing the importance of Aristophanes, among others) (Zupančič 2008a). In all of this, it is also clear that the relation between psychoanalysis and philosophy is crucial. For the Ljubljana troika, psychoanalysis at its best is a form of philosophy, understood as an acute critique of the psyche and of politics.

In his recent texts, we have seen Žižek introduce the thematic of future directions, suggesting certain limitations in the philosophies of Lacan and Hegel. But (for and) against Malabou's powerful critique of the inadequacy of psychoanalysis to deal with contemporary 'nonmeaning', Žižek has argued eloquently that sensitivity to the limits of meaning and epistemological truth are precisely central to contemporary psychoanalysis, as it continues to reinvent Freud and Lacan for 'philosophy in the present', and philosophy in the future. Here, no radical rereading of the psychoanalytical tradition would be required but simply attention to the detail of Lacan's own texts on truth, where Lacan at his own most radical moment avers his very lineage with Freud: 'A hole in truth: it is the negative aspect that appears in anything to do with the sexual, namely its inability to aver. That is what a psychoanalysis is all about. We can feel that what Freud called "sexuality" takes on a new meaning from the very beginning' (Lacan 2008: 22). For Žižek, then, the very radicality and contemporaneity of Malabou's philosophical intervention in *The New Wounded* (Malabou 2012) would lead all the way back not simply to Lacan, but to Freud.[1] As Lacan notes, 'Freud's terms come back to life, take on a different import' (Lacan 2008: 23). And this rebirth of Freudianism and psychoanalysis would paradoxically, and somewhat against Malabou's active reading, be there 'from the very beginning' (Lacan 2008: 22).

NOTES

Introduction

1 While the 'popularity' of Žižek is seen by many professional philosophers as proof of the superficiality of his thought, it also can be seen more positively in the light of a politicized emphasis on 'popular consciousness'. The 'critique of ideology' in Žižek vehemently opposes any simple opposition between philosophical knowledge and (popular) 'false consciousness'. The connections between the Ljubljana School of Psychoanalysis and elements of so-called 'low culture,' such as punk, similarly practice a subversion of traditional, institutional and professional divisions. In leftist thinking, this brings Žižek, Dolar and Zupančič far closer to thinkers such as Gramsci and Freire (Freire 1972) and further away from thinkers such as Althusser and Marcuse (Althusser 1994). Lacan is also an interesting and somewhat paradoxical example in this case. While his work is supposedly extraordinarily 'difficult' (Derrida 1988), it also is famous for its slogans, jokes and popular examples (Lacan 2008). In the film Žižek! (Žižek 2007b), directed by Astra Taylor, Žižek is keen to stress the 'simple' and 'direct' message which lies behind his thinking, contrasting it for example with the endless qualifications of 'deconstructionism'. He gives the comical example of Judith Butler struggling to describe the phenomenon of love or even the existence of a bottle of iced tea (Žižek 2007b).

Chapter 1

1 Beforehand, a necessary disclaimer has to be made – in what is proverbially called a 'typical Slovenian way' – namely, by saying what this introduction is not, or rather, what it will not or cannot aspire to be. First, it will not be a *clavis* of any sort, a key to what Žižek is all about, it will not uncover the secrets of the recent Yugoslav history, it will not attempt to sort out and simplify the vivid

variety of what Slovenian or Yugoslav 'alternative culture' was in the 1960s, 1970s and 1980s, and it will certainly refrain from resorting to the level, as Mladen Dolar elegantly phrased it at our first meeting concerning this book, of 'who slept with whom'. Secondly, it will not jump on the contemporary bandwagon of classifying the people, groups and movements of the time into the 'left' and 'right', into the true 'independentists' and the 'yugophiles', the freedom fighters and the traitors, the discourse too frequently misused and abused by Slovenian politicians and intellectuals today. Finally, it will not provide either an inside view or an outside view, but will try to balance on the narrow edge between the two.

2 Namely, Slovenians, Croats, Serbs, Macedonians, Montenegrians and awkwardly named 'Muslims', that is, Bosniacs and two nationalities, Albanians in Kosovo and the Hungarians in Vojvodina. The criteria for distinguishing the two statuses was that the nationalities, unlike the nations, were those that belonged to a nation that had a nation state *outside* of Yugoslavia, in these two cases Albania and Hungary.

3 Before 1991, the parliament was still officially called the 'Sociopolitical assembly' and the government was the 'Executive Council', while the federal republic was presided over by a collective presidency of four members, led by a president of the presidency. Žižek, who is often mistakenly said to have been a presidential candidate, was actually running for one of these four seats in the collective presidency as a candidate of the ZSMS, but did not succeed.

4 The dates in brackets specify the time when each of these proclaimed independence. The degree to which each of this is internationally recognized, is a separate issue.

5 Žižek was supposed to have started teaching years before that, but was suspended from doing so after he refused to alter his master's thesis in order to better suit the official line (Dolar et al. 2014).

6 Institutions and organizations were establishing centres for the study of Marxism at different levels. Žižek, for example, worked for the Marxist Centre at the Central Committee of the League of Communists of Slovenia in the late 1970s.

7 The poem *Duma* (Word) by Tomaž Šalamun (an excerpt of which serves as the epigraph to the book), which is a parody of an older Oton Župančič poem with the same title that starts 'I walked our land and drank its beauty'. Šalamun rewrote it as: 'Fucked by the Absolute/ fed up with virgins and other dying sufferers/ I love you o neighbors, meek fantasies of God the Father/ I love you o integral characters of sweet gazing/ in my mind grace yielded/

o proud possessors of anxieties/ o trained intellectuals with sweaty little hands/ o logicians, vegetarians with the thickest glasses/ o muzzled rectors/ o ideologues with your whoring ideologies/ o doctors munching on punctuation marks and Skofja Loka pastries/ o mummified academicians patting passion and pain/ Pascal who tried and Bach who pulled it off/ o lusty inexpressible dried-up lyricist/ o horticulture, the enlightened and the happy swallows/ o socialism à la Louis XIV or how to shelter the poor little creatures/ o one hundred thirty-five constitutional bodies or how to keep/ a dead cat from stinking/ o the revolutionary zeal of the masses or/ where is the sanatorium to cure our impotence/ I walked our land and got an ulcer/ land of Cimpermans and pimply groupies/ land of serfs myths and pedagogy/ o flinty Slovenians, object of history crippled by a cold/' (translated by Tomaž Šalamun and Christopher Merrill, http://www.writinguniversity.org/index.php/main/author/tomaz_salamun1/).

8   Allegedly, the problem was that the staff of the printing shop fell mysteriously ill, machines were all suddenly broken and the mechanic was called overnight to join the army.

9   In the post-war period, Nietzsche was perhaps the most unwelcome of authors, being associated with the rise of fascism and national-socialism. In the mid 1950s, the first texts on his work were starting to be published again (cf. Vuko Pavićević's *Filozofija Fridriha Ničea*, Rad, Belgrade, 1955), staying true to the official line of criticizing his thought, but already introducing a differentiation between his ideas and those of his Nazi admirers.

10 A line from a Pankrti song, with a pun on the socialist custom that no one should be called 'gentleman' for this represented bourgeois upper class, but should instead be called 'comrade'.

Chapter 2

1   We might compare Klossowski's invocation of concepts such as 'evil' with a similar trajectory in Bataille. In his text *Literature and Evil*, for example, (a text written during this period and with which Lacan would have been familiar), Bataille also seeks to critique moralism through the notion of 'evil'. Significantly, in relation to the Lacanian project, Bataille also seeks to defend a notion of the ethical not unrelated to that of Lacan, although Bataille refers to it as 'hypermorality': 'I believe that the Evil – an acute form of Evil – which it [literature] expresses, has a sovereign value for us. But this

concept does not exclude morality: on the contrary, it demands a hypermorality [*mais cette conception ne commande pas l'absence de morale, elle exige une hypermorale*]' (Bataille 2001: 8).

2 This jettisoning of the notion of the 'ethical' is sometimes associated with Nietzsche's *On the Genealogy of Morals* (Nietzsche 1967). It is perhaps surprising that Nietzsche does not figure more significantly in the Lacanian analysis (it is known, for example, that Freud thought highly of Nietzsche's critique of morality and religion). While there are clear tensions between Nietzsche and Lacan, for example, in relation to concepts such as 'evil' (which Nietzsche reads as exclusively Christian), nonetheless there are also powerful affinities. Nietzsche's description of the 'anti-nihilist' in *On The Genealogy of Morals* is not far removed from Lacan's own perspective on a breakthrough of the current moralistic (and religious) impasse: 'This man of the future, who will redeem us not only from the hitherto reigning ideal but also from that which was bound to grow out of it, the great nausea, the will to nothingness, nihilism; this bell-stroke of noon and of the great decision that liberates the will again and restores its goal to the earth and his hope to man; this Antichrist and antinihilist; this victor over God and nothingness – *he must come one day*'. (Nietzsche 1967).

Chapter 3

1 Benjamin, in conclusion to this essay also says something significant concerning the relation between surrealism and materialism. We will see that Dolar stresses strongly the 'materialist' element of Lacan's work, very much in line with the discussion, for example, in Seminar XI from Lacan on the 'critique of idealism' (Lacan 1994). In the case of Benjamin, there is an emphasis on the gap between materialism and anthropology, again anticipating the significant critique of humanism in psychoanalysis. Kafka, and Dolar's employment of Kafka here (Dolar 2006), would also be a very effective *antihumanist* gesture. As Benjamin puts it: 'For it must in the end be admitted: metaphysical materialism, of the brand of Vogt and Bukharon, as is attested by the experience of the Surrealists, and earlier of Hebel, Georg Buchner, Nietzsche and Rimbaud, cannot lead without rupture to anthropological materialism. There is a residue' (Benjamin 1979: 239). One might see, for example, the Ljubljana School of Psychoanalysis as precisely taking up these two key thematics of 'rupture' and 'residue'. The lineage from surrealism back to Nietzsche and Rimbaud is striking here, but the lineage can also be seen as extending (in)directly to Lacan.

Epilogue

1. One can make an analogous argument that Derrida's work also anticipates very clearly this philosophical dimension. In *On Touching* (Derrida 2005), for example, Derrida reads the work of Nancy in terms of a problematic of 'plasticity and technicity' (*'en compte de la plasticité et de la technicité'*) (Derrida 2000: 249, 2005: 220). Derrida seems to be arguing against the notion that one can draw the boundaries of touch at the organic limits of bodies. Rather, we now have to consider a whole new dimension of 'touch' and 'sense', which has evolved from 'the intertwining of *techne* and the body [*verflectung*]' (Derrida 2005: 237). The affinities with the thematic of *The New Wounded* are clear. Derrida's work also owes a significant debt to Bataille in this regard, especially in the context of a technics or a 'writing' of embodiment (Irwin 2010, especially Chapter 2; Bataille 1988a), a debt Derrida readily acknowledges, for example, in his seminal essay, 'From Restricted to General Economy: A Hegelianism Without Reserve' (in Derrida 1972).

BIBLIOGRAPHY

Primary References

Dolar, M. (1978), 'O nekaterih vprašanjih in protislovjih v marksističnih analizah fašizma'. *Problemi, Razprave*, year 16, 177/180: 49–111.
—(1982), *Struktura fašističnega gospostva. Marksistične analize fašizma in problemi teorije ideologije*. Ljubljana: DDU Univerzum.
—(1989), 'The Unconscious is Structured as Yugoslavia', in *Mladina*, Ljubljana, pp. 15–30.
—(1992a), 'Hitchcock's Objects', in Žižek, S. (ed.), *Everything You Always Wanted to Know about Lacan but Were Afraid to Ask Hitchcock*. Verso: London.
—(1992b), 'A Father Who Is Not Quite Dead', in Žižek, S. (ed.), *Everything You Always Wanted to Know about Lacan but Were Afraid to Ask Hitchcock*. London: Verso.
—(1998), 'Cogito as the Subject of the Unconscious', in Žižek, S. (ed.), *Cogito and the Unconscious*. Durham and London: Duke University Press, pp. 11–40.
—(2003), 'The Punk Movement and the Rituals of Ideology', in IRWIN (ed.), *IRWIN Retro Princip. 1983–2003*. Berlin: Inke Anni, pp. 155–6.
—(2006), *A Voice and Nothing More*. Cambridge, MA: MIT Press.
Dolar, M. and Žižek, S. (2002), *Opera's Second Death*. New York: Routledge.
Dolar, M., Irwin, J. and Motoh, H. (2014), 'From Structuralism to Lacan – Interview with Mladen Dolar', in Irwin, J. and Motoh, H. (eds), *Žižek and His Contemporaries. The Emergence of the Slovenian Lacan*. London/New York: Bloomsbury.
Žižek, S. (1981), Editorial in: *Problemi*, year 19, no. 205/206, Ljubljana.
—(1989), *The Sublime Object of Ideology*. London: Verso.
—(1991a), *For They Know Not What They Do: Enjoyment as a Political Factor*. London: Verso.
—(1991b), *Looking Awry: An Introduction to Jacques Lacan Through Popular Culture*. Cambridge, MA: MIT Press.

—(1992a), *Enjoy Your Symptom: Jacques Lacan in Hollywood and Out*, First edition. London: Routledge.
—(ed.) (1992b), *Everything You Always Wanted to Know about Lacan but Were Afraid to Ask Hitchcock*. London: Verso.
—(ed.) (1994a), *Mapping Ideology*. London: Verso.
—(1994b), 'Introduction: The Spectre of Ideology', in Žižek, S. (ed.), *Mapping Ideology*. London: Verso, pp. 1–33.
—(1994c), *The Metastases of Enjoyment: On Women and Causality*. London: Verso.
—(1997), *The Plague of Fantasies*. London: Verso.
—(ed.) (1998a), *Cogito and the Unconscious*. Durham and London: Duke University Press.
—(1998b), 'Introduction: Cogito as a Shibboleth', in Žižek, S. (ed.), *Cogito and the Unconscious*. Durham and London: Duke University Press, pp. 1–10.
—(1998c), 'Four Discourses, Four Subjects', in Žižek, S. (ed.), *Cogito and the Unconscious*. Durham and London: Duke University Press, pp. 74–116.
—(1998d), 'The Cartesian Subject versus the Cartesian Theatre', in Žižek, S. (ed.), *Cogito and the Unconscious*. Durham and London: Duke University Press, pp. 247–74.
—(1999a), *The Ticklish Subject – The Absent Centre of Political Ontology*. London: Verso.
—(1999b), *The Žižek Reader*, edited by Elizabeth Wright and Edmond Wright. Oxford: Blackwell.
—(1999c), 'There is No Sexual Relationship', in Elizabeth Wright and Edmond Wright (eds), *The Žižek Reader*. Oxford: Blackwell, pp. 174–205.
—(1999d), 'Kant with (or against) Sade', in Elizabeth Wright and Edmond Wright (eds), *The Žižek Reader*. Oxford: Blackwell, pp. 283–301.
—(1999e), 'Burning the Bridges', in Elizabeth Wright and Edmond Wright (eds), *The Žižek Reader*. Oxford: Blackwell, pp. vii–x.
—(2000), *The Fragile Absolute – or, Why is the Christian Legacy Worth Fighting for?*. London: Verso.
—(2001a), *Enjoy Your Symptom: Jacques Lacan in Hollywood and Out*. London: Routledge. [Including new introduction and new chapter 6]
—(2001b), *The Fright of Real Tears: Krzysztof Kieślowski Between Theory and Post-Theory*. London: BFI.
—(2002), 'The Real of Sexual Difference', in Barnard, S. and Fink, B. (eds), *Reading Seminar XX. Lacan's Major Work on Love, Knowledge and Feminine Sexuality*. Albany: State University of New York Press, pp. 57–76.

—(2003a), *The Puppet and the Dwarf. The Perverse Core of Christianity*. Cambridge, MA: MIT Press.
—(2003b), 'The Enlightenment in Laibach', in IRWIN (ed.), *Irwin Retro Princip*. 1983–2003. Berlin: Inke Anni, pp. 42–8.
—(2003c), 'A Letter From Afar', in IRWIN (ed.), *Irwin Retro Princip*. 1983–2003. Berlin: Inke Anni, pp. 65–6.
—(2005), 'Foreword: They Moved The Underground', in Monroe, A. (ed.), *Interrogation Machine: Laibach and NSK*. Cambridge, MA: MIT Press, pp. xii–xv.
—(2006a), *Lacan*. London: Granta.
—(ed.) (2006b), *Lacan: The Silent Partners*. London: Verso.
—(2006c), *The Parallax View*. Cambridge, MA: MIT Press.
—(2006d), *The Universal Exception*. London: Continuum.
—(2007a), 'The big Other between Violence and civility'. Preface to Žižek, S., in Butler, R. and Stephens, S. (eds), *The Universal Exception*. London: Continuum (paperback), pp. vii–xxxii.
—(2007b), *Žižek!* (film). Directed by Astra Taylor. London: ICA Films.
—(2007c), 'Why Laibach and the Neue Slowenische Kunst Are Not Fascists', in Žižek, S. (ed.), *The Universal Exception*. London: Continuum.
—(2007d), 'Easter European Liberalism and its Discontents', in Žižek, S. (ed.), *The Universal Exception*. London: Continuum, pp. 13–32.
—(2008a), 'Enjoyment within the Limits of Reason Alone'. Foreword to the Second Edition of *For They Know Not What They Do: Enjoyment as a Political Factor*. London: Verso, pp. xi–cvii.
—(2008b), 'Preface: Enjoy your Symptom – or Your Fetish?', in Žižek, S. (ed.), *Enjoy Your Symptom: Jacques Lacan in Hollywood and Out*. London: Routledge. [Routledge Classics Edition], pp. ix–xvi.
—(2008c), *Violence*. London: Profile Books.
—(2009), *First as Tragedy, Then as Farce*. London: Verso.
—(2010), *Living in the End Times*. London: Verso.
—(2012a), *Less Than Nothing: Hegel and the Shadow of Dialectical Materialism*. London: Verso.
—(2012b), *The Year of Dreaming Dangerously*. London: Verso.
Žižek, S. and Badiou, A. (2009), *Philosophy in the Present*. Cambridge: Polity Press.
Žižek, S. and Daly, G. (2003), *Conversations with Žižek*. Cambridge: Polity Press.
Žižek, S. and Milbank, J. (2009), *The Monstrosity of Christ. Paradox or Dialectic*. Cambridge, MA: MIT Press.
Žižek, S. et al. (eds) (1984), *Filozofija skozi psihoanalizo*. Ljubljana: DDU Univerzum.
Žižek, S., Butler, J. and Laclau, E. (2000), *Contingency, Hegemony, Universality: Contemporary Dialogues on the Left*. London: Verso.

Žižek, S., Irwin, J. and Motoh, H. (2014), 'From Lacan to Hegel' – Interview with Slavoj Žižek', in Irwin, J. and Motoh, H. (eds), *Žižek and His Contemporaries. The Emergence of the Slovenian Lacan*. London/New York: Bloomsbury.

Zupančič, A. (1992), 'A Perfect Place to Die: Theatre in Hitchcock's Films', in Žižek, S. (ed.), *Everything You Always Wanted to Know about Lacan but Were Afraid to Ask Hitchcock*. London: Verso.

—(1998), 'The Subject of the Law', in Žižek, S. (ed.), *Cogito and the Unconscious*. Durham and London: Duke University Press, pp. 41–73.

—(2000), *Ethics of the Real: Kant, Lacan*. London: Verso.

—(2003), *The Shortest Shadow: Nietzsche's Philosophy of the Two*. Cambridge, MA: MIT Press.

—(2008a), *The Odd One In: On Comedy*. Cambridge, MA: MIT Press.

—(2008b), *Why Psychoanalysis?: Three Interventions*. Aarhus: Aarhus University Press.

Zupančič, A., Irwin, J. and Motoh, H. (2014), 'Encountering Lacan in the Next Generation – Interview with Alenka Zupančič', in Irwin, J. and Motoh, H. (eds), *Žižek and His Contemporaries. The Emergence of the Slovenian Lacan*. London/New York: Bloomsbury.

Secondary References

Ades, D. and Bradley, J. (2006), *Undercover Surrealism: Georges Bataille and Documents*. London: Hayward Gallery.

Althusser, L. (1994), 'Ideology and Ideological State Apparatuses (Notes Towards an Investigation)', in Žižek, S. (ed.), *Mapping Ideology*. London: Verso.

Aristotle (1976), *Ethics*, translated by J. A. K. London: Penguin; Thomson.

Arms, I. (ed.) (2006), *Irwin retroprincip*. Ljubljana: Mladinska knjiga.

Badiou, A. (2000), *Ethics*. London: Verso.

—(2006), 'Lacan and the Presocratics', in Žižek, S. (ed.), *Lacan: The Silent Partners*. London: Verso, pp. 1–15.

—(2009), *Pocket Pantheon; Figures of Postwar Philosophy*. London: Verso.

Badiou, A. and Žižek, S. (2009), *Philosophy in the Present*, edited by Peter Engelmann. Cambridge: Polity Press.

Balibar, E. (2007), *The Philosophy of Marx*. London: Verso.

Barnard, S. (2002), 'Introduction', in Barnard, S. and Fink, B. (eds), *Reading Seminar XX. Lacan's Major Work on Love, Knowledge and Feminine Sexuality*. Albany: State University of New York Press, pp. 1–20.

Barnard, S. and Fink, B. (2002), *Reading Seminar XX. Lacan's Major Work on Love, Knowledge and Feminine Sexuality*. Albany: State University of New York Press.
Barnes, J. (1990), *Early Greek Philosophy*. London: Penguin.
Bataille, G. (1988a), 'The Psychological Structure of Fascism', in Allan Stoekl (ed.), *Visions of Excess: Selected Writings 1927–1939*. Minneapolis: University of Minnesota Press.
—(1988b), *Visions of Excess: Selected Early Writings*, translated by Alan Stoekl. Minnesota: University of Minnesota Press.
—(2001), *Eroticism*. London: Penguin.
Baugh, B. (2005), *French Hegel: From Surrealism to Postmodernism*. London: Routledge.
Benjamin, W. (1979), 'Surrealism: The Last Snapshot of the European Intelligentsia', in Benjamin, W. (ed.), *One Way Street*. London: Verso, pp. 225–39.
Bersani, L. (2002), 'Introduction' to Freud, S. *Civilisation and Its Discontents*. London: Penguin, pp. vii–xxii.
Bookchin, M. (1974), 'Paris, 1968', in G. Woodcock (ed.), *The Anarchist Reader*. London: Fontana, pp. 25–47.
Bowie, M. (1991), *Lacan*. London: Fontana.
Bowman, P. and Stamp, R. (2007), *The Truth of Žižek*. London: Continuum.
Butler, J., Laclau, E. and Zizek, S. (2000), *Contingency, Hegemony and Universality: Contemporary Dialogues on the Left*. London: Verso.
Butler, R. (2005), *Slavoj Žižek: Live Theory*. London: Continuum.
Chiesa, L. (2007), *Subjectivity and Otherness: A Philosophical Reading of Lacan*. Cambridge, MA: MIT Press.
Daly, G. (2003), 'Introduction: Risking the Impossible', in Žižek, S. and Daly, G. (eds), *Conversations with Žižek*. Cambridge: Polity Press, pp. 1–22.
Debord, G. (2000), *Society of the Spectacle*. London: Rebel Press.
De Kesel, M. (2009), *Eros And Ethics: Reading Jacques Lacan's Seminar VII*. New York: State University of New York Press.
Deleuze, G. and Guattari, F. (2004), *Anti-Oedipus*. London: Continuum.
Derrida, J. (1972), *Writing and Difference*, translated by Alan Bass. Chicago: Chicago University Press.
—(1977), *Margins of Philosophy*, translated by Alan Bass. Chicago: Chicago University Press.
—(1978), 'From Restricted to General Economy: A Hegelianism without Reserve', in Bass, Alan (ed.), *Writing and Difference*. Chicago: University of Chicago Press, pp. 251–77.

—(1981a), 'Plato's Pharmacy', in *Dissemination*, translated with an introduction by Barbara Johnson. Chicago: University of Chicago Press, pp. 61–172.
—(1981b), 'The Double Session', in *Dissemination*, translated with an introduction by Barbara Johnson. Chicago: University of Chicago Press, pp. 173–286.
—(1982), 'The Ends of Man', in *Margins of Philosophy*, translated by Alan Bass. Chicago: University of Chicago Press, pp. 109–36.
—(1987), *The Postcard: From Socrates to Freud and Beyond*. Chicago: University of Chicago Press.
—(1988), 'The Purveyor of Truth', in John P. Muller and William J. Richardson (eds), *The Purloined Poe: Lacan, Derrida and Psychoanalytic Reading*. Baltimore: John Hopkins, pp. 173–212.
—(2000), *Le Toucher, Jean-Luc Nancy*. Paris: Éditions Galilée.
—(2005), *On Touching – Jean-Luc Nancy*. Stanford: Stanford University Press.
Drolet, M. (2004), *The Postmodernism Reader: Foundational Texts*. London: Routledge.
Dufresne, T. (1997), *Returns of the 'French Freud': Freud, Lacan and Beyond*. New York: Routledge.
Eagleton, T. (1994), 'Ideology and its Vicissitudes in Western Marxism', in Žižek, S. (ed.), *Mapping Ideology*. London: Verso, pp. 179–226.
—(2003), *Figures of Dissent*. London: Verso.
Fink, B. (2004), *Lacan to the Letter: Reading Écrits Closely*. Minneapolis: University of Minnesota Press.
Flahault, F. (2003), *Malice*. London: Verso.
Foster, H. (1996), *The Return of the Real*. Cambridge, MA: MIT Press.
Freire, P. (1972), *Pedagogy of the Oppressed*. London: Penguin.
Freud, S. (1977), *On Sexuality: Three Essays on the Theory of Sexuality and Other Works*. London: Penguin.
—(2002a), *Civilisation and Its Discontents*. London: Penguin.
—(2002b), *The Joke and Its Relation to the Unconscious*. London: Penguin.
—(2009), *The Interpretation of Dreams*. London: Sterling.
—(2010), *The Psychopathology of Everyday Life*. London: Penguin.
FV (2008), *Alternative Scene of the Eighties*. Ljubljana: Mednarodni Grafični Likovni Center.
Gantar, P. (1993), 'Discussions on Civil Society in Slovenia', in Graziano, G. and Bilic, A. (eds), *Civil Society, Political Society, Democracy*. Ljubljana: Slovenian Political Science Association, pp. 350–65.
Gramsci, A. (1988), *The Antonio Gramsci Reader: Selected Writings 1916–1935*, edited by D. Forgacs. London: Lawrence and Wishart.
Graziano, G. and Bilic, A. (1993), *Civil Society, Political Society, Democracy*. Ljubljana: Slovenian Political Science Association.

Hallward, P. (2000), 'Introduction', in Badiou, A. (ed.), *Ethics*. London: Verso.
—(2003), *Badiou. Subject to Truth*. London: Verso.
Hegel, G. W. F. (1979), *Phenomenology of Spirit*, translated by A. V. Miller. Oxford: Oxford University Press.
Homer, S. (2005), *Jacques Lacan*. Oxon: Routledge.
Hribar T., Lovšin, P., Vidmar, I. (eds) (2003), *Punk je bil prej: 25 let punka pod Slovenci*. Ljubljana: Cankarjeva založba, Ropot.
Hurst, A. (2008), *Derrida Vis-à-vis Lacan: Interweaving Deconstruction and Psychoanalysis*. New York: Fordham University Press.
IRWIN (1993), *Neue slowenische Kunst. Irwin*. Ljubljana: Moderna galerija.
—(2003a), *IRWIN Retro Princip*. 1983–2003. Berlin: Inke Anni.
—(2003b), 'WAS IST KUUNST?', in IRWIN (ed.), *IRWIN Retro Princip*. 1983–2003. Berlin: Inke Anni, pp. 147–8.
Irwin, J. (2010), *Derrida and the Writing of the Body*. Surrey: Ashgate.
—(2012), ' "We Don't Know What Will Become Of This Psychoanalysis" – On a Malabou/Žižek Encounter'. Issue on *The Unconscious*, Avello 1(2): 1–24.
Johnston, A. (2009), *Badiou, Žižek and Political Transformations: The Cadence of Change*. Illinois: Northwestern University Press.
Kalan, V. (2009a), 'Seznam predavanj v letih 1919–1969'. *Anthropos* 3–4 (215–16): 201–43.
—(2009b), 'Oddelek za Filozofijo', in *Zbornik Filozofske fakultete Univerze v Ljubljani, 1919–2009*. Ljubljana: Znanstvena založba Filozofske fakultete Univerze v Ljubljani, pp. 130–49.
Kay, S. (2003), *Žižek: A Critical Introduction*. Cambridge: Polity Press.
Khader, J. and Rothenberg, M. A. (2013), *Žižek Now: New Perspectives in Žižek Studies*. Cambridge: Polity Press.
Kierkegaard, S. (1992), *Either/Or: A Fragment of Life*, translated by Alastair Hannay. London: Penguin.
Klossowski, P. (1991), *Sade, My Neighbour*, translated by Alphonso Lingis. Illinois: Northwestern University Press.
Kotsko, A. (2008), *Žižek and Theology*. London: T&T Clark.
Kreft, L. (1998), *Zjeban od absolutnega: perspektivovci in perspektivaši: portret skupine*. Ljubljana: Znanstveno publicistično središče.
Krnc, P. G., Jeffs, N. and Neven, K. (2008), *FV: Alternativa osemdesetih = alternative scene of the eighties*. Ljubljana: Mednarodni grafični likovni center.
Lacan, J. (1992), *The Ethics of Psychoanalysis. 1959–1960. The Seminar of Jacques Lacan Book VII*, edited by Jacques-Alain Miller, translated with notes by Dennis Porter. London: W. W. Norton.
—(1994), *The Four Fundamental Concepts of Psychoanalysis*. London: Penguin.

—(1998), *On Feminine Sexuality. The Limits of Love and Knowledge, 1972–1973. ENCORE. The Seminar of Jacques Lacan Book XX*, edited by Jacques-Alain Miller, translated with notes by Bruce Fink. London: W. W. Norton.
—(2002a), *Écrits*, translated by Bruce Fink. London: Norton.
—(2002b), 'Kant with Sade', in Lacan, J. (ed.), *Écrits*, translated by Bruce Fink. London: Norton, pp. 645–70.
—(2008), *My Teaching*. London: Verso.
Laclau, E. (1989), Preface to Žižek, S. *The Sublime Object of Ideology*. London: Verso, pp. ix–xv.
Leader, D. and Groves, J. (1995), *Lacan for Beginners*. London: Totem books.
Lear, J. (2005), *Freud*. London: Routledge.
Lyotard, J. F. (1993), *Political Writings*, translated by Bill Readings and K. P. Geiman. Minneapolis: University of Minnesota Press.
Lyotard, J. F. and Deleuze, G. (1993), 'On the Department of Psychoanalysis at Vincennes', in Lyotard, J. F. (ed.), *Political Writings*, translated by Bill Readings and K. P. Geiman. Minneapolis: University of Minnesota Press, pp. 20–6.
Macey, D. (1988), *Lacan in Contexts*. London: Verso.
—(1994), 'Introduction', in Lacan, J. (ed.), *The Four Fundamental Concepts of Psychoanalysis*. London: Penguin, pp. vii–xxxiii.
Malabou, C. (2004), *Counterpath: Travelling with Jacques Derrida*. Stanford: Stanford University Press.
—(2012), *The New Wounded: From Neurosis to Brain Damage*. New York: Fordham University Press.
Malabou, C. and Vahanian, N. (2008), 'A Conversation with Catherine Malabou'. *Journal for Cultural and Religious Theory* 9: 1–13.
Marcuse, H. (2002), *One-Dimensional Man: Studies in the Ideology of Advanced Industrial Society*. London: Routledge.
Marx, K. (1992a), 'Theses on Feuerbach', in Karl Marx (ed.), *Early Writings*, translated by R. Livingstone and G. Benton. London: Penguin, pp. 421–3.
—(1992b), 'Economic and Philosophical Manuscripts (1844)', in Karl Marx (ed.), *Early Writings*, translated by R. Livingstone and G. Benton. London: Penguin, pp. 279–400.
Mastnak, T. (1988), 'The Implosion of the Social: Beyond Radical Democracy', in Mastnak and Rado Rika (eds), *The Subject and Democracy*. Ljubljana: Freedom Press, pp. 113–25.
Močnik, R. (1993), 'How we were fighting for the victory of reason and what happened when we made it', in Irwin (ed.), *A Nonveteran Reflection. NSK Embassy Moscow*. Piran: Obalne Galerije Piran, pp. 88–90.
Monroe, A. (2005), *Interrogation Machine: Laibach and NSK*. Cambridge, MA: MIT Press.

Motoh, H. (2012), 'Punk is a Symptom': Intersections of Philosophy and Alternative Culture in the '80s Slovenia. *Synthesis Philosophica* 53(1): 285–96.
Mouffe, C. (2005), *The Return of the Political*. London: Verso.
Muller, J. P. and Richardson, W. J. (1988), *The Purloined Poe: Lacan, Derrida and Psychoanalytic Reading*. Baltimore: John Hopkins Press.
Mundy, J. (ed.) (2006), *Surrealism Unbound*. London: Tate.
Myers, T. (2003), *Slavoj Žižek*. London: Routledge.
Nancy, J. L. (2005), 'Salut to you, salut to the blind we become', in Derrida, J. (ed.), *On Touching – Jean Luc Nancy*. Stanford: Stanford University Press.
Nietzsche, F. (1967), *On the Genealogy of Morals*, translated by W. Kaufmann and R. J. Hollingdale. New York: Vintage.
Pearson, D. (2013), 'Žižek and Theology in a Post-Secular Age'. Phd Thesis. Submitted June 2013, St Patrick's College, Dublin City University.
Pirjevec, J. (1995), *Jugoslavija: [1918-1992]: nastanek, razvoj ter razpad Karadjordjevićeve in Titove Jugoslavije*. Koper: Lipa.
Plato (1961), *The Collected Dialogues of Plato*, edited by E. Hamilton and H. Cairns. New York: Pantheon.
Porter, D. (1992), 'Translator's Introduction' to Lacan, J. (1992), *The Ethics of Psychoanalysis. 1959–1960. The Seminar of Jacques Lacan Book VII*, edited by Jacques-Alain Miller, London: W. W. Norton, pp. i–vi.
Pound, M. (2008), *Žižek: A (Very) Critical Introduction* (Interventions). Grand Rapids: Eerdmans.
Repe, B. (2002), *Jutri je nov dan: Slovenci in razpad Jugoslavije*. Ljubljana: Modrijan.
Sade, M. De (1980), *Philosophy in the Bedroom*. London: Penguin.
Seery, A. (2008), 'Slavoj Žižek's Dialectics of Ideology and the Discourses of Irish Education'. *Irish Educational Studies* 27(2): 13–28.
Sharpe, M. (2004), *Slavoj Žižek, a Little Piece of the Real*. London: Ashgate.
Sontag, S (2001), 'The Pornographic Imagination', in Bataille (ed.), *Story of the Eye*. London: Penguin.
Strajn, D. (1991), 'On Walter Benjamin'. *Filozofski Vestrik* 1: 109–20.
Taylor, C. (2007), *A Secular Age*. Cambridge, MA: Harvard University Press.
Vahanian, N. (2008), 'A Conversation with Catherine Malabou'. *Journal for Cultural and Religious Theory* 9: 1–13.
Weatherill, R. (2011), *Forgetting Freud: Is Psychoanalysis in Retreat?* Dublin: Academica Press.
Wollheim, R. (1971), *Freud*. London: Fontana.
Zgaga, P. (1991), 'Democracy, culture, education as a question of form'. *Filozofski Vestrik* 1: 160–70.

INDEX

Adam, F. 28
Adorno, T. W. 29
Alajbegović, Z. 31
Althusser, L. P. 6, 25, 29, 52, 97, 99, 127, 132, 197
Aristotle 43, 71–5, 90, 133, 155, 164

Badiou, A. 41–8, 58–9
Balibar, E. 29, 39–40, 84, 89, 115, 131
Bataille, G. 9, 51–3, 56, 59, 62, 67, 70, 92, 96, 110, 121, 153, 189, 199, 201
Baugh, B. 54, 88
Benjamin, W. 57–8, 78–80, 85, 200
Bersani, L. 64, 70, 73, 77, 85–6, 155, 187
Beseda (*Word*) 26
Bilic, A. 9
Borghesia 31
Bosnia and Herzegovina 21–2, 127
Bowie, M. 39–40, 51, 86, 90
Božovič, M. 28
Butler, R. 11, 111, 197

Časopis za kritiko znanosti, domišljijo in novo antropologijo see *Journal for the Critique of Science, Imagination and the New Anthropology*

Croatia 21–2, 97, 127
Croatian Democratic Union (HDZ) 21

Debenjak, B. 25
De Kesel, M. 123, 156
Deleuze, G. 25, 29, 48–9, 100–1, 105, 111, 129, 131, 162
Derrida, J. 6, 10–11, 25, 29, 34, 39–40, 49, 51, 65, 73–4, 77–9, 83, 86, 88, 90, 97–8, 100, 105, 120, 127, 129–32, 138, 156, 162, 188–91, 197, 201
Djilas, M. 19
Dolar, M.
   affirmation of Lacanianism 112–13
   art and philosophy movements 102–3
   civil society and alternative culture 104–5
   cogito and voice 37
   development and growth 84–5
   differences among the troika 109–10
   friendship with Žižek 84
   Hegelian influence 87–9, 110–12
   ideology critique 113–15
   on Lacan 87
   Lacan's intellectual influence 98–100
   Lacanian philosophy, conceptualization 106–7

Marxism influence 89
metamorphic approximations 89–90
'objectively subjective' Lacanianism 107–9
object voice 37, 86, 113
oeuvre 92–3
relation to alternative culture 113
similarities among the troika 109–10
as Slovenian philosopher 93–6
Socrates and Plato 90–2
structuralist and Marxist fusion 96–8
study at Vincennes in Paris 100–2
ultraorthodox Lacanianism 105–6

Eagleton, T. 43

Foucault, M. 6, 29, 52, 97, 99–101, 127, 132
Freire, P. 197
Freud, S.
  Civilisation and Its Discontents 11
  influence on the Ljubljana 10–11, 29
  Jokes and Their Relations to the Unconscious 7
  The Interpretation of Dreams 13
  The Psychopathology of Everyday Life 13
FV art movement (FV 112/15) 9, 20, 26, 29–31, 33, 37, 103, 137, 151, 183, 195

Gantar, P. 9, 34–8, 46, 84, 93, 112, 118, 125, 127, 137, 141, 195, 208
Gramsci, A. 25, 29, 197, 208
Graziano, G. 9
Gržinić, M. 31
Guattari, F. 29, 49, 101

Hallward, P. 42, 130
Hegel, G. W. F. 23, 54–5, 86–9, 98, 100, 102, 108, 120–3, 133–5
Heidegger, M. 25, 27, 29, 94, 98, 127–8, 130, 132, 137, 167
Hitchcock 54, 92
Horkheimer, M. 29
Hurst, A. 79, 188, 191
Husserl, E. G. A. 24–5, 29, 34

Ivančić, A. 31

Journals
  Beseda (*Word*) 26
  Journal for the Critique of Science, Imagination and the New Anthropology 27
  Mladina 8, 13
  Nova revija (*The New Journal*) 27
  Perspektive (*Perspectives*) 26
  Praxis 23
  Razpol (*The Journal of the Freudian Field*) 27
  Revija 57 (*Journal 57*) 26
  Vestnik (later *Filozofski Vestnik*) 24

Kafka, F. 6, 84–5, 200
Kant, I. 10, 21, 25, 40, 44, 53–62, 64–5, 67–70, 72, 74, 76, 78–9, 86, 89, 92, 100–1, 108–9, 121, 123, 131, 138, 145, 152, 161–2, 164–5, 170–2, 175, 180, 185, 195, 204, 206, 210
Kay, S. 6, 8, 10, 83, 121, 209

INDEX

Kierkegaard, S.   42, 55, 112, 190
Klossowski, P.   9–10, 51, 53,
    59–63, 67, 69, 72, 79, 121
Kojève, A.   54–5, 66, 88, 100,
    110–11, 131, 134
Korčula Summer School
    (1963–74)   16, 23
Korda, N.   31
Kotsko, A.   86
Kristeva, J.   6, 83, 95, 97, 130
Kučan, M.   20–1

Lacan, J.
    and Derrida   11, 78–80
    The Ethics of Psychoanalysis
        10, 64–77 (see also *The
        Ethics of Psychoanalysis*)
    *The Four Fundamental Concepts
        of Psychoanalysis*   7, 40,
        42, 44, 48, 53, 56, 70, 84,
        124, 133, 147, 152, 154,
        159, 185
    Lacan's militancy   186
    Lacan's philosophy   10, 185
    and the Ljubljana troika   80–1
    from structuralism   93
Lacan in Contexts   9, 46
The Lacan effect
    affirmative ethical and political
        understanding   65–6
    Aristotelian ethics   74–6
    Badiou's impressions   41–8,
        58–9
    context-specific importance of
        Ljubljana   147
    deadocks of Lacanianism
        188–90
    the death drive   60–1, 73
    Derrida's critique   65–6, 77–80
    and Dolar   106–7, 112–13
    'esotericism' of his approach
        188
    ethics and morality   67–9
    Freudian influence   64

influence on Slovenian society
    9, 76–7
influence on French thought
    39–40
later Lacanianism   186
liberation of desire   59–60
Ljubljana School of
    Psychoanalysis   9, 39–81
the Ljubljana troika   80–1,
    187
Macey's critique   46–53
radical critique of ideology   58
Slovenia's Lacanianism   2, 5,
    17, 20, 33, 52, 56, 76–7,
    118, 181
versus Sadean thought   58–61
and Žižek   132–3, 145–6
and Zupančič   68, 158, 160–1
Lacan's Silent Partners   6
Laclau, E.   40, 46, 106, 117–18,
    125, 138, 147, 194–5
Laibach   2, 9, 20, 29, 31–3, 36,
    78, 84, 102–6, 126, 135,
    140, 148–9, 158, 184,
    195
*Less than Nothing: Hegel and the
    Shadow of Dialectical
    Materialism*   4, 11
Ljubljana School of Psychoanalysis
    early years   3–10, 183
    evolution of thought   5
    future directions   194–6
    genealogy of philosophy   22
    journals and their influence
        27–8
    the Lacan effect   9, 39–81
        (*see also* The Lacan
        effect)
    Lacanian–Marxism   24–5
    Yugoslavian culture and
        politics   14–15
Logar, C.   22, 39–40, 44, 46–7
Lyotard, J. F.   48–9, 62, 101,
    129, 162

Macedonia 16–17, 21–2
Macey, D. 9, 39–40, 44, 46–53, 57, 59, 66, 76, 78, 80, 88, 121
Majer, B. 24
Malabou, C. 11, 73, 179, 190–6, 209–11
Mandič, D. 31
Marcuse, H. 29, 44, 58, 113, 127, 129, 197, 210
Marx, K. 16, 23, 46, 84, 86, 89, 97, 103, 112–19, 122, 131–5, 143, 195
Marxism 23
  Lacanian–Marxism 24
Mastnak, T. 3, 34–7, 84, 104, 210
Miller, J-A. 29, 48, 66, 108, 118, 129
Milošević, S. 19–21, 84, 141, 185
Mladina 8, 13, 185
Močnik, R. 3, 20, 26–7, 30–7, 40, 47, 84, 92, 112–13, 118, 125–6, 135, 141, 149, 181, 183–4, 186, 189
Montenegro 21–2, 30
Mouffe, C. 40, 59, 68, 117

Nancy, J. L. 11, 201, 208, 211
Neue Kunsthandlung/Novi kolektivizem 31–3
Neue Slowenische Kunst (NSK) 2, 9, 20, 31–2, 40, 84, 118, 135, 151, 183
Nietzsche, F. 29, 90, 109–10, 112, 139, 153, 161, 166–70, 172, 175, 199–200, 206, 211
Nova revija (The New Journal) 27
NSK *see* Neue Slowenische Kunst (NSK)

Occupy Wall Street movement 11, 135
Orwell, G. 29

Perspektive (Perspectives) 26, 28–9, 33, 94
Plato 8, 43, 47, 60, 66, 87, 90–2, 100, 107–8, 123, 137, 143, 146, 155–7, 176–7, 196
Political and social climate
  Arab Spring movement 3, 11, 135, 184
  authors' and editors' role 33–7
  avant garde literary trends 26
  development of critical thought 29
  emergence of Nationalism 18–22
  foreign authors, translations 28–9
  Group FV 112/15 30
  impact on academic institutions 22
  importance of publication 28
  Laibach 31
  literary journals 26–9
  new generation thinkers 28
  philosophical and cultural trends 28
  Praxis movement 16
  theatre and music 31–3
Porter, D. 65–7, 73
Praxis, the journal 23
Praxis movement 8, 16, 89, 93–4, 107
Praxis school (group) 89, 96–7, 99, 107, 126, 130, 132, 137
Problemi group
  cultural involvement 29, 97
  and Dolar 84, 95
  Lacanian orientation 27
  and Marxism 96
  'Nazi scandal' 38, 135
  official troubles 28–30, 114, 128

Pankrti (Bastards)   30
and *Perspektive* writers   26
Punk Problemi affair   24,
    102–3, 119, 148
theory and literature/arts
    link   26
Pučnik, J.   26
Punk Problemi affair   9, 18, 24,
    28, 30, 102, 119, 148

Ranković, A.   15, 18
Razpol (*The Journal of the
    Freudian Field*)   27–8
Revija 57 (*Journal 57*)   23, 26
Riha, R.   27–8, 162, 199
Rus, V.   23–4

Sade, M. De
    comparison with Kant   9–10,
        67–79, 121–3, 131, 138,
        171
    importance of philosophy for
        Lacan   53–5
    with Kant   56–65
    for Zupančič   161, 180
Sadean legacy   10, 54–61, 64, 69
Šalamun, T.   33, 199
Sartre, J-P.   23, 29, 65, 94,
    100–1, 111
SASA *see* Slovenian Academy of
    Sciences and Arts (SASA)
Saussure, F.   29
Scipion Nasice Sisters' Theatre
    2, 31–2
Serbia   17, 21–2, 30
Serbian League of Communists
    (LC)   19
Sereval, D.   31
Slovenia
    Slovenian Academy of Sciences
        and Arts (SASA)   25, 27
    Slovenian Peasant Union   20
    Slovenian People's Party   20
    Slovenian neo-Lacanianism

academic influence   6
concrete universality   4
and *doxa* or commonsense   8
joke and the unconscious
    wish   7
political and cultural
    movements   20
psychoanalysis and
    sociopolitical life   7–8
relation to the unconscious   7–8
Sadean anti-moralism   10
Scientific Research Centre of
    SASA   25
Socialist Federal Republic of
    Yugoslavia (SFRY)   17,
    19, 21–3
Sontag, S.   53, 59–60, 62, 121

Taylor, C.   53, 121
The Ethics of Psychoanalysis
    10, 40
the 'desire' principle   145, 172
and *The ethics of the Real*
    170–4
history of ethical thought   164
influence of Freud on Lacan
    122
Lacan's differences with
    Freud   75–80
the thematic of ethics   55–68
The New Wounded   11
Tribuna   24–5

Vestnik (later Filozofski
    Vestnik)   27
Vidnana, I.   38

Wahl, J.   54–5, 88
Weiss, B. L.   14

Yugoslavia
    Basic Organizations of
        Associated Labour
        (TOZD)   17

coalition of oppositional
  parties 20–1
complex political prehistory 8
Dayton Agreement in 1995 22
DEMOS 20–1
economic crisis 15, 17
economic prosperity 15
ethnicity issues 16
international events 16
international relations 18
League of Communists of
  Yugoslavia (LCY) 18
Marxism 8
nationalist tendencies 19
Non-Aligned Movement 15,
  17–18
political liberalization 15
Punk Problemi 9
Yugoslav National Army 19
Yugoslav People's Army
  (YPA) 22

Zgaga, P. 36
Žižek–Malabou encounter 179,
  190–4
Žižek, S.
  critique of ideology 148–50,
    184, 197n. 1
  differences among the troika
    139–40
  French structuralism
    influence 127–31
  Freudian revolution 120–1
  on Hegel 133–4
  ideology 37, 118–20
  interpretation of Lacan 143–6
  key Lacanian concepts 132–3
  on Lacan 123–45
  and Lacanianism 123–4
  Laclau and Lacanianism
    117–18
  *Less Than Nothing: Hegel and
    the Shadow of Dialectical
    Materialism* 4, 9

Ljubljana connection 125–7
Malabou, encounter with 179
Marxist influence 134
  orthodox Lacanianism 139
  as a philosopher 142
  philosophical inheritance 120
  philosophical relations to the
    troika 137–8
  philosophy and literature 143
  psychoanalytical principles
    124, 138–9
  range of influence 134–5
  relation to alternative culture
    135–7, 140–1, 148
  *The Sublime Object of
    Ideology* 27
  versus Malabou 190
  writing and exposition style
    120–3
Zupančič, A.
  Aristophanes' speech 176–7
  'the body more than body'
    concept 169–70
  'desire' and 'drive' concepts
    173–5, 178
  distinction between life and
    death drives 153
  ethics and comedy 37, 151–2,
    178
  ethics and political critique
    152
  ethics of the real 153–4, 178
  *Everything You Always Wanted
    to Know About Lacan
    But Were Afraid to Ask
    Hitchcock* 5, 54, 92,
    117, 144
  evolution as a Slovenian
    thinker 158–9
  Freudian influence 154–5
  future of Lacanian
    philosophy 177–8
  interpretation of Kantian
    ethics 171–2

Lacan and the next
    generation 158
Lacanian dogmatism 160–1
love and sexual difference
    175–6
Marxist influence 156
Nietzsche's influence 167–9
notion of embodiment 166–7
philosophical and psycho-
    analytical work 151–3
philosophy versus
    psychoanalysis 162–5,
    179–81
Plato to psychoanalysis
    155–6
professional growth 161–2
real versus symbolic 172
sexuality and
    psychoanalysis 156–8,
    165–6